# THE
# MURDER

Marilyn Monroe as she appeared in *The Seven Year Itch*. Corbis-Bettmann/UPI.

# THE MEN WHO MURDERED MARILYN

by

## MATTHEW SMITH

BLOOMSBURY

First published in 1996
This paperback edition first published 1997

Bloomsbury Publishing Plc
38 Soho Square, London W1V 5DF

Copyright © 1996 by Matthew Smith

The moral right of the author has been asserted

The author would like to express his gratitude to those listed
below for their co-operation and kindness:

Excerpts from *Marilyn: The Last Take* (Dutton, 1992) are reproduced
by kind permission of Patte B Barham.

Excerpts from *The Marilyn Files* (SPI Books, 1992) are reproduced
by kind permission of Robert F. Slatzer.

Excerpts from *Marilyn and Me* (Doubleday, 1992) are reproduced
by kind permission of Susan Strasberg.

Excerpts from *Coroner* (Simon & Schuster, 1983) are reproduced
by kind permission of Thomas T. Noguchi.

Extracts from *Kennedy* (HarperCollins Publishers, 1965) are reproduced
by kind permission of Theodore C. Sorensen, HarperCollins Publishers
and Hodder & Stoughton.

Extracts from *Marilyn* (Warner Paperback Library, 1975) are
reproduced by kind permission of Norman Mailer.

Extracts from *Robert Kennedy and His Times* (Houghton Mifflin Company, 1978)
are reproduced by kind permission of Arthur M. Schlesinger Jr and Houghton
Mifflin Company.

A CIP catalogue record for this book
is available from the British Library

ISBN 0 7475 3094 7

10 9 8 7 6 5 4 3 2 1

Typeset by Hewer Text Composition Services, Edinburgh
Printed in Great Britain by Cox & Wyman Limited, Reading

**To Margaret**

# CONTENTS

# ACKNOWLEDGEMENTS

Without the assistance of many people this book would never have been written. At the top of the list I must place my wife, Margaret, without whose help and encouragement I could never have coped with the enormous volume of work involved in investigating a 1962 mystery.

It was with great pleasure that I talked for some hours with Bob Mitchum, who knew Marilyn in the era of the big studios and deepened my understanding of those days. I especially appreciate his writing an introduction to this book, and the interest he takes in seeking a resolution of the Marilyn mystery.

Robert E. Slatzer and his wife Debbie were a wonderful support to me, a source of many valuable documents and a mine of information, and merit my special thanks. I shall not forget their kindness, nor Robert's generosity in providing many pictures for this book.

Another of my sources, close to the Greensons, was also kind and extremely helpful. I promised I would not name the person, but that is no excuse for not saying how much I appreciated the valuable information given me.

Natalie Jacobs went to a great deal of trouble to help me and after innumerable telephone conversations I felt we had become firm friends. A valued friendship was also the result of long discussions I had with lawyer John Miner.

Dr Cyril Wecht, one of America's most respected and distinguished pathologists, offered me his expert advice unhesitatingly, in spite of the enormous demands made upon his time.

Chief of Police Tom Reddin, now retired, and his wife Betty were a pleasure to meet. Tom lives very much in the present, but has a clear memory of the time of Marilyn Monroe's death and the gift of accurate recall. I much appreciated his help.

With Jack Clemmons I spent some happy hours chewing the fat over the case. First-hand testimony is rare, and Jack's has a special value. I particularly remember Jack taking me to see the house at Fifth Helena Drive in which Marilyn lived and died.

I also had the pleasure of meeting Jeanne Carmen, Marilyn's close friend and neighbour. She was a valuable witness and I was extremely fortunate to have her help.

For being kind enough to see me and offer help I am indebted to Pat Newcomb, who was Marilyn's press secretary. I am grateful also to Dr Thomas Noguchi, Dr Robert Litman and Dr Norman Farberow, who took the time to assist me. Ted Landreth, Chris Olgiati and Patte Barham all contributed to my work and I appreciate their kindness. I owe a debt of gratitude to many others too, in particular Milo Speriglio, Mike Rothmiller, Lee Israel, Evelyn Moriarity and Antoinette Giancana. John Rudd and Chris Mills were kind enough to lend me books.

Finally, I must acknowledge the help I received from the management and staff of the Hollywood Plaza Inn when I was doing research in the USA.

# INTRODUCTION
## Robert Mitchum

In 1941 I was working the graveyard shift in the sheet metal department of Lockheed Aircraft in Burbank, California. My workmate was a decent, good-humoured, helpful fellow named Jim Dougherty. He looked like a large brick, red-haired, square-shouldered and solid all the way down. He carried with him a picture of his wife greeting him at the garden gate, clad only in a tiny French apron. The subject was so innocent and vulnerable that it generated tender amusement rather than lust.

A group of us workers went to a company dance at the old Palladium Ballroom where the Dorsey Brothers Orchestra was performing. Jim's wife was a very pretty, very shy young lady (very young), who did not smoke or drink. That is how I met Norma Jean Dougherty, later to be known as Marilyn Monroe.

Next time I saw her was on the RKO lot when I was working there. She was working there also, and a few of us were sitting around watching her walk across the lot. One of the group said, 'Just think, we could have adopted that little girl.'

Over the next few years I saw her from time to time, mainly through her friendship with Jane Russell, who is a dear friend of mine. When we worked together our association was more or less limited to the set, as each night we retreated to our respective cabins in the Canadian woods. During that time I did learn, however, that she suffered severe menstrual disorders that were very painful, embarrassing and disabling. She had been treated extensively for this condition but it seemed to persist. Also, she was falling deeper into the prison of agoraphobia. This condition was not well known at the time, and was responsible for many of the behavioural oddities with which she was charged.

Once outside her own room and amongst other people she had to assume the manufactured identity which had been foisted upon her and which was totally foreign to her true nature. She had to play Marilyn Monroe, and was terrified she would miss a cue or fail to deliver as expected.

I was in New York the night she sang at John Kennedy's birthday party. She came up to my hotel room and told me that she was not going to Madison Square Gardens. I convinced her that she *must* go and took her down to the lobby into a swarm of Secret Service agents. Later she called me and seemed anxious to talk to me. For some shallow and selfish reason I regarded her concern as trifling and begged off. I never saw her again.

After her death I had a long luncheon with Pat Newcomb in Washington, DC, at which time she told me, 'Marilyn *really* wanted to talk to you.' I have never shed the guilt I felt at hearing that. Ironically, Ms Newcomb, formerly Marilyn's press secretary, was at that time employed as secretary to Ethel Kennedy, Bobby's wife.

I find it difficult to accept the suicide ruling on Marilyn's death. She was a confused, troubled lady who, confronted with living the life of an artificial stranger, felt inadequate to the demands of deportment expected of her, but was never morose or despondent. I never saw her take a drink, and know nothing of any association with pills.

Matthew Smith's book probably begs more questions than it answers, but it is a masterly review of an occurrence which has troubled our consciences for years. Perhaps it will trigger some latent, long-sleeping recollection which may help clarify the contrived muddle which has served as an explanation of the death of Marilyn Monroe. If so, he has performed a signal act of kindness to the confused world who loved her, and I for one applaud his efforts and thank him for allowing me to be consulted.

# 1

# A DEATH SURROUNDING
# MANY PROBLEMS

In the middle of a Saturday night Sergeant Jack Clemmons found himself driving along Sunset Boulevard in the direction of Fifth Helena Drive, and if the almost uncanny absence of traffic was anything to go by it was a relatively peaceful night. It was half past four, and just five minutes earlier he had received, as Watch Commander of Western Division, a phone call telling him that Marilyn Monroe had committed suicide. It was not usual for a Watch Commander to drop everything at receiving a report of a suicide and to drive without delay to the scene of the death. But lately the Police Department had been embarrassed by acting on reports which later proved to be hoaxes. And, after all, this was Marilyn Monroe – and as stars went, there were few bigger.

Jack Clemmons went to Marilyn Monroe's home on Fifth Helena Drive primarily to ascertain whether the call was genuine. As it was, he spent some ninety minutes there in an atmosphere decidedly odd and rather uncomfortable, and he was not sorry when his colleagues eventually arrived and he could hand over to them. The three people he found at the house were Marilyn's psychiatrist, Dr Ralph Greenson, her housekeeper, Mrs Eunice Murray, and her physician, Dr Hyman Engelberg. It had been Dr Greenson who had telephoned him.

Mrs Murray answered the door, and Clemmons asked her how long it was since the two doctors had arived. He was amazed to be told that they had been there since soon after the body had been discovered by Mrs Murray, at about midnight, and his first question to them all was therefore why they had

delayed contacting the police. They tried to fob him off and
Clemmons had a hard time getting a response. It was Dr
Greenson who finally offered the explanation that they were
unable to act without the permission of the publicity department
at Marilyn's studio, and he had contacted the police as soon as
Twentieth Century-Fox had cleared it. Sergeant Clemmons was
distinctly dissatisfied with this story but decided it was one for
the investigating officers. Both Greenson and Engelberg knew
the law relating to the reporting of these things; they could
hardly claim ignorance.

Mrs Murray took him to see the body, which was lying face
down, arms by its sides, diagonally across the bed, toes to bottom
right and head to top left (the opposite way to that described by
many people). It lay across the telephone wire and the phone,
which Clemmons was told had been found off the hook, was
now in place. On the bedside table was an assortment of bottles
which had contained the dead star's prescription drugs. Dr
Greenson pointed to one of them and said, 'She must have
taken the whole bottle.' In other respects Dr Greenson was
not very forthcoming; but then the others were even less so. It
did not take long for Clemmons to realise that very little was
being volunteered, and when there was anything to say it was
Greenson who did most of the talking, almost as though he had
been elected spokesman. Usually in a case of suicide the people
around had plenty to say: sometimes it was remorse they were

Sergeant Jack Clemmons answered a call from the house.

giving voice to, sometimes guilt, and sometimes sheer horror and frustration. Clemmons linked the reticence in the Monroe household to the oddball atmosphere.

When the sergeant asked who had discovered the body, it was Mrs Murray who spoke up. She had gone to bed about ten o'clock, she said, and had noticed Marilyn's bedroom light showing under the door and the telephone wire disappearing under it too. She assumed Marilyn was either telephoning friends or reading. Waking up again at about midnight, she passed the bedroom door as she went to the bathroom and noticed that the light was still on and the telephone wire still there. It was unusual for Marilyn to be awake so late so she knocked at the door, which was locked on the inside. When she could not rouse Marilyn, she became alarmed and rang Dr Greenson, she said. Dr Greenson lived nearby and he came over at once to join her in trying to rouse Marilyn. When they did not succeed, he walked round the side of the house and peered through the bedroom window. Seeing Marilyn lying naked on the bed, he had broken a window and climbed in.

When Greenson had drawn Clemmons' attention to the empty medication bottles he had also inadvertently drawn the policeman's attention to the absence of a glass which Marilyn could have used to help her swallow so many pills. Greenson said they were Nembutal capsules and that she had been taking them regularly to help her to sleep. He joined Clemmons in the search for the missing glass, as did Dr Engelberg and Mrs Murray, but they drew a complete blank: there was no receptacle of any kind anywhere in the bedroom. Clemmons also established that there was no water supply in the bathroom because of renovations that were being carried out, so there could be no answer to the riddle there. The mystery remained unsolved and, indeed, deepened when Clemmons learned that Marilyn found liquid essential when swallowing pills of any kind.

While he was looking around Clemmons heard the noise of a washing machine and a vacuum cleaner, and at first thought how odd that was. But then he reminded himself how many people were likely to be coming to the house during the next day, and accepted it as fastidiousness on Mrs Murray's part: no doubt she did not want Marilyn's house to look a mess. But beyond neatness and tidiness, Clemmons recognised a house which had been prepared for his own visit. The bedroom was extremely tidy, and in his experience suicides were not people concerned with appearances; in fact they were notoriously messy. He wondered whether Marilyn had left a note explaining her suicide, but there was none to be found.

Clemmons used his radio to summon back-up and an investigator while he was on his way to Fifth Helena Drive. First to arrive was Sergeant Marvin Iannone, who would control the expected deluge of traffic. Detective Sergeant R. E. Byron would soon join Iannone as the investigating officer.

It was already light as Clemmons made his way back to West Los Angeles Division, where he would spend the rest of his shift dealing with telephone enquiries from the world's press. So that was the way life had ended for the Hollywood sex symbol, he mused – pretty girl who seemed to have the world at her feet. No family near when she had reached the point of no return,

The bedside table with its array of bottles. The mystery was how Marilyn was supposed to have swallowed a large number of pills without any water – there was no sign of a glass when Clemmons was there. *AP Wide World.*

not even one of her circle of friends – only a housekeeper who would be joined at the discovery of her body by her doctors. Clemmons would hear later about Marilyn's complaint to her psychiatrist, Ralph Greenson, in a telephone call to him earlier on the day she had died: 'Here I am, the most beautiful woman in the world, and I have no date for Saturday night.'

But when it came to his own experiences that night Jack Clemmons had a lot to think about. He was puzzled about a number of things which had happened at Marilyn's home. He was not confident that he had hit on the true reason why the washing machine and vacuum cleaner were being used in the middle of the night, and the idea of a housekeeper and two doctors sitting around a corpse for four hours waiting for a call from Fox before ringing the police was ludicrous. Then he had had a curious feeling that the people he spoke to were not the only ones in the house when he was there. He felt that one or more people were secreted in one of the rooms he did not enter, and he had had no occasion to make a search. Then, of course, there was the mystery of the missing glass, which was an absolute imponderable . . . It would not be long before he came to question everything he had learned at the Monroe house that night. The mystery was just beginning.

Sergeant Byron's enquiries did not add up to much. By the time he got round to Mrs Murray, Dr Greenson and Dr Engelberg they had had more time to get their act together and the statements he obtained from them differed from what they had originally told Clemmons. Dr Greenson now said he had not been called until 3.30 a.m., which relieved him of the necessity of telling the story about having to wait four and a half hours for permission from the studio before he could call the police. Mrs Murray supported this by changing her account of the timescale and saying it was 3.30 a.m. when she had woken up and seen the light under the door. She later added that when she got no answer after knocking on the door she took a fireplace poker outside and pushed the closed bedroom curtains back through an open window which was protected by security bars. Seeing Marilyn lying on the bed, she had telephoned Dr Greenson at once and he had come over quickly. Dr Greenson had then broken a window to gain entry and, after a delay of a couple of minutes, had opened the bedroom door and declared, 'We've lost her.'

Though Byron did not know that what he was being told contradicted the statements made to Clemmons, he drew the conclusion that it had been somewhat rehearsed. He quickly became aware that Mrs Murray, for one, was not telling him what he should know and said so in the death report:

> It is this officer's opinion that Mrs Murray was vague and possibly evasive in answering questions pertaining to the activities of Miss Monroe during this time. It is not known whether this is or is not intentional. During the interrogation of Joe DiMaggio Jr [her stepson], he indicated he had made three phone calls to the Monroe home, only one of which Mrs Murray mentioned.

What Mrs Murray meant, no doubt, was that though Joe

Marilyn's psychiatrist, Dr Ralph Greenson, was on the scene soon after the tragedy.

DiMaggio Jr, the son by a previous marriage of her former husband, had telephoned at 2 p.m. and again at 4.30 p.m., she told him that Marilyn was out, and indeed Marilyn had not spoken to young Joe on those occasions. It was, therefore, just as she had said: Marilyn had spoken to him only once, when he rang again about 7.30 p.m. In this instance she was accused of being unhelpful over the wrong things. More importantly, Byron apparently did not notice the discrepancy between two statements made by Mrs Murray. The housekeeper told him that she had passed DiMaggio Jr's call to Marilyn *in bed* at 7.30 p.m., when on another occasion she had said that Marilyn had gone to bed at 8 p.m. Incredibly, both these statements were included by Byron in the same report. For whatever reason, he seems not to have pursued the truth with Mrs Murray. He simply noted that she was being evasive and left it at that. It is also worth noting that not one of the senior personnel at Police Headquarters or in the coroner's office who read Byron's report appears to have taken him to task for its shortcomings or brevity.

The whole timeframe of events was the basic problem. The first version, given to Sergeant Clemmons – that Mrs Murray had gone to bed at 10 p.m., visited the bathroom at midnight, seen the light on under the door and called Dr Greenson soon after twelve – had led to the problem of why the call to the police had been delayed until 4.25 a.m. The second version, given to Sergeant Byron – that Mrs Murray had not discovered the body until 3.30 a.m. – was more realistic as far as the call to the police was concerned, but the problem with this scenario was that Dr Greenson obviously needed time to get dressed and drive to Fifth Helena Drive, after which he said he called Dr Engelberg. Dr Engelberg also needed time to get dressed and drive to Marilyn's house and yet, after examining the body, he timed the death certificate at 3.50 a.m. This was totally unrealistic if Mrs Murray had made her call to Greenson only twenty minutes before. It was another riddle which Byron let by him, and it too was not challenged by higher authority.

By the time Engelberg carried out his examination of the body rigor mortis had set in, which should have told the doctor that Marilyn had been dead for several hours. If he was, in fact, at the scene by 3.50 a.m. it was misleading of him to show this time on the death certificate without commenting on the rigor mortis. But while the question must arise as to whether he could have reached the house by that time, it may be far more pertinent to ask whether he was – perhaps earlier, perhaps later than 3.50 a.m. – drawn into some kind of conspiracy to conceal the truth.

Byron, when conducting his investigation, was apparently not aware of the absence of the drinking glass, and it seems that Dr Greenson, Dr Engelberg and Mrs Murray, who had all joined in the search for it, did not enlighten him. He did not note its absence. But then it seems that the Investigating Officer did not even look at the floor, where he would have seen at once that, since Marilyn had had a new thick pile carpet laid only a few weeks before, when her bedroom door was closed light could not be seen underneath it. It seems, also, that not one of the other policemen who were in and out of the house noticed this either. It was Robert Slatzer, who had been married to Marilyn briefly and who had remained her lifelong friend, who had spotted this when he had gone over to her house after hearing that she was dead.

It is hard to believe that Sergeant Byron did not explore the geography of the house during his investigation, when he would have discovered that Mrs Murray had a bathroom en suite to her bedroom. He might have asked why she had needed to be passing Marilyn's bedroom door at all, let alone why she claimed to have seen light under a door beneath which no light would show. (See plan of house, p. 220.)

Slatzer spotted something else which went unnoticed by the police. The glass from the window supposedly broken by Dr Greenson to gain entry into Marilyn's locked bedroom had fallen outside the house, indicating that the window had been broken from inside. This in turn raised the whole issue of whether Marilyn's door had been locked at all. She normally did not lock it, according to her friends.

To add to the growing number of mysteries surrounding the death of Marilyn, another teaser would appear with the toxicologist's report. When Sergeant Clemmons had had his attention drawn to the various pill containers by Dr Greenson, the doctor had indicated the bottle nearest the bed and said,

'She must have taken the whole bottle.' The phial tops lay on the bedside table. Clemmons told me, 'I thought to myself, that's a lot of pills,' and he remembers looking into the eight containers and finding them all empty. When the toxicologist's report appeared, however, to his amazement he saw that varying numbers of pills were listed as being present in all but two. Who removed the remaining pills in the first place? And who returned them to the containers before they went to the coroner's office? And why? This was not the only shock for Clemmons, however. He was dumbfounded to see, among photographs of the death scene taken for the coroner, one of the bedside table which now showed a drinking vessel present.

But this does not represent all the peculiarities, irregularities and discrepancies which arose in the Marilyn Monroe investigation. The case was full of problems of one kind or another. Fingerprints, for instance, provide another example. One source states that when the police dusted the house for prints not a single print was found, whilst another claims that prints were

Dr Greenson said he broke the window to gain access into Marilyn's bedroom. *Corbis-Bettmann/UPI.*

lifted. It would be interesting to know which is right, but far more interesting to know why fingerprints were dusted for at all. In an open-and-shut case of suicide where no crime has been committed – and the police claimed that this was so here – fingerprints do not enter into consideration.

It is hard to believe that, had all the above peculiarities been observed by those responsible for the investigation into Marilyn's death, it could so readily have been assumed to be a case of suicide. But even from the first news of the tragedy the authorities called it such. When Ralph Greenson telephoned the news of Marilyn's death to Los Angeles Police West Division at 4.25 on Sunday morning, 5 August 1962, he called it suicide, and it could be believed that from that time on this view was never questioned. Or could it have been that, for some reason, this was the verdict that the authorities wanted and were determined to promote?

It might be thought that it was the autopsist who first cracked the façade, when he softened plain suicide to 'probable' suicide. But on the other hand it could just as easily be regarded as the first hint that Miss Monroe's death was to be seen as no more than a *slight* case of suicide.

# 2

# STATE OF AFFAIRS

When a suicide occurs, it is the deceased's general state of mind which is usually revealing and which evokes from those around the response, 'I should have seen it coming.' In particular, it is the state of mind during the period immediately before their death which is of paramount importance to fully understanding what led to such a sad event. To ascertain both the general and specific state of mind it is customary for the police or the coroner's staff to probe the deceased's circumstances and ask many questions of their nearest and dearest.

As indicated in Chapter 1, the strange thing about the death of Marilyn Monroe was that no one waited for the outcome of an enquiry; as early as the time when her body was discovered a decision seemed to have been made that she had taken her own life. In the telephone call made to the police by her psychiatrist, he announced not only that she had died but that she had committed suicide. On reflection, it is strange that it was Dr Greenson who could instantly call it suicide, because he was in the best possible position to know her state of mind. Apart from sinus problems and a susceptibility to colds, the only ongoing problem Marilyn had with her health was insomnia. But during the period before her death this problem was gently abating, and Ralph Greenson had been weaning her off the medication upon which she had become so dependent.

It is true that Marilyn had been fired by her studio, Twentieth Century-Fox. The almost bankrupt Fox had *Something's Got to Give* on the stocks, the most expensive of their current productions, and Marilyn was wearing them down by feuding with George Cukor, the director. Spitting fire and endlessly arguing over the script, she repeatedly failed to appear on the set, costing them more and more money. The last straw appeared to have been when she called in sick, then flew to New York to perform at President Kennedy's forty-fifth birthday party in Madison Square Garden. Fox threw the book at her, slapping a $500,000 writ on Marilyn Monroe Productions Inc. for 'wilful violation of contract'. However Lena Pepitone, her New York maid, wrote of her dismissal, 'Being fired by the studio she detested didn't bother her at all. "Good riddance!" she declared.' This was putting the expected brave face on it, however. It was not true.

Undaunted, she replied by marshalling ace photographers George Barris, Bert Stern and Douglas Kirkland to take the kind of pictures which would make her more desirable than ever to the ailing studio – and the ploy worked. Negotiations were entered into which resulted in the writ being dropped and Marilyn being reinstated at almost three times her previous

Mrs Eunice Murray was the keeper of secrets as well as of Marilyn's house.
*Robert F. Slatzer.*

salary. As far as the period immediately before her death was concerned, therefore, her relationship with the studio could not be construed as depressing or likely to drive her to suicide: quite the opposite.

From a professional point of view Marilyn's present looked secure and healthier than ever, and her future rosy. She was currently negotiating with Jules Styne a remake of *A Tree Grows in Brooklyn* as a musical with Frank Sinatra. On Sunday, 5 August, the day her death was reported, she was due to meet Sidney Skolsky to discuss a proposal for a film life story of blonde bombshell Jean Harlow, who had been Marilyn's ideal as a girl, and on the Monday afternoon she had an appointment with Gene Kelly to discuss plans for filming a story which was later released as *What a Way to Go*. Additionally, she had been offered an extremely lucrative deal with an Italian-based film company. There was no doubt that at this time life was full of promise for her.

To add to all this, Marilyn, who had always been an apartment

The house on Fifth Helena Drive was the first that Marilyn had ever owned, and she was very proud of her 'hacienda'.

dweller, had moved into the first house she had ever owned. It was a modest bungalow, far removed from the glitzy residences usually associated with top-ranking stars, but it was the right price and was built in the Mexican adobe style which she adored. She had still not furnished it fully when she died, but this did not stop her inviting her friends. Among her frequent visitors were her devoted make-up man Allan (Whitey) Snyder and her wardrobe lady, Marjorie Plecher, later to become Allan's wife, who often called in for a drink in the evening.

Her many other friends at this time included her coiffeur, the legendary Sydney Guilaroff, and her personal masseur, Ralph Roberts, who was by now a trusted friend. She maintained a firm friendship with Marlon Brando, with whom she had had an affair, and she and her ex-husband, Joe DiMaggio, remained on good terms. Frank Sinatra, who had been a friend of Joe DiMaggio's until they had fallen out, was close to her, and she included the other members of the 'rat pack'

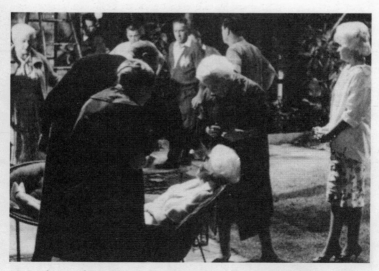

On the set of *Something's Got to Give* are acting coach Paula Strasberg (left), Whitey Snyder (behind) and, adding a touch to Marilyn's make-up, Agnes Flanagan; on the far right is Evelyn Moriarity, Marilyn's stand-in. *Robert F. Slatzer Collection.*

– Dean Martin, Sammy Davis Jr and especially Peter Lawford – among her friends. Until recently, when the relationship had become strained, her acting coaches, Lee and Paula Strasberg, had been firmly part of her inner circle. And then there were Pat Newcomb, her press secretary, Eunice Murray, her housekeeper-companion, and her doctors, Ralph Greenson and Hyman Engelberg.

But it has to be said that the make-up of the complex personality which was Marilyn Monroe also had a dark side. She was at times moody and morose. She experienced an unhappiness which penetrated her very bones and in her blackest moments found little solace in her friends, although those who have traced her life back to its unhappy roots find nothing surprising in this. She had overdosed several times, and though on each occasion she had carefully ensured that she would be discovered it was, superficially, these traumas which persuaded some people to regard her as suicidal. They had not considered the fact that those who really want to kill themselves make sure they will not be prevented from doing so. They had not recognised in these occurrences the classic cry for help which has long been acknowledged by psychologists.

There was much talk of a crisis of some sort during the weekend before Marilyn died. She had accepted an invitation to spend it at the Cal-Neva Lodge at Lake Tahoe. The place, owned by Frank Sinatra in partnership with Mafia figure Sam Giancana, was situated on the border between Nevada and California – hence its name. Sinatra was present, as were Peter Lawford and his wife, Pat, who was President Kennedy's sister. Dean Martin was there too and Marilyn took the opportunity to discuss with him *I Love Louisa*, a new film in which they were both due to appear. Giancana and another Mafia figure, Johnny Roselli, are commonly believed to have been there as well, though there are those who hotly deny this.

Her ex-husband Joe DiMaggio was also present at the Cal-Neva Lodge, but the details vary between accounts. One source records him and Marilyn being close and keeping a low profile; another, perhaps more realistically, says they were distinctly separate, since Joe was at loggerheads with Sinatra and not a guest. Joe was mad at Sinatra for inviting Marilyn to weekend parties of this kind which offered opportunities for sex, booze and drugs. In fact, accounts of the entire weekend vary. Some offer lurid reports of Marilyn being raped by Sam Giancana and overdosing as a consequence, while another scenario has her overdosing by accident and being walked about supported by the Lawfords and Frank Sinatra to offset the effects of the drugs. Whether there is truth in any of the stories is hard to say. It is even harder to see the weekend as some kind of composite of all these features, since DiMaggio was extremely jealous of any other man being involved with Marilyn and none of the events was feasible if she were in his company. But since Marilyn was a guest of the Lawford–Sinatra party, Joe being in her company at all must be most unlikely. More likely is the account in which they only saw each other at a distance, rendered by an employee of the Cal-Neva and described by Anthony Summers. Marilyn was standing there barefoot, swaying on the edge of the pool and staring upward. Her gaze, according to the employee, led to DiMaggio, standing in the driveway, staring back. Though

Mafia boss Sam Giancana was for a while co-owner with Frank Sinatra of the Cal-Neva Lodge.

it was said by some that she was quiet and withdrawn during the weekend, she nevertheless managed to be quite drunk when she was flown home in Sinatra's private plane.

The week which was to follow – her last week – was not stated to be anything other than a normal, busy week. It was rumoured by some that she planned to remarry Joe DiMaggio and was happy about that, which might be supported by an unfinished letter found in her possessions after she died.

Dear Joe,
If I can only succeed in making you happy – I will have succeeded in the bigest [sic] and most difficult thing there is – that is to make *one person completely happy*. Your happiness means my happiness and

Contradiction comes in the form of José Bolanos, a handsome Mexican fan with whom she had been romantically linked for some time. He had accompanied Marilyn to the Golden Globe awards on 5 March, and claimed to have spoken to her on the telephone the night she died. It would seem odd for her not to have broken off such a relationship if she intended remarrying Joe DiMaggio. None the less, the rumours were strong and the wedding was said to have been set for the Wednesday following the day she died, though Joe said nothing on the subject.

It was Joe DiMaggio who claimed Marilyn's body and made arrangements for the funeral and for her burial in a crypt at the small Westwood Memorial Park. But the funeral was something of a bitter affair, with many of Marilyn's friends excluded. Joe would not admit Sinatra, even though he, Ella Fitzgerald and Sammy Davis Jr turned up with security personnel to assert that they had permission to go into the chapel. Pat Lawford, a particularly close friend, was in tears. She had flown back to Los Angeles from Hyannis Port on the East Coast to join her husband at the funeral, but both were refused admission. A determined Joe had said to one of the funeral director's staff, 'Be sure that none of those damned Kennedys come to the funeral.' The night before the burial took place DiMaggio had spent a long time kneeling beside Marilyn's coffin.

Hundreds of reporters and photographers were in attendance and about a thousand fans gathered to watch the proceedings. A non-denominational minister said a few brief words and Lee Strasberg delivered the eulogy. 'Marilyn never liked goodbyes,' he said, 'but in the peculiar way she had of turning things around so that they faced reality, I will say *au revoir . . .*' Marilyn had been a fan of Judy Garland and this inspired the playing of 'Over the Rainbow'. Wreaths were sent by Frank Sinatra and comedian Jack Benny among others, and flowers arrived from another ex-husband, Arthur Miller, and his children. The twenty-four mourners admitted included Allan Snyder, Marjorie Plecher, the Greenson family and old friends the Kargers, the Strasbergs, Ralph Roberts and Pat Newcomb. Marilyn's lawyer Milton Rudin was also there.

Three times every week for the next twenty years, two red roses were delivered to Marilyn's crypt from Joe DiMaggio. When they ceased, long-time friend Robert Slatzer ordered white roses to be sent in an arrangement which will continue long after he dies.

\*

Marilyn's coffin is taken for burial in a crypt at Westwood Memorial Park. *AP Wide World.*

With a few notable exceptions, those who were close to Marilyn simply did not consider her a potential suicide. It was strange of Ralph Greenson to promote the idea of suicide and to say she had been 'very despondent' when her other friends – including friends who had spoken to her on that last day – were shocked and horrified by the news. It was true Marilyn had complained of not having a date for that Saturday night, but that was hardly an indication of desperation. Greenson's comments were stranger still when it is considered that, asked about Marilyn's disposition the last time they had seen her, both Pat Newcomb and Eunice Murray said she was in good spirits. Newcomb, who had stayed overnight on the Friday and did not leave until late afternoon, is quoted as saying that she was gay and happy, sunbathing and looking over film scripts. Murray was presumably in Marilyn's presence until she retired in the evening. She heard her talking to Joe DiMaggio Jr on the telephone as late as 7.30 p.m., when she was quite elated at the news that he had decided not to marry his girlfriend. And both Newcomb and Murray were in the house when Greenson was visiting Marilyn. Were they talking about the same woman?

When Arthur Miller was informed that she had taken her own life he responded, 'It had to happen . . . it was inevitable.' He did not apparently mean that he expected suicide, but rather that he would not have been surprised if one of her overdoses had gone wrong. 'It would have been easy if she had been simple: you could have helped her,' he said.

Since signing her revised contract with Fox Marilyn had bought a whole new wardrobe – hardly the act of someone so depressed that she was contemplating suicide. The same might be said of her appointment with Sidney Skolsky for the day on which she was found dead, not to mention a dinner date that night with Frank Sinatra and the internationally known restaurateur Mike Romanov and his wife, Gloria. She had also planned a busy day for Monday, the following day – apart from seeing Gene Kelly on business she had a date to play golf with her friend Jeanne Carmen. Looking ahead, she had made plans with Lena Pepitone for a Labor Day party at her Sutton Place apartment in New York. Marilyn's whole demeanour was one of a busy person absorbed in her daily affairs and, if anything, exhilarated by her new terms with Fox and her other prospects.

Something of a mystery surrounds the whereabouts of Paula Strasberg at the time Marilyn died. It seems that the rift between Marilyn and her old friend was not about to be healed, for just a few days before she died Marilyn signed a cheque for $205.59 to a travel agent for a plane ticket – a contractual obligation – for Paula to travel from Los Angeles to New York. The cheque was awaiting clearance at the City National Bank at Beverly Hills when Marilyn's death was announced, but though this suggests Paula Strasberg had just flown out of Los Angeles, there is no indication that she had been in touch with Marilyn before she died.

Shortly before she died Marilyn had expressed the intention of 'taking control of her life' and getting rid of some of those whom she no longer found helpful to have around. What did she mean by that? One possibility is that she was going to pull her love life out of the doldrums by remarrying Joe DiMaggio, as has been suggested, and that as a consequence certain people would become surplus to requirements. Another is that she intended making changes among those who were managing her business affairs. The departure of Paula Strasberg, at Marilyn's expense, may have been her marching orders and could have represented the first round fired. Her friend Jeanne Carmen has no doubt, however, that there was something else in the wind. She is convinced, she told me, that Marilyn had become disenchanted with her domestic arrangements and in particular Mrs Murray.

Her housekeeper was recommended to Marilyn by Ralph Greenson, her psychiatrist, and it appears that Mrs Murray was charged by Greenson with keeping a weather eye on her employer, though Marilyn knew nothing of this arrangement. Murray kept Greenson informed of her movements and activities. According to Robert Slatzer, Marilyn told a friend she felt she was being 'spied on' in her own home. Mrs Murray clearly had considerable influence on the star, soon introducing another member of her family into Marilyn's household. When Marilyn wanted a handyman she recommended her son-in-law, Norman Jeffries, and Marilyn took him on. This, however,

Marilyn's friend and neighbour Jeanne Carmen said that Marilyn came to dislike having Mrs Murray around. *Jeanne Carmen.*

was not the only 'in-breeding' among those who surrounded Marilyn. Frank Sinatra had recommended his lawyer, Milton (Mickey) Rudin, to her, as well as Ralph Greenson, who was Rudin's brother-in-law.

It was also strongly felt that Marilyn had decided to change her relationship with Ralph Greenson, upon whom she had been leaning excessively in the period before she died. She was seeing him as much as twice daily. Greenson had become more than a psychiatrist: he intruded into her business affairs, assuming the role of negotiator, and was known to make guarantees to the studio that he could 'deliver' her to the set ready for work. He had failed to prevent Fox from firing Marilyn, however, and she did not like failure. This, with a realisation that the psychiatrist kept her on too tight a rein, may have combined to make her anxious to make a fresh start.

'Marilyn couldn't walk across a room without advice and counsel and people with vested interest,' was the comment made by Peter Levathes, a Fox executive. Whatever the case, her resolution came too late.

# 3

# CORONER'S VERDICT

Five days after Marilyn had been found dead, Los Angeles County Coroner Theodore Curphey announced that she had died from barbiturate poisoning. On 17 August he declared, '. . . it is my conclusion that the death of Marilyn Monroe was caused by a self-administered overdose of sedative drugs and that the mode of death is probable suicide'.

The autopsy report was amended in the light of the coroner adding the word 'probable' to the verdict. Dr Noguchi, the autopsist, assured me in a recent conversation that when there is no suicide note and no clear intention of suicide can be

Los Angeles Medical Examiner-Coroner Theodore Curphey. He told the press he thought Marilyn had taken the capsules 'in one gulp, within – let's say – a period of seconds'. It was believed she had taken about forty Nembutals and a huge volume of chloral hydrate tablets. *Robert F. Slatzer Collection.*

the case report, written up and signed by a coroner's deputy, 'C. Pace', there may be an indication of doubt about suicide having existed earlier in the proceedings. The column entry heading 'Reported As' was responded to with a question mark against the 'suicide' sub-heading. Whatever the case, the authorities found no difficulty in firmly stonewalling on the suicide issue.

There is no doubt that a blanket of secrecy was thrown over Marilyn Monroe's death. A very few people, some friends, some journalists, realised this, but the great majority of people did not. Little more than a year later the same kind of thing happened with the John F. Kennedy assassination and, as in that tragedy, it would take years for the few who knew what was happening to be listened to. In the sixties the people of America had confidence in their government and trusted local officialdom. They believed what they were told and saw no reason for challenging the word of those who represented the authorities. By and large this went for the media too, and it was regarded as dishonest and even disloyal to give voice to doubts. Most people in the United States would now agree that it was the gradual exposure of a conspiracy to kill President Kennedy, and with it the revelation that the government had not told them the truth, which changed all this, and to this day confidence in government has not been restored. But at the time when Marilyn Monroe died it was taken for granted that what was announced by the Los Angeles authorities on the subject was correct and true. It was assumed that a competent investigation had been carried out by the police and that all avenues had been explored before finalising the matter as a version of suicide.

This was, of course, far from the truth. The Police Department merely scratched the surface – a shameful apology for an investigation. It was only the extremely successful cloak of secrecy which prevented the sham from being recognised then and for a long time afterwards. There was not so much as a coroner's inquest, which would have exposed the shortcomings in the police enquiries as well as the labyrinth of contradictions which had emerged. The coroner did not even establish the time of death. The police showed their hand very early in the proceedings by referring the death to the then recently formed

Suicide Prevention Team, whose terms of reference limited them to enquiring into the 'how' and the 'why' of a suicide, and not to delve into whether or not the death actually was suicide.

It was not the autopsy which justified closing the book on the Monroe case; far from it. The coroner at first asserted that a large volume of drugs had been ingested at once. The stomach, however, was empty. And despite the fact that the victim had supposedly taken a huge number of Nembutal capsules, neither the remnants of the gelatine capsules nor the tell-tale traces of the dye which colours them were found in the intestinal tract. Although this was by no means unique in cases of overdose, it was sufficiently unusual to warrant further investigation. It was explained away, however, by a later assertion that she must have ingested the large number of pills over a long period of time on the Saturday: in such cases the digestive system has time to dispose of the signs.

This, of course, did not explain how the victim survived long enough to ingest the large volume of drugs which they said was missing from her bedside. In the first place she would have succumbed long before she had taken the number of capsules involved, and since it is impossible for a body to continue to digest the contents of the stomach after death it ought to have shown the remains of gelatine and dye. In any case, thorough questioning of all those who spoke to and saw Marilyn during Saturday, 4 August, would have disposed of the idea that she spent a large part of the day ingesting drugs. This is not to say that she took none, but the shape and content of her day hardly permitted the kind of drug-taking which would have resulted in her death.

Yet Marilyn had certainly died from the effects of a massive drug overdose. It was interesting that analysis established that she had consumed no alcohol, which precluded her having died from an unfortunate mix of drugs and booze (she frequently washed down pills with champagne). Samples sent by Noguchi to toxicologist Raymond Abernathy, however, revealed that her blood contained 4.5 milligrams per cent of barbiturates – Nembutal – and 8 milligrams per cent of chloral hydrate. Further, her liver contained 13 milligrams per cent of pentobarbital, which also translates into Nembutal.

Taken separately, the barbiturates alone represented a very high drug intake. The number of Nembutal capsules required to produce 4.5 milligrams per cent in the blood is estimated as anything up to ninety. Similarly, the amount of chloral hydrate – also frequently used as a sedative and famed as 'knock-out drops' – was many times the recommended dosage.

Dr Noguchi quickly saw the two problems: that the drugs could not all have been taken at one time or all the tell-tale signs would have been present in the stomach, and that they could not have been taken gradually either, or she would have been dead long before the volume of drugs found in her liver could have been taken. At the start of the autopsy every inch of Marilyn's skin had been searched – a routine check against the possibility that she might have been injected with the fatal dosage. But though Noguchi used a magnifying glass and worked very hard he found no needle mark, and this theory had been abandoned.

Dr Thomas Noguchi conducted the autopsy, but when he wanted to follow up on his work he found that all the samples had been disposed of. *Thomas T. Noguchi (photo Judith Gordon).*

Some days after the initial autopsy Dr Noguchi decided he would conduct further tests on the samples taken of Marilyn's organs, but when he asked toxicologist Raymond Abernathy for them he was told they had been disposed of. Noguchi was nonplussed, but was told it seemed appropriate to get rid of them after a verdict had been reached. Whatever might have been deemed appropriate, it was by normal standards extremely unusual for specimens to be discarded in that way. Nevertheless, Noguchi's guns were well and truly spiked and further investigation was impossible.

Marilyn's last day displayed no vital clues which might have helped either Noguchi or the coroner. Certainly the terms in which Theodore Curphey appeared to see an open-and-shut case of suicide were not supported. Marilyn did not lock herself away in her bedroom during Saturday. Mid-morning she was grizzling at Pat Newcomb, who had stayed on Friday night and had just got up. It seems that the insomniac Marilyn envied Pat because she slept like a log. Marilyn, who had been awake a large part of the night and had started the day telephoning her friend Jeanne Carmen at 6 a.m., was not in the best of moods. But although Marilyn may have started the day aggressively, it could not be called suicidally.

Pat Newcomb was suffering from bronchitis and had thought of going into hospital for a rest, but Marilyn had persuaded her to stay the night instead since she could take the sun on her patio and have all the privacy she needed. They had had 'dinner at a quiet restaurant near her home' on the Friday night, according to Pat, and on Saturday she had found Marilyn quite happy as the day went on. Mrs Murray, notoriously unreliable in her testimony, said the same. Even in the evening, when Joe DiMaggio Jr had telephoned, she was bright and had sparkled at Joe Jr's news because she had apparently viewed his plan of marriage to the girl he had just broken from as a disaster waiting to happen. She was delighted when he told her he had changed his mind.

There were, however, a number of problems noted that day. Ralph Greenson made a statement to the effect that he had found her 'very despondent' and appearing somewhat drugged when he had visited her on Saturday afternoon. He claimed to have sent her off to the beach, driven by Mrs Murray, to cheer her up. Mrs Murray changed her mind about saying that Marilyn was in good spirits and supported Greenson in his version of things, as she always did, and Pat Newcomb also agreed with them later on. There may, however, have been a strong reason for this group to be inventive on the subject, as will be seen later. Ralph Greenson also said, however, in a conflicting statement, that Marilyn sounded 'quite pleasant' in a mid-evening phone call he had with her; in yet another statement, made a few days after she had died, he completely reversed on the subject and said that he did not believe Marilyn had committed suicide.

Peter Lawford said he telephoned at about 5 p.m. that Saturday afternoon with an invitation for Marilyn to join him and a few friends for supper; she had declined, saying she did not feel up to it. This was odd in the light of her ringing Greenson earlier in the day complaining that she did not have a date for that night. Lawford claims to have spoken to Marilyn again later that evening, at about 7.30 p.m., when her speech was thick and slurred and he had difficulty catching what she said. He said he asked her what the trouble was and tried to rouse her by shouting her name at her. Deborah Gould, to whom Peter Lawford was later married, said he confided to her that during that call Marilyn had said it would be best for everybody if she died, and she was going to kill herself. Gould reports Lawford's callous response as being, 'Nonsense, Marilyn, pull yourself together but . . . whatever you do don't leave any notes behind.' In another version, Lawford quotes Marilyn as saying, 'Say goodbye to Pat, say goodbye to the President, and say goodbye to yourself, because you're a nice guy.' She stopped speaking and there was no further noise on the line, said Lawford. He hung up and tried the number again, but got a busy signal.

The timing and content of Lawford's second call gives much cause for concern, since Joe DiMaggio Jr was calling Marilyn at about that time. The clash in timing seems to have been resolved by placing Joe Jr's call a little earlier and Lawford's call a little later than had been stated, for Joe Jr found he could check his timing with the particular stage reached in a baseball game which was on television while he made the call. This may resolve the problem of two calls supposedly made at the same time, but it contributes nothing towards explaining the apparent differences in Marilyn's state of mind between the two calls. Mrs Murray had said she sounded happy talking to Joe Jr, and this was confirmed by Joe Jr himself who said she was 'happy, gay and alert' and not depressed. Also, immediately after hanging up Marilyn called Greenson, and this was when he said she sounded 'quite pleasant' and 'more cheerful'. Could such a gross change possibly have occurred in the space of the few minutes which elapsed between these calls and Lawford's?

It is true that some of the people she spoke to on the telephone that evening picked up indications that she was not as bright and cheerful as she had been earlier in the day. Henry Rosenfeld, for instance, a wealthy garment manufacturer whom Marilyn had met in New York, rang at about 9 p.m. and reported her as sounding 'groggy'. Sydney Guilaroff, her coiffeur, spoke to her not long after Rosenfeld and said she had told him she was 'very depressed'. She hung up on him, he said. After this José Bolanos called and said she had simply placed the receiver down without hanging up at the end of the conversation, though he said it was not the first time she had done this. And Ralph Roberts, her masseur, said he thought she had tried to reach him when he was out and had been intercepted by his answering service. The answering service said he had received a call from someone with a slurred voice.

On the other hand, Marilyn rang Jeanne Carmen for the third time that day at about 10 p.m. – one of the last calls she is known to have made – and Jeanne did not find her speaking in a slurred voice or sounding incredibly low. Marilyn had been asking her to come over to see her all day, and in one of the earlier calls had asked her to bring a 'bag of pills' with her. Jeanne Carmen told me she did not find this unusual, for she had on occasions shared Nembutals and other pills with Marilyn. They were not, she said, difficult to obtain in those days and they had a lot to learn about messing with drugs. But on that day she had had misgivings about taking pills over. Besides, it was her birthday that day and she had a pretty full day planned. When she received the third call so late, she cried off because she was by then tired. Marilyn, she said, sounded 'nervous' and 'on edge', but she would not accept that she sounded worse than this. Deborah Gould revised the timing of the second call that Lawford made, placing it this time at a little after 10 p.m. but in view of Carmen's testimony it made no more sense then than it had at 7.30 p.m.

If Lawford's second call was made as late as ten o'clock it produced different timing problems. He claimed that it was after this call, in something of a panic, that he rang his manager and friend Milton Ebbins, who was also vice-president of the film production company he ran. He told him he thought something terrible was happening to Marilyn and he thought he should go over. Ebbins, he said, persuaded him not to go, since if the problem was drink and drugs it would be unseemly for the brother-in-law of the President to get involved and would create unwanted headlines. Better that Ebbins call her lawyer, Milton Rudin, he said, and have Rudin check it out. According to Rudin, Ebbins managed to locate him at 8.45 p.m. and he was calling the Monroe house at about 9 p.m. He asked Mrs Murray about Marilyn's physical wellbeing and, after a brief delay in which he believed Mrs Murray went off to see her employer, received the answer that she was all right. A police interview with Milton Rudin at the time of the investigation records, 'Believing that Miss Monroe was suffering from one of her despondent moments, Mr Rudin dismissed the possibility of anything further being wrong.' Since Rudin confirmed Ebbins' timing of the call to him and Mrs Murray confirmed the timing of Rudin's call to her, Deborah Gould's revised timing of Lawford's second call was obviously quite erroneous. This places Lawford's call almost straight after Joe DiMaggio Jr's call once again, with the impossible differences between the two unresolved. And there was a final twist to the tale of the Lawford account of telephone calls that evening.

For whatever reason Lawford was again panicking over Marilyn at about 11 p.m. and rang the Naarrs, his supper guests, who by then had got home and were going to bed. He told them he feared she had overdosed and Joe Naarr offered to go across to Fifth Helena Drive to check out what was happening. Before he left the house, however, he received another call from Peter Lawford telling

him it was a false alarm and there was no need to go
after all.

As will later be revealed, evidence exists which suggests that
Marilyn was dying by eleven o'clock, and if this is so it raises
many questions about the telephone calls from Lawford to
Naarr. What did he learn which prompted him to ring Naarr
in the first place, and what happened to make him cancel
everything a few minutes later? Did he obtain information he
was not revealing? Was he being updated on events at Marilyn's?
And was he trying to establish witnesses to a timescale which
suggested that all was well with Marilyn at 11.30 p.m.?

From out of the mass of contradictory detail which surrounds
the death of Marilyn Monroe, there is identifiable evidence of
the existence of a small group of people who were promoting
the idea of suicide. It was psychiatrist Ralph Greenson who
first pressed the suicide verdict. He called it such from first
reporting her death, with physician Hyman Engelberg keeping
a low profile on the subject. Greenson reinforced the idea when
he spoke of her being very low when he had visited her during
Saturday afternoon. As already noted, Mrs Murray and Pat
Newcomb changed their testimony and faithfully supported
him in his assertion, which clearly suited those in the Police
Department. With one exception, the telephone calls she made
and received during the evening which appeared to indicate that
Marilyn was disturbed only did so in the light of the evidence
of Greenson and company. By themselves they gave rise to no
alarm. None of those who spoke – later – of irregularities saw
the need to take any action: not Guilaroff nor Bolanos, nor
Rosenfeld nor Roberts. And all of these were people devoted
to Marilyn who would certainly have started alarm bells ringing
had they considered she was in any real trouble.

The odd call out, of course, was the second call from Lawford.
Peter Lawford was perhaps the most prominent member of this
group promoting the idea of suicide. Marilyn had been drawn
into the circle of people which surrounded him, and for this
reason she was frequently in his company. It seems she did not
especially like Lawford but was happy enough to spend time
with those to whom he was linked, and she was no stranger to

his impressive beach house which had once been owned by film magnate Louis B. Mayer. The conversation with Lawford in the second telephone call more than spelled out suicide, however: it bludgeoned the message home. 'Say goodbye to Pat, say goodbye to the President, and say goodbye to yourself, because you're a nice guy.' This left nothing to the imagination. But taking into account the rest of what Lawford said about the voice which came and went and which eventually trailed away to nothing, we are left with the enormous problem of how she could have been so obviously well and happy speaking to Joe DiMaggio Jr and Ralph Greenson, and so patently suicidal just a few minutes later.

As explained already, there were complications attached to moving this telephone conversation to another time in the evening. It seems that Deborah Gould tried to do this, and it clashed with a telephone call to Jeanne Carmen. In fact any other time between 7.30 p.m. and 10 a.m. would be questionable because of that late call to Carmen. Marilyn might have sounded

The Lawford beach house at Santa Monica had once belonged to movie magnate Louis B. Mayer. *Robert F. Slatzer.*

'nervous' and 'on edge', but by then she was betraying no signs of the trauma that Lawford attributed to her. There is no doubt that the locating of Lawford's second call is decidedly problematic. Given the various difficulties, it would be easy to believe that the call never in fact took place.

In 1985 a new complexion was put on the matter of the troublesome Lawford call. Detective Fred Otash was interviewed by the *Los Angeles Times*, and he had some interesting information about a telephone call between Lawford and Marilyn. It seems that within a short time of Marilyn dying, Lawford contacted Otash for certain help he needed and, to use the detective's own words, he looked 'half crocked and half nervous'. In this state he spoke about a phone call in which Marilyn had said, 'Tell him [the President] goodbye from me,' in an altogether different context from the one he spun around it for the press and the world. No goodbyes for Pat, no goodbyes for him. Nothing about suicide, no trailing voice, no phone going dead. She sounded normal. Lawford, in being inventive about this call and describing Marilyn as suicidal, was not aware of the telephone calls she had made and received that Saturday evening, neither did he know the times of them. He could not, therefore, slot the 'deterioration' into a time when her supposed state of mind was not contradicted by another call.

The Otash story, therefore, shed new light on a thorny problem. The temptation to throw out the story of Lawford's second call altogether had been resisted because of the checkable calls which were made between Lawford and Ebbins, Ebbins and Rudin, Rudin and Mrs Murray and all the way back down the line. This series of calls in turn produced their own mysteries, however. The basic reason for Lawford not dealing instantly with any problems that Marilyn might have had was full of holes. The idea of ringing Ebbins in the first place did not allow for the normal instinct to hop into the car and get across to Marilyn's as quickly as possible. If, of course, he really felt that proximity to drugs and drink might have been compromising for a brother-in-law of the President he could always have called the police. That way he need have been no more than a caller who became alarmed at what he had heard. And all things considered, when it came to booze and drugs Hollywood reporters had long been aware that Lawford had a very close acquaintance with them both.

Instead, according to the story given – and here is the real mystery relating to the series of calls – there was a delay before Lawford made contact with Milton Ebbins and a further delay of about an hour before Ebbins eventually contacted Rudin at a party. Had the whole thing been genuine, Marilyn might have been dead long since. The story rings hollow. It smacks of Peter Lawford using those around him to establish a case for suicide. And if this is so, then Lawford knew a whole lot more than he ever revealed about Marilyn's death. Here are two obvious questions. Exactly what did Peter Lawford know about Marilyn's death? And why was he so anxious to create 'evidence' that Marilyn planned to take her own life?

The answer to the first question remains obscure. The answer to the second can be summed up in the mention of two names: John F. and Robert F. Kennedy.

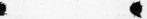

File # 81128

## OFFICE OF COUNTY CORONER

Date Aug. 5, 1962      Time 10:30 a.m.

I performed an autopsy on the body of   MARILYN MONROE
at the Los Angeles County Coroner's Mortuary, Hall of Justice, Los Angeles,
and from the anatomic findings and pertinent history I ascribe the death to:

ACUTE BARBITURATE POISONING

DUE TO      INGESTION OF OVERDOSE

(final 8/27/62)

### ANATOMICAL SUMMARY

EXTERNAL EXAMINATION:

1. Lavidity of face and chest with
   slight ecchymosis of the left side
   of the back and left hip.

2. Surgical scar, right upper quadrant
   of the abdomen.

3. Suprapubic surgical scar.

RESPIRATORY SYSTEM:

1. Pulmonary congestion and minimal
   edema.

LIVER AND BILIARY SYSTEM:

1. Surgical absence of gallbladder.

2. Acute passive congestion of liver.

UROGENITAL SYSTEM:

1. Congestion of kidneys.

DIGESTIVE SYSTEM:

1. Marked congestion of stomach with
   petechial mucosal hemorrhage.

The complete six-page autopsy report as submitted by Dr Noguchi.

2

2. Absence of appendix.

3. Congestion and purplish discoloration

of the colon.

EXTERNAL EXAMINATION:

The unembalmed body is that of a 36-year-old
well-developed, well-nourished Caucasian
female weighing 117 pounds and measuring
65½ inches in length. The scalp is covered
with bleached blond hair. The eyes are
blue. The fixed lividity is noted in the
face, neck, chest, upper portions of arms
and the right side of the abdomen. The
faint lividity which disappears upon pressure
is noted in the back and posterior aspect
of the arms and legs, A slight ecchymotic
area is noted in the left hip and left side
of lower back. The breast shows no significant lesion. There is a horizontal 3-inch
long surgical scar in the right upper
quadrant of the abdomen. A suprapubic
surgical scar measuring 5 inches in length
is noted.

The conjunctivae are markedly congested;
however, no ecchymosis or petechiae are
noted. The nose shows no evidence of
fracture. The external auditory canals
are not remarkable. No evidence of trauma
is noted in the scalp, forehead, cheeks,
lips or chin. The neck shows no evidence
of trauma. Examination of the hands and
nails shows no defects. The lower extremities show no evidence of trauma.

BODY CAVITY:

The usual Y-shaped incision is made to
open the thoracic and abdominal cavities
The pleural and abdominal cavities contain

Marilyn Monroe
# 81128
Aug. 5, 1962

3

no excess of fluid or blood. The mediastinum
shows no shifting or widening. The diaphragm
is within normal limits. The lower edge
of the liver is within the costal margin.
The organs are in normal position and
relationship.

## CARDIOVASCULAR SYSTEM:

The heart weighs 300 grams. The pericardial
cavity contains no excess of fluid. The
epicardium and pericardium are smooth and
glistening. The left ventricular wall
measures 1.1 cm. and the right 0.2 cm.
The papillary muscles are not hypertrophic.
The chordae tendineae are not thickened or
shortened. The valves have the usual number
of leaflets which are thin and pliable.
The tricuspid valve measures 10 cm., the
pulmonary valve 6.5 cm., mitral valve 9.5
cm. and aortic valve 7 cm. in circumference.
There is no septal defect. The foramen
ovale is closed.

The coronary arteries arise from their usual
location and are distributed in normal
fashion. Multiple sections of the anterior
descending branch of the left coronary artery
with a 5 mm. interval demonstrate a patent
lumen throughout. The circumflex branch
and the right coronary artery also demonstrate
a patent lumen. The pulmonary artery contains
no thrombus.

The aorta has a bright yellow smooth intima.

## RESPIRATORY SYSTEM:

The right lung weighs 465 grams and the left
420 grams. Both lungs are moderately congested
with some edema. The surface is dark red
with mottling. The posterior portion of the
lungs shows severe congestion. The tracheo-
bronchial tree contains no aspirated material
or blood. Multiple sections of the lungs

Marilyn Monroe
# 81128
Aug. 5, 1962

4

show congestion and edematous fluid exuding
from the cut surface. No consolidation or
suppuration is noted. The mucosa of the
larynx is grayish white.


LIVER AND BILIARY SYSTEM:

The liver weighs 1890 grams. The surface
is dark brown and smooth. There are marked
adhesions through the omentum and abdominal
wall in the lower portion of the liver as
the gallbladder has been removed. The
common duct is widely patent. No calculus
or obstructive material is found. Multiple
sections of the liver show slight accentuation
of the lobular pattern; however, no hemorrhage
or tumor is found.


HEMIC AND LYMPHATIC SYSTEM:

The spleen weighs 190 grams. The surface
is dark red and smooth. Section shows dark
red homogeneous firm cut surface. The
malpighian bodies are not clearly identified.
There is no evidence of lymphadenopathy.
The bone marrow is dark red in color.


ENDOCRINE SYSTEM:

The adrenal glands have the usual architec-
tural cortex and medulla. The thyroid glands
are of normal size, color and consistency.


URINARY SYSTEM:

The kidneys together weigh 350 grams. Their
capsules can be stripped without difficulty.
Dissection shows a moderately congested
parenchyma. The cortical surface is smooth.
The pelves and ureters are not dilated or
stenosed. The urinary bladder contains

Marilyn Monroe
# 81128
Aug. 5, 1962

5

## GENITAL SYSTEM:

The external genitalia shows no gross
abnormality. Distribution of the pubic
hair is of female pattern. The uterus
is of the usual size. Multiple sections
of the uterus show the usual thickness of
the uterine wall without tumor nodules.
The endometrium is grayish yellow, measuring
up to 0.2 cm in thickness. No polyp or
tumor is found. The cervix is clear,
showing no nabothian cysts. The tubes are
intact. The openings of the fimbria are
patent. The right ovary demonstrates
recent corpus luteum haemorrhagicum. The
left ovary shows corpora lutea and albicantia.
A vaginal smear is taken.

## DIGESTIVE SYSTEM:

The esophagus has a longitudinal folding
mucosa. The stomach is almost completely
empty. The contents is brownish mucoid
fluid. The volume is estimated to be no
more than 20 cc. No residue of the pills
is noted. A smear made from the gastric
contents and examined under the polarized
microscope shows no refractile crystals.
The mucosa shows marked congestion and
submucosal petechial hemorrhage diffusely.
The duodenum shows no ulcer. The contents
of the duodenum is also examined under
polarized microscope and shows no refractile
crystals. The remainder of the small
intestine shows no gross abnormality. The
appendix is absent. The colon shows
marked congestion and purplish discoloration.
The fecal contents is light brown and formed.
The mucosa shows no discoloration.

The pancreas has a tan lobular architecture.
Multiple sections shows a patent duct.

Marilyn Monroe
# 81128
Aug. 5, 1962

6

SKELETOMUSCULAR SYSTEM:

The clavicle, ribs, vertebrae and pelvic
bones show no fracture lines. All bones
of the extremities are examined by palpation
showing no evidence of fracture.

HEAD AND CENTRAL NERVOUS SYSTEM:

The brain weighs 1440 grams. Upon reflection
of the scalp there is no evidence of contusion
or hemorrhage. The temporal muscles are
intact. Upon removal of the dura mater the
cerebrospinal fluid is clear. The superficial vessels are slightly congested. The
convolutions of the brain are not flattened.
The contour of the brain is not distorted.
No blood is found in the epidural, subdural
or subarachnoid spaces. Multiple sections
of the brain show the usual symmetrical
ventricles and basal ganglia. Examination
of the cerebellum and brain stem shows no
gross abnormality. Following removal of
the dura mater from the base of the skull
and calvarium no skull fracture is demonstrated.

Liver temperature taken at 10:30 a. m.
registered 89° F.

SPECIMEN:

Unembalmed blood is taken for alcohol and
barbiturate examination. Liver, kidney,
stomach and contents, urine and intestine
are saved for further toxicological study.
A vaginal smear is made.

T. NOGUCHI, M. D.
DEPUTY MEDICAL EXAMINER

TN:ag:G

# 4

# OUT OF CONTROL

For many years the biggest argument about Marilyn Monroe raged around the question of whether she had been romantically involved with Attorney General Robert Kennedy, brother of the President. In the sixties the name of Kennedy was greatly revered and the relatively few top writers who dared broach the subject of such a relationship moved with stealth and spoke only of 'an important man' in Marilyn's life. To have mentioned the man by name would have resulted in the wary editors not cooperating at any price. The editors had their own special fears: not the obvious ones about costly legal wrangles – which alone might have been justified – but rather fears about Internal Revenue probes and other forms of harassment which might suddenly have descended upon them.

To tell the story without actually mentioning the name was termed using a 'blind item' technique. Walter Winchell and Dorothy Kilgallen, two of the nation's top newspaper columnists, adopted such tactics, Kilgallen leading with: 'Marilyn Monroe is cooking in the sex appeal department. She has appeared vastly alluring to a handsome gentleman. A handsome gentleman with a bigger name than Joe DiMaggio in his heyday – so don't write her off.' In 1962, only a few months after Marilyn died, *Photoplay* magazine printed a feature story in which the man was all but named. He was described as someone whose career had reached heights beyond what he had expected and who would achieve even greater things; he was also credited with being 'free of scandal' and an otherwise devoted husband. In the story Marilyn was said to have called the man the night she died, when he told her he could not leave his wife and would not be able to see her any more. The feature was a sensation, creating ripples which reached high places. It was quite obvious that it was talking about Robert F. Kennedy.

J. Edgar Hoover, no doubt with a degree of malicious pleasure – for there was no love lost between the head of the FBI and the Attorney General, his boss – gave warning of the intended bombshell to Robert Kennedy, who could do little about it. A few months later Hoover returned to RFK to report that a hard-hitting booklet written by an extreme right-wing activist, Frank A. Capell, was about to be published. Capell had no compunction about naming the Attorney General as the man who had had a relationship with Marilyn Monroe, and he also hinted in his slim volume that Robert Kennedy was with Marilyn shortly before she died. The single-minded Capell, however, was more interested in discrediting Robert Kennedy than in resolving what had happened to Marilyn Monroe, and his political sympathies diluted the effect of his book. In fact it only had a very limited circulation and was not released to the public.

When it came to books for the mass market by known authors, two early works by Fred Lawrence Guiles created a great deal of curiosity about the possible involvement of Robert Kennedy. In his earliest writings on the subject, in about 1967, Guiles moved a little closer than the columnists to identifying Kennedy when he spoke of 'The Easterner'. But even in 1967 he did not use the name in *Norma Jean* since he was not, he later said, prepared to blow Kennedy out of the political water with revelations about his liaison with Marilyn while he was a candidate for the presidency. Had Guiles felt differently, there is no doubt that this is what would have happened in view of his standing as a writer. Revisions to editions which appeared after Robert Kennedy's death, however, included the mention of his name.

While the 'blind item' articles remained 'blind items' they were ignored. An unsuspecting public could regard the reports as juicy gossip or tasteless tittle-tattle. However, some people could place them in context and see the importance of what was being implied, while others read between the lines and, though they were unaware of the details, recognised that here was an enormous scandal just waiting to break. In this latter group were the power brokers and the politicians – politicians who were the Kennedys' friends and politicians who were their enemies.

The Kennedy family, for their part, have always staunchly ignored any claims that Robert was involved in any other way but casually, and entirely properly, with Marilyn Monroe. But then, as far as steamy relationships were concerned, denials were required not only for Robert; there was also Jack.

It was no secret to Washington correspondents that something was going on between John F. Kennedy and Marilyn Monroe. Hollywood's gossip columnists were also in the know, and it was not uncommon knowledge among New York journalists. The press knew about other women, too, but chose to remain silent for a variety of reasons. One was that some editors were simply wary of crossing the Kennedys, and they also had to make allowances for the political persuasions of the owners of their papers. The argument that journalists saw the President's

John F. Kennedy. *US National Archives*.

private life as his own concern, which has been put forward by some of the more recent writers as an explanation for them doing and saying nothing about Kennedy's indiscretions, is hard to believe. Even in this age of moral laxity the behaviour of the US President is constantly under scrutiny, while in the fifties and early sixties it was infinitely more so. A full-blown scandal would have demolished the Kennedy presidency and the press corps knew it, but there were huge problems in reporting such philanderings. The public would not have swallowed casual reports about the misbehaviour of their President: to make any impact would have required a whole campaign based on cast-iron evidence – hearsay and the drawing of conclusions would certainly not have been enough. And then, not the least of the editors' problems was the risk of such a campaign rebounding on them if it was seen as an anti-Kennedy smear. It would have been enough to wipe out a whole newspaper.

Jack Kennedy first met Marilyn in the mid-fifties, long before he became President, when their paths crossed at a Hollywood party thrown by Charles Feldman, a friend of JKF's, who had become Marilyn's agent. At the time Marilyn was married to Joe DiMaggio and their early relationship was purely social. It was not until 1961 that things changed.

In June that year Marilyn had accepted an invitation to attend Frank Sinatra's opening at the Sands in Las Vegas. She rarely attended such occasions, but this time had gone along in the company of Peter Lawford and his wife Pat, John F. Kennedy's sister. Another of John F.'s sisters, Jean Smith, joined the party which occupied a ringside table. The festivities went on for days, and when they finally ended Marilyn flew back to Los Angeles with the Lawfords. At the same time Jack Kennedy, now President of the United States, flew out to Los Angeles, and it would seem that this marked the time when the relationship between him and Marilyn became something else.

It was also in the summer of 1961 that President Kennedy was in New York and stayed at the Hotel Carlyle, where he had a suite. Marilyn was brought to him there for what was supposedly a secret meeting – one of the most publicised best-kept secrets in the history of journalism. Following this there were numerous clandestine meetings, some of which were arranged by 'beards'. The beard, whover he was, was there to give the impression that he was dating Marilyn, although in fact he was bringing her secretly to Jack Kennedy. When JFK visited the West Coast Peter Lawford acted as a beard, inviting Marilyn to his beach house when Jack Kennedy was visiting.

Marilyn and Jack were said to have flown off together on holiday in the *Caroline*, the President's aircraft, and were known to meet on various other occasions, Marilyn sometimes disguising herself by wearing a wig and carrying a stenographer's pad. It is well known that Jack Kennedy had liaisons with many other women, though it seems that his relationship with Marilyn was the only one which became serious. She was heard to remark, 'I wish he hadn't married Jackie. I'd like to be his wife.' The relationship, then, was obviously serious to Marilyn too.

The most public manifestation of their relationship was at the glittering celebration of the President's forty-fifth birthday at Madison Square Garden on 19 May 1962. This was the

The President's forty-fifth birthday party at Madison Square Garden. Marilyn placed her relationship with Twentieth Century-Fox on the line to fly to New York to sing 'Happy birthday, Mr President'. *John F. Kennedy Library.*

occasion on which Marilyn ducked out of her responsibilities at Twentieth Century-Fox to fly to New York to sing 'Happy birthday, Mr President', wearing a rhinestone-embroidered silk gown into which, if not poured, she was sewn, and left little to the imagination.

There is no doubt that for a President of the United States who purported to be a happily married family man to conduct himself in such a manner carried enormous risks, and Kennedy knew it. He was ever conscious of his need to improve on the ultra-slim margin of votes which had placed him in the White House, and a sex scandal in the hands of his political enemies on the run-up to the next election could easily have been his undoing. And this was not the only problem caused by Jack Kennedy's relationship with Marilyn. It was believed that Jackie knew what was going on and had, for instance, stayed away from the birthday celebration for that reason. It was even reported that she was theatening divorce; the break-up of their marriage would have spelt certain political ruin for John F. Kennedy, and he decided that it was time to call a halt.

Calling a halt was no easy thing with Marilyn, and according to interviews given by Deborah Gould, Peter Lawford's third wife, Jack sent his brother Robert to placate her and to explain matters. It was simple for a meeting to be arranged by their mutual friend Peter Lawford, and it took place at a party at the actor's beach house. But it seems that Robert, who had no reputation for womanising, fell under Marilyn's spell and one dangerous liaison was replaced by another.

Accounts vary on when Robert Kennedy first became friendly with Marilyn. Some think the affair began about a year before she died, and her friend Jeanne Carmen said in an interview with me that it could have been as long as a year, though to her memory it was more likely to have been about six months. 'I saw them together at least half a dozen times – in her apartment, at the beach, at Lawford's beach house – during that time.' Marilyn tried hard to please Robert. Because the subjects he raised in conversation were sometimes unfamiliar to her, after their meetings she made notes. Details of topics and terminology went into a red dairy so that she could remind herself of them before future meetings.

As with Jack, Marilyn grew serious about Robert, and it would appear that this was not without encouragement. She told her old friend Robert Slatzer that Robert had said he intended divorcing Ethel and marrying her. Unbelievable as this was, it seems that Marilyn had lost touch with reality in regard to her relationship with the Attorney General. As for Robert, it was all something of a new experience for him. He did, however, appear to enter into it with gusto and became somewhat careless and even unconcerned about being seen with Marilyn. Her friend Jeanne Carmen, her studio maid Hazel Washington and the housekeeper Eunice Murray all saw them together, and they are by no means the only ones. This was strange behaviour for a man who had been named Father of the Year. It was also strange behaviour for an astute politician who knew it led in a straight line to political embarrassment, even disaster.

A most revealing letter from Jean Kennedy Smith was discovered among Marilyn's effects many years after her death.

Dear Marilyn
Mother asked me to write and thank you for your sweet note to Daddy – he really enjoyed it and you were very cute to send it.
Understand that you and Bobby are the new item!
We all think you should come with him when he comes back east.
Love,
Jean Smith

Jean Kennedy Smith did not admit until much later that the letter was genuine – in 1994, when the letter was auctioned, raising public eyebrows – but scorned it being taken seriously. She said it was a joke.

But this interpretation was most unlikely, and the letter appeared to imply a degree of approval on the part of certain family members. It is hard to imagine Rose Kennedy sharing any enthusiasm that the others may have felt, however, as she sternly disapproved of the philandering of her sons. This reached

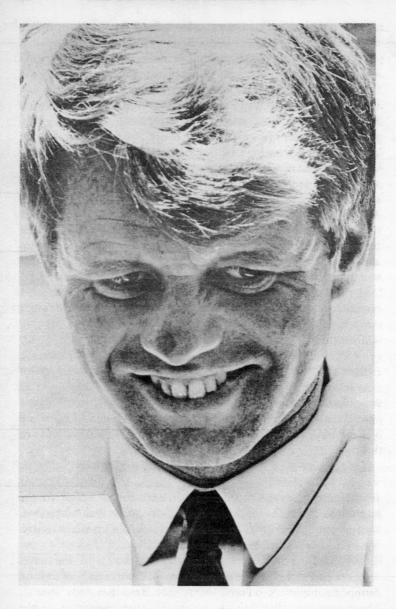

Marilyn grew serious about Robert Kennedy. *John F. Kennedy Library.*

crisis point when she was recruited to help in the campaign being mounted by youngest son, Edward, in his bid for the Senate. She put her foot down and called a halt to the brothers' extra-marital activities in view of the risk of adverse publicity.

If their mother thought in such terms, it is rather incredible that her sons in high office could not put their dangerous activities in perspective. Robert would never know it, but during his campaign for the party nomination for the presidency just a few years later taped evidence of his affair with Marilyn was being sought by a 'cross-party group' in order to discredit him. I obtained the full story from Washington-based Ralph de Toladeno, who was commissioned by the group to locate the tapes. He told me he had done so, but then news of Robert Kennedy's murder broke and the acquisition of this evidence did not take place.

As with Jackie Kennedy in relation to Jack's affair with Marilyn, so with Ethel Kennedy: it was only a queston of time before she got to know what was going on. It was natural that she would challenge him and demand that he abandoned the relationship. Some people believe she threatened divorce, which would probably have brought his political career to an ignominious end – particularly since he was the holder of the Father of the Year accolade. This may not have been the entire reason for his sudden decision to end the affair, however. The enormous risks he was taking finally, it would seem, penetrated his awareness. The perilous predicament that he had forged for himself was a powder keg ready to blow, and he was well aware that his political enemies carried matches . . .

There was probably one indication, if Marilyn recognised it, that he had decided to call it a day. Jeanne Carmen told me of an occasion when she was at Marilyn's apartment while Robert Kennedy was visiting. He saw the red diary and yelled at Marilyn, 'Get rid of this!', throwing the book across the room. Marilyn was nonplussed and her friend embarrassed. In Jeanne's view this marked the end of the relationship.

And when Robert Kennedy called it a day he called it a day: he dropped completely out of Marilyn's life, leaving her bewildered. There were no calls from him to explain matters, neither could she reach him anywhere. The special number he had given her at the Justice Department did not respond; she discovered it had been disconnected, and his office would not accept her calls. She was beside herself. After all, this was no casual relationship. He had promised to marry her when he divorced Ethel, and Marilyn had entertained ideas about becoming a member of the revered Kennedy family. Her thoughts had perhaps even strayed as far as one day becoming America's first lady. To treat her this way was unthinkable. What had she done? Why was he doing this to her? When the silence continued, she became furious.

She wanted to ask Robert's sister, Pat Lawford, with whom she was on best friend terms, how to reach her brother, but Pat was out east at the Kennedy compound at Hyannis Port in Massachusetts. Peter Lawford had gone to earth when Robert Kennedy had signalled the end of the affair, but Marilyn sought him out and obtained a number on which she could reach his wife. Whether Pat ever told her what she wanted to know is uncertain, but we know she obtained the information that the Attorney General was flying to the West Coast that Friday with Ethel and four of their children. He was delivering an address to the American Bar Association convention early the following week and in the meantime having a break at the ranch of an attorney friend, John Bates, south of San Francisco.

Marilyn also knew that when RFK spent time on the West Coast he stayed at the St Francis Hotel in San Francisco and, indeed, the Bar Association had booked a suite for him there to use as an office. The *San Francisco Chronicle*, covering his arrival at the airport, commented on the absence of his 'usual flashy smile' and suggested that the cares of the administration may have been 'weighing heavily on him'. The switchboard at the St Francis Hotel now became the target for Marilyn's telephone calls, but not one of her messages received any response. She was livid. Could he not have called her to explain and to say goodbye? This was the second Kennedy to dump her unceremoniously. But she would have her moment. She would take the initiative and call the shots. She would bring Robert Kennedy to heel by spreading the word that she intended to call a press conference for 11 a.m. the following Monday, at which she would blow the whistle on both the Kennedy brothers to the nation's press.

That did it. The news reached the ears of Justice Department staff, who called Robert Kennedy in San Francisco. 'You'd better get your ass down to LA because she's out of control,' was the undiplomatic signal he received. Presumably having left Ethel and the children at the Bates ranch, Kennedy flew into Los Angeles. Accounts vary on whether it was later on the Friday or on the Saturday that he went by helicopter to the Fox lot, from where he was whisked to the Beverly Hilton Hotel in a limousine. An employee at the hotel is quoted as saying that he spent the Friday night there, though in fact it may have been that he booked and paid for the suite for that night and did not arrive until the following morning. Marilyn's dinner arrangements would suggest this.

At about seven on Friday evening food was delivered to Marilyn's house by Briggs' Delicatessen. Clearly her intention was to entertain someone for dinner and since delicacies of various kinds, hors d'oeuvres and champagne were included, a special guest was indicated. There is no doubt about either the delivery of the food or the items in question, for in order to be paid Briggs were obliged to make a claim for the sum of $49.07 against Marilyn's estate. (This has been quoted elsewhere as £150 but I have taken the lower figure.) In 1962 values $49.07 was quite a large sum, so no expense had been spared. The problem lay with the guest, who failed to turn up. Marilyn and Pat Newcomb were seen out dining at a restaurant on the Sunset Strip a little later that evening and Marilyn was reported as being the worse for drink. As Robert Slatzer pointed out in his book *The Marilyn Files*, since no one has ever admitted to being the guest who never showed, there is a strong indication that it was Robert Kennedy who was expected and, perhaps because his schedule had broken down and he never reached Los Angeles that Friday night, he failed to appear. Perhaps, also, that was the reason for Marilyn being a little tipsy.

When Marilyn spoke to journalist Sidney Skolsky on the telephone on Saturday morning she told him she was going to see Robert Kennedy that evening. The manner in which she bandied the Kennedy name about made Skolsky nervous, though there was little he could do except keep his own tongue silent. But it is clear that if the arrangements for them to meet came adrift as the day went on since Marilyn, strangely, made a

Creditor's Claim No. P-458935

Affidavit of creditor, D. J. Briggs, subscribed and sworn to on April 26, 1963,

before William G. Sharp, County Clerk, Superior Court of California, in and for

the County of Los Angeles.


            IN THE SUPERIOR COURT OF THE STATE OF CALIFORNIA IN AND
                  FOR THE COUNTY OF LOS ANGELES

In the Matter of the Estate of                              CREDITOR'S CLAIM
     Marilyn Monroe
                 Deceased.

Date of death:  August 5, 1962.
Date of first pub. notice to creditors:   March 4, 1963.

Don J. Briggs, Incorporated                        , whose address is
   (if claimant is executor or administrator, must so state)

13038 San Vicente Boulevard, Los Angeles 49, California

is a creditor of the above named decedent and presents the following claim:

| Date of Item | Description of Item | Amount Claimed |
|---|---|---|
| | Merchandise sold and delivered in accordance with attached invoice. | 215.41 |

---

BRIGGS   wines                                              EXbrook 5-9997
  "      spirits          13038 San Vicente, Los Angeles 49   GRanite 6-1223
         unusual foods

         Marilyn Monroe
         12305 - 5th Helena Dr.
         Los Angeles 49, Calif.

| Date | Charges | Credits | Balance |
|---|---|---|---|
| Balance forward | | | |
| July 11, '62 | 65.28 | | |
| 19 | 57.75 | | |
| 30 | 43.31 | | |
| Aug. 3 | 49.07 | | 215.41 |

                                          Your balance is
                                          last amount in
                                          this column

   Payments are due on or before the 10th of the month following the date of
                                                           purchase.
BRIGGS                          13038 San Vicente Blvd., Los Angeles, 49

T R U E
      C O P Y

   The Briggs food store claim submitted for payment after Marilyn's death.
     On Friday, 3 August, she had expensive food delivered.

half-arrangement to have dinner on the patio with her masseur, Ralph Roberts, to whom she also spoke on the telephone that morning, but presumably long after she had spoken to Skolsky. Roberts agreed to call her again in the early evening to confirm arrangements, though when he rang at about 6.30 p.m. Dr Greenson, who was paying a house call at that time, curtly told him that Marilyn was not in. By all indications the dinner date with Robert Kennedy was originally quite firm but then cancelled, though nothing is known of a call from Kennedy in the late morning.

A possible solution lies in the cause of Marilyn being quite upset and somewhat depressed during the late morning and early afternoon. When hairdresser Agnes Flanagan was at the house during the morning, a special delivery package arrived which contained a stuffed toy tiger. She saw Marilyn clutching it and observed that she was clearly upset, but did not know why. It so absorbed Marilyn that Flanagan, no doubt feeling something of an intruder, left. Could the tiger have accompanied a note, perhaps cancelling the evening arrangement? Or was the tiger itself the message? A message of goodbye? From Robert Kennedy?

Had Robert Kennedy made an arrangement to have dinner with Marilyn that Friday night and, finding it necessary to cancel, made a Saturday dinner date which he also broke? If so, it is small wonder she was upset. But then why, if he would not have dinner with her, did he visit her house that Saturday? He paid two visits: the time of the first, in the afternoon, is uncertain, but a neighbour was witness to him being there. He was seen arriving at about 7 p.m. If certain accounts of what happened at their meetings, derived from a bug, are accurate, it would seem that the events encapsulated everything that their relationship had now become. Kennedy went to Marilyn's house to carry out an essential chore and, failing to complete it, went back. He had apparently decided that a romantic dinner did not provide the setting for what he had to do. The soft soap was out; the hard man was in.

He was angry, but then her threat to go public had hit its mark. She reminded him of his promise to marry her but he was more concerned, it seemed, with locating and removing

her red diary with its notes about their discussion, which was
at least politically dangerous and possibly constituted a security
risk. By all indications these were bitchy, ill-tempered meetings,
and Robert Kennedy, by reputation, was capable of excelling
at both. He did not find the diary and, since Marilyn did not
enlighten him as to its whereabouts, he left empty-handed. He
had seen Marilyn for the last time.

After spending a little time at the beach house Robert Kennedy
called at his hotel to pick up his things, and was soon whirring
to the airport in a helicopter that Peter Lawford had hired for
him. From here he made his way to San Francisco. Within a
very few hours, Marilyn was dead.

# 5

# ABSENCE OF TRUTH

The mystery which lies behind the death of Marilyn Monroe has been well concealed by the Los Angeles Police Department. As though this were not enough, it would seem that those nearest to Marilyn and involved in the discovery of her body made false or misleading statements. Had certain statements been made to a coroner's court those involved would have been lucky to escape with a warning and might well have been prosecuted for perjury. Enquiries, such as they were, were conducted by the police, who were not seeking false statements. But the coroner saw fit not to hold an official inquest, and at his behest the police quickly deferred to the newly formed Suicide Team, set up to investigate primarily the circumstances and state of mind of suicides and to evolve a strategy for suicide prevention.

Dr Ralph Greenson was, of course, the first to muddy the waters by changing his various statements. He first claimed he was called to the Monroe house at about midnight, but this left an awkward, unexplained gap until 4.25 a.m. when the police were called. For midnight he then substituted 3.30 a.m. which resolved the problem of the gap but created new problems relating to the signing of the death certificate. That certificate was signed by Dr Hyman Engelberg at 3.50 a.m. which now meant that Dr Greenson was claiming that he dressed and drove to Fifth Helena Drive, then called Engelberg, who dressed and drove to Fifth Helena Drive, examined the body and signed the death certificate – all in the space of twenty minutes. This was quite impossible. (The time of 3.50 a.m. was shown on Sergeant R. E. Byron's Follow-Up Report. On his first report the time was shown as 3.35 a.m. which would have been an even greater impossibility. The statement made to Sergeant Jack Clemmons that Marilyn was pronounced dead shortly after 12.30 a.m. was totally incompatible with the revised timings for events given by Mrs Murray and Dr Greenson.)

In one contradictory claim which was made, it was Mrs Murray who called Dr Engelberg and, indeed, Dr Engelberg himself said it was Mrs Murray who had telephoned him. Had Mrs Murray called Engelberg immediately after calling Greenson this would have relieved the timescale slightly, but would not have accounted for the apparent absence of Engelberg during the sequence of events said to have led to the discovery of the body. In all the accounts of Dr Engelberg arriving it was later than Greenson and *after* the discovery of the body.

When the coroner's official, Guy Hockett, collected the body at 5.30 a.m. he commented that rigor mortis was so advanced that he had to bend her arms in order to strap her on to the gurney. His estimate was that she had been dead for several hours. Had the police obtained this information, it should

Dr Hyman Engelberg. *Robert F. Slatzer Collection.*

have suggested to them that Greenson's claim of a midnight call was more realistic than 3.30 a.m., reintroducing the long time delay problem. From an interview with a well-informed source close to the Greenson family, who has asked not to be named, I learnt that Dr Greenson, having been out with his wife for dinner that evening, was in fact called to the Monroe house by Mrs Murray shortly after midnight.

The changes made to the timescale by Dr Greenson were, perhaps, more significant than has been realised, since he was a man of great integrity and must have felt he had a compelling reason for the discrepancies he introduced. The same might be said about the fact that three days after her death he contradicted his original adamant claim that Marilyn had committed suicide. During questioning by Deputy District Attorney John Miner, he admitted that he did not believe it was true. Had something occurred in that brief period to make him change his mind, or had he been engaged in deception from the beginning? Had he decided to come clean? Could Dr Greenson have been entrapped in some wider conspiracy? Noticeably everyone else who was at the Monroe house at the time the police were called went along with his changing timescales and the suicide theory.

Ralph Greenson's story about breaking Marilyn's bedroom window to gain entry from outside when he found her dead is also seen as a fabrication in the light of Robert Slatzer's discovery that the broken glass had fallen on to the ground *outside* the window; this claim was supported by Eunice Murray's handyman son-in-law, who also noticed the glass. Mrs Murray was, of course, his main support in this assertion, but she was not a pillar of reliability or consistency.

Mrs Murray was perhaps the ace deceiver when it came to describing Marilyn's final hours and the discovery of her body. She introduced a tissue of lies into the story, beginning with the events of the Saturday when she strongly denied seeing Robert Kennedy at the house. She admitted this deception in 1985 when participating in a BBC television documentary. After giving her usual story to camera, Mrs Murray was unaware that she was still wired for sound. She suddenly said, 'Why, at my age, do I still have to cover this thing?' and admitted she had been lying about Robert Kennedy's presence at the house.

He had indeed been there. Evidence of this has been obtained from elsewhere, but when Mrs Murray finally admitted it she was virtually confirming that there had been a conspiracy of silence, as had long been suspected.

Another statement made by Mrs Murray related to a question which she said Marilyn had asked on that Saturday. Marilyn had apparently enquired whether there was any oxygen in the house. This would have constituted strong indication of an intention to attempt a 'cry for help' suicide, but, since Marilyn never kept oxygen in the house and there was no reason why she should believe that her housekeeper had put it on a shopping list, it sounded like an invention of Mrs Murray's designed to underpin a suicide theory.

Mrs Murray supported Dr Greenson in his first statement that he was called about midnight and also in his second statement that he was called at about 3.30 a.m. She supported him also in the broken window story, which was linked to her claim to Sergeant Jack Clemmons that, after going to bed at 10 p.m. she woke at about midnight and was making her way to the bathroom when she saw a light under Marilyn's bedroom door with a telephone wire running beneath it. She said she knocked on the door and, alarmed when she received no response, called Dr Greenson. He came to the house promptly, and when he too could not rouse Marilyn they both went outside and looked through the bedroom window. Seeing her lying face down on the bed he broke a pane, opened the window and climbed into the room. Finding that she was dead, Greenson had immediately called Dr Engelberg.

The story was adjusted when later told to investigating officer Sergeant R. E. Byron, in order to fit in with Greenson's new timescale. She had woken at about 3.30 a.m. and had tried to rouse Marilyn, but without success; a little later she tried again, but still without success. Though consistent in saying that it was Dr Greenson who had broken the window for access, in this account it was Mrs Murray who had first gone outside and looked through the window to see Marilyn lying there. It is small inconsistencies of this kind in repeating stories which challenge the reliability of a witness.

In a third version, for the police follow-up report, the time now remained constant but she had called Dr Greenson twice. The first time was when she could not rouse Marilyn, the second time was to report what she saw through the window – which, in this version, she did on Dr Greenson's instruction in the first call.

In an interview with Robert Slatzer, Marilyn's neighbour Abe Landau revealed yet another dimension to Eunice Murray's array of accounts relating to how her employer had died. Some days after Marilyn's death Landau and his wife bumped into Mrs Murray, who told them all about it. It was an accident, the housekeeper had said. She would take pills and go to sleep, then wake up and take more, forgetting that she had already taken some.

Altogether, Mrs Murray revealed herself to be unreliable from the beginning. In her book *Marilyn: The Last Months*, which was published in 1975, she changed her story once more by claiming that she had not seen a light or telephone wire under Marilyn's door, but it had been a 'sixth sense' which had made her knock. Later, in 1982, when she gave an interview to researcher Justin Clayton, she told him she had found Marilyn's door ajar, then hastily tried to correct herself, but it was too late. The question of the broken window was finally laid to rest. If the door was open there was no need for Dr Greenson to have gained entry by breaking a window.

To dispose completely of the subject of the window, the question of how Mrs Murray – or Ralph Greenson – could have seen anything through Marilyn's bedroom window was inviting challenge. It will be recalled that Marilyn had not long moved into the house at Fifth Helena Drive and had not finished furnishing it. One of the things she had not got round to was curtains for her bedroom window. A sheet had been pinned across as a temporary solution: certainly it could not have been drawn and would have been extremely difficult to pull aside. It would have been remarkable if Mrs Murray had been able to pull it aside with a poker through a small, open window at the top, even if she had had a ladder to enable her to stand at the same height as the window; but she had no ladder. All the references to the window would therefore appear to have been red herrings.

The window may have been broken to support the stories which were to be told, although it strikes me as odd that neither Mrs Murray nor Ralph Greenson was smart enough to realise that a pane broken on the inside would fall outwards, a sure sign that it had been broken from within. The question must be asked, therefore, whether the window was in fact broken by others and the stories, which were quite unnecessary to the discovery of Marilyn's body, concocted to explain the breakage and conceal its true cause.

Little is ever said about the important role played by Dr Hyman Engelberg in the drama surrounding the discovery of Marilyn's body. He appeared to abdicate to Dr Greenson all responsibility for statements regarding his actions, exposing him to the charge of complicity in the misleading statements that Dr Greenson made. In fact, though they were not heavily publicised, Engelberg did make statements contradicting Dr Greenson's timescale. He spoke of the alarm being raised at 'about eleven or twelve', and said he was called to the house between 2.30 and 3.00 a.m. He appears to have acquiesced in regard to the timescale officially attributed to him, however, making no fuss and issuing no challenge. It was Dr Engelberg who signed the death certificate, and it is the time it was signed which raises problems. It shows 3.50 a.m. which does not fit the timescale presented by Mrs Murray and Dr Greenson. It might be considered reasonable, however, to accept 3.50 a.m. as an accurate time, ignoring the Murray–Greenson timescale anomalies.

All the indications are that Marilyn's body would have been greatly affected by rigor mortis by 3.50 a.m., however, and if so, Dr Engelberg did no favours to the cause of truth by not indicating it in some way on the death certificate. Although the time shown on a death certificate is not essentially a record of the actual time of death, it might be expected to be accompanied by an indication of the time of death. Certainly if Dr Engelberg was aware that there was a huge difference between the time of death and the time when the death certificate was signed he might have been expected to note this. In recent years Dr Engelberg has refused to speak on the subject of Marilyn's death. Refusal to speak in circumstances such as these often indicates that something is being withheld. It would be very interesting to have Dr Engelberg lay out the timescale for the whole sequence of events and to comment on the state of the body when he examined it.

In an interview with me Pat Newcomb, another who has remained silent on the matter, claimed that she was called to the Monroe house by lawyer Milton (Mickey) Rudin at about 4 a.m. It should be noted that this was before the police were called; they, of course, should have been the first to be called. The call to Pat Newcomb indicated that Rudin was already at the house and fully primed on what was happening. Milt Ebbins, Peter Lawford's agent, confirmed that Rudin was there in a statement quoted by Anthony Summers in *Goddess*. He asserted that at 4 a.m. he too received a call from Rudin in which he said, 'I'm at Marilyn's house now and she's dead.' Milton Rudin is yet another who will not speak about his knowledge of the events surrounding her death.

Three of Marilyn's neighbours reported that soon after dawn on Sunday, 5 August, a woman ran out of the house screaming, 'Murderers! Murderers! Are you satisfied now you've killed her?' Most of the reporters outside the house heard about the event, and there cannot be any doubt that it occurred. Celebrated Hollywood reporter Florabel Muir was determined to identify the woman who had uttered the screams, and, having satisfied herself that it was not Mrs Murray, she turned to the question of whether it was Pat Newcomb. 'There had to be a reason why Newcomb was the last called,' said Muir, who suspected that when she arrived at the house shortly after 4 a.m. Pat Newcomb found herself at what she regarded as a murder scene. Muir got no further with the matter, and when I raised the subject at an interview with Pat Newcomb I received no comment. But were there not only two women at the Monroe house that night, Murray and Newcomb?

The man who could probably have answered all the questions about Marilyn's death was Peter Lawford. His all-consuming preoccupation, however, was with keeping the names of Jack and Bobby Kennedy from being linked to Marilyn. This was hypocritical in the extreme, since it was he who had been the means of both Jack and Robert conducting their liaisons with her. But Lawford would not budge when it came to answering any question which might even remotely link Marilyn with the Kennedy brothers, a position which he maintained until he died in 1984.

This did not of course prevent the relationships from being discovered by other means, but in defending the Kennedys he remained mute on the many other things he could have told us about her death. Lawford was another of those who was on the scene long before the police. He was anxious to have the place 'swept' of documents, tapes or anything else which could link the dead star with the Kennedys. To assist him in this emergency operation he requested the services of private detective Fred Otash, which was ironic – Otash had bugged Lawford's Malibu mansion for Bernard Spindel (see Chapter 10) and had supplied him with technicians for bugging the very house he now wanted 'sweeping'. Otash said he was too well known for such work, but provided one of his men to go over with an off-duty police officer. Otash later said, 'When they got there,

Pat Newcomb outside Marilyn's house a few hours after the tragedy.
*Corbis-Bettmann/UPI.*

from what they tell me, the place was swarming with people. They were incapable of sweeping the place or anything.' But in spite of what Otash heard they seem to have got the job done, for when Sergeant Clemmons arrived as the first police officer on the scene he thought it odd that there were no documents or letters lying around. He told me the house appeared to have been cleaned up before he got there.

Before the police came the house was 'cleaned up' by other interested parties too. Ace publicist Arthur Jacobs and two Twentieth Century-Fox publicists combed the files in Marilyn's house, removing some documents wholesale and destroying others. In Peter Harry Brown's and Patte B. Barham's book *The Last Take*, Marilyn's studio maid Hazel Washington is quoted as saying, 'Honey, those agents burned documents in the fireplace.'

Lawford openly maintained that Robert Kennedy was back East during this time, which was sheer nonsense in the light of the public announcements that he was to be in San Francisco to deliver an address to the American Bar Association. In reality, however, he was in Los Angeles on the day Marilyn died. Retired Chief of Police Tom Reddin, who was an Assistant Chief at the time, assured me that there was no doubt about it: his men informed him that the Attorney General had been sighted in Los Angeles. As recounted in Chapter 3, Lawford's phone calls to Marilyn on the day she died smacked strongly of scenario engineering, raising support for the idea of her taking her own life.

On that last day of her life it would seem that Marilyn was reluctant even to speak to Robert Kennedy. He, on the other hand, appeared desperate to see her in order to sort things out. Apparently the original plan was that Lawford would have them meet at his house that night for dinner. Marilyn seems to have resisted this arrangement though it would appear that she eventually agreed to see the Attorney General at her own home. Kennedy, for his part, was equally resistant to the idea of their meetings becoming social occasions; indeed, the indications were that they were acrimonious occasions.

Accounts of the events of that Saturday have been strongly influenced by Lawford's insistence that he made a second telephone call to Marilyn that day, though, for reasons already identified, neither he nor his third wife could settle on a time for it which did not clash with calls made by Marilyn to others who gave a conflicting account of the way she sounded. This had to raise the question of whether the call was ever made, though Fred Otash's account of the call, as rendered to him by a 'half crocked and half nervous' Lawford, made it clear a call had been made. The trouble was that the actor had later placed a different construction on it. The question centred on why he was so determined to make it appear that she had planned to commit suicide.

Knowledge of the full content of the call would be vital to an understanding of the truth, but would not emerge until the mid-eighties. Lawford's embroidered version was accepted and ranked as the only call made to Marilyn which advertised an intention of suicide; unchallenged by the coroner's suicide team, it became the only real indication that Marilyn had died

Tom Reddin, who later became Chief of Police himself, knew Chief Parker well. Parker's ambition was likely to encourage him to be very helpful to Robert Kennedy. *Tom Reddin.*

by her own hand. The account of the call rendered years later by Lawford's wife Deborah Gould was fuller than Lawford's version, though it is interesting to note that before he died Lawford denied most of what Gould attributed to him.

Fred Otash, however, offered in his 1985 interview an account of the controversial phone call which explained everything. 'According to Lawford, he had called her and she had said to him that she was passed around like a piece of meat. She had had it. She didn't want Bobby to use her any more. She called the White House and there was no response from the President. She was told he [John Kennedy] was in Hyannisport and she didn't connect with him. She kept trying to get him. He [Lawford] had tried to reason with her to quiet down and come to the [Lawfords'] beach house and relax. She said, "No I'm tired. There is nothing more for me to respond to. Just do me a favour. Tell the President I tried to get him. Tell him goodbye for me. I think my purpose has been served."' Lawford tried to get back to Monroe, but she had either left the phone off the hook or was making another call.

This is a more realistic version of what took place in the so-called second telephone call, for whose timing there were ample openings. The first comment made to the press by Lawford a few days after Marilyn's death and before he concocted the imaginative 'Say goodbye to the President' version of things was, in relation to her actual state of health and wellbeing as revealed in the Otash version of the call, far more accurate. He said, 'There didn't seem to be anything wrong with Marilyn. She sounded fine.'

Lawford's 'nervousness' regarding Marilyn's welfare, which led him to telephone the couple who had been his dinner guests, merits suspicion. Joe Naarr offered to go to see if there was any problem with Marilyn. Minutes later and before he had left, Lawford rang again saying there was no need to go after all: he now knew that all was well. Unless he knew a lot more than he ever said, what led Lawford to think that anything was amiss with Marilyn so late at night in the first place? And what relieved his mind so quickly, causing him to ring Joe Naarr again to cancel his trip to Fifth Helena Drive? He clearly appeared keen for the Naarrs to know of his anxiety over Marilyn, but then equally keen for Joe Naarr *not* to go to the house.

Someone else who appears quickly to have gone along with the idea of suicide was Arthur Jacobs. Starting from a lowly job with Metro Goldwyn Mayer he had become one of Hollywood's top publicists. He was one of the first – if not the first – on the scene the night Marilyn died. Jacobs had the opportunity to assess at first hand what was happening, and he went ahead with accidental suicide announcements. It is interesting to note at this point, however, that a publicist can handle suicide with a great deal more ease than, for instance, murder, and from a professional viewpoint, therefore, suicide would suit the publicity machine which started up the moment he arrived at Marilyn's house. Jacobs, probably with Pat Newcomb, planned the 'campaign' and was personally involved in selling it to Hollywood, the United States and, indeed, the world.

It is quite clear that in the late evening of 4 August and early morning of 5 August 1962 some sort of conspiracy was hatched at Fifth Helena Drive which, through the efforts of Jacobs' press campaign, held sway for years and for many people still does. The conspiracy has not held together completely, however. Marilyn's psychiatrist, Ralph Greenson, was the first to break from it, declaring as early as the Wednesday following Marilyn's death that he did not believe that she had committed suicide. At this time no one wanted to hear his statement, and it is doubtful that any wider coverage of it in the following days would have made any impact against the clamour of the Jacobs publicity machine. Any changes that Greenson made to the views he expressed were kept very quiet, and the overall effect was that the 'probable suicide' verdict at the heart of the detailed press statements was not challenged.

As explained earlier, Mrs Murray blew the gaff in her interview with Justin Clayton by saying that the bedroom door was not locked, and later while making the BBC programme *Say Goodbye to the President*. She admitted that Robert Kennedy was indeed in Marilyn's house that last day, that there was no locked bedroom door, no light under the bedroom door and no need for a window to be broken to gain entry. Mrs Murray was, of course, only confirming what had already been found out or deduced.

Known only to those people privy to the conspiracy – and more than those immediately close to Marilyn were involved in it – the reasons for it ever being hatched slipped into a dark abyss, swallowed by the Jacobs publicity machine and the suicide theory. And apart from a few journalists who guardedly wrote about certain aspects of them, they remained hidden for years.

# 6

# THE AMBULANCE

In 1982, Los Angeles District Attorney John K. Van de Kamp conducted a review of the circumstances surrounding Marilyn's death. It mostly let sleeping dogs lie, but one event did shed new light on the case. It was the testimony of Ken Hunter, who in 1962 had been a driver for the Schaefer Ambulance Company, which ran Los Angeles' biggest fleet of ambulances. Hunter claimed he had taken an ambulance to the house on Fifth Helena Drive on the night that Marilyn died. He told how when he and his partner arrived they found her dead, and added that the police were arriving as they departed. Hunter's testimony created a stir. It inspired hope that other features of the case would come to light, and underlined the feeling that the mystery surrounding it was the result of a cover-up.

It was not until 1985 that Hunter's claims received confirmation. Walt Schaefer, the owner of the company, having previously denied supplying an ambulance to the Monroe house, now admitted that Hunter had been right. Schaefer also added to Hunter's story, with which he did not totally agree. Marilyn was still alive when the ambulance reached her house, Schaefer said, and she was taken to Santa Monica Hospital. He had no knowledge of her being returned home, he said, and could not remember who had ordered the ambulance. His records would not help, he explained, because he destroyed everything after five years. Attempts to find corroboration in the records of Santa Monica Hospital also failed: they had long since disposed of their files for 1962.

Ken Hunter claimed that his partner in the ambulance

that night had been Murray Liebowitz, but Liebowitz disclaimed all knowledge of the event, declaring that he had been off duty that night. Schaefer was adamant that Liebowitz had been there, though at one point he confused him with Hunter and said he was the driver. There was further confusion when Schaefer said that another driver named James Hall had never worked for him, when it was proven beyond doubt by researchers that he had. And when it came to the matter of who had driven the ambulance to Marilyn's house on the night she died, James Hall put the cat among the pigeons.

Hall claimed that in fact *he* had been the driver of the ambulance in question, and he too claimed Liebowitz had been his partner. He timed the arrival of the ambulance at about 3.30 a.m. and spoke of the trouble Pat Newcomb had given him. She was hysterical, he said, screaming, 'She's dead! She's dead!' and trying to climb across him while he worked. Marilyn, he said, was in the bed in the guest room and, although comatose, was still alive. He explained that CPR (cardiopulmonary resuscitation) cannot be carried out on a patient in bed because the body is simply pressed into the soft surface. He and his partner had to move Marilyn on to the floor, therefore, and in doing so she was accidentally dropped. It was this which had caused the bruise on her hip that had later been observed by the autopsist, he claimed. 'Dead bodies don't bruise,' said Hall, 'so she was definitely still alive.'

In Hall's story mouth-to-mouth resuscitation was proving successful and she was responding. His activity was quickly halted, however, by the arrival of a man who announced that he was Marilyn's doctor. Hall looked across at Pat Newcomb and took his cue from her, he said. Since she was not contradicting the newcomer, Hall allowed him to take over. The doctor tried to revive her and, according to Hall, when he was unsuccessful produced from his bag a hypodermic with a long needle already in place. He pushed her breast to one side and roughly administered the injection. When the needle would go no further, presumably because of encountering a rib, he pushed and something snapped. 'It was quite a snap,' said Hall. One minute later she was dead. Hall says that for years he assumed that he had watched her being given an adrenalin shot, but now believes he saw her being murdered. Although he did not know who the man was at the time, he later identified Ralph Greenson as the murderer.

Hall's father, ex-wife and brother have all said he told his story to them soon after Marilyn died, and this lends support to what he now says. But why did he wait thirty years to go public with his account? After all, he claimed to have been a witness to murder, and his silence made him an accessory after the fact. This is the first and most obvious weakness in James Hall's story, but there are numerous other flaws too.

According to Hall the time of death must have been soon after 3.30 a.m., which creates all kinds of problems. Guy Hockett, the coroner's man, said that by 5.30 a.m., when he collected the body, it was in the advanced stages of rigor mortis. He had to bend her arms forcibly to be able to strap her to the gurney. Though rigor was likely to have begun it would not have been so advanced if she had died shortly after 3.30 a.m. Hockett estimated several hours had elapsed since her death, and it has been said elsewhere that it would have taken as much as six hours, given the temperature of the house, for the body to become so rigid.

Dr Hyman Engelberg provides another stumbling block to Hall's story, for he signed the death certificate at 3.50 a.m. Regardless of changes made to the accounts and timescales rendered by Mrs Murray, Engelberg must have been at the house for some time before he signed the certificate, and Hall's story tends to suggest either complicity to murder or criminal neglect on the doctor's part. Engelberg was either there in the bedroom watching Marilyn being murdered or – just as bad – in some other room while his patient was being treated by an ambulance driver and then murdered by a colleague. This will not do at all. Engelberg was neither party to murder nor neglectful of his patients.

Ralph Greenson, an eminent psychiatrist, would also have been stepping entirely out of character to commit a murder – and would have been acting totally irrationally into the bargain. After all, he had no motive: quite the reverse, in fact. Since Marilyn was Greenson's patient, she represented part of his livelihood. It has been said that he was annoyed because Marilyn planned to sever her connections with him, but in the first place there is no evidence that this was the case, and in the second a doctor simply does not take offence and kill off those patients who leave him.

It must also be remembered that, although Greenson had qualified as an MD, he practised only as a psychiatrist. He was engaged as such by Marilyn, which explains why she was also treated by Dr Engelberg, who was a physician. Engelberg had been sent for at roughly the same time as Greenson, for they had separate functions; and Greenson was no more likely to open a bag and administer an injection than Engelberg was to sit her down and enquire about her emotional state. Besides, if Hall's timescale is even approximately correct, both doctors were on hand when he arrived.

The statement regarding the production of a syringe complete with large needle from a doctor's bag merits challenge of itself. It would have been highly unlikely. Doctors do not carry syringes around in their bags already fitted with needles of any kind: to do so would be dangerous, unhygienic and risking breakage.

In Hall's story Greenson calmly murdered Marilyn in front of a number of witnesses, which completely defies belief. Had he ever wanted to take Marilyn's life, he would have done so when they were alone. But then for any doctor to take a patient's life without reason represents him taking leave of his senses, and there has never been the remotest suggestion that Ralph Greenson was less than completely sane, logical and reasonable at any period of his life. Greenson has been outrageously maligned in this absurd story.

When interviewing autopsist Dr Thomas Noguchi I obtained physical evidence to contradict the Hall story. Dr Noguchi was asked whether, in the careful magnifying-glass examination of Marilyn's skin which he carried out with the assistance of Deputy District Attorney John Miner, there was any indication of a roughly administered injection near Marilyn's breast. He assured me that there was none. Furthermore he told me that, as part of the autopsy, he had removed the ribcage and a broken or damaged rib was not likely to have escaped his attention. I asked John Miner about this at a separate interview and he gave me the same answers. Miner qualified as a doctor before entering law and his observation was, therefore, like Dr Noguchi's, entirely professional. Since his time as a deputy DA Miner had become a lawyer specialising in medical malpractice cases. Both doctors were aware of James Hall's story and appeared glad to be able to refute his version of Marilyn's death with medical evidence based on their own observations.

No credence can be given to the James Hall story, therefore. Even minor points made by him in the telling of it tend to militate against its credibility. He spoke, for instance, of a police officer and a figure whom he later identified as Peter Lawford being present, thus adding another two who were witnesses to a brutal murder and another two who have kept silent.

Hall's story does not detract from the fact that a mystery surrounds the calling of an ambulance to Fifth Helena Drive and Walt Schaefer's claim that it transported Marilyn to Santa Monica Hospital. Whilst driver Ken Hunter does not go along with the hospital story, Schaefer was not likely to invent it, for in doing so he introduced a big question to which he had no answer. He cannot explain, he said, how the body of Marilyn Monroe was returned to her house. There were, of course, differing cross-motives which might compel both Hunter and Schaefer to introduce discrepancies into their respective versions of what happened. Walt Schaefer, for instance, was asked why he had previously denied supplying an ambulance to the Monroe residence and gave quite a startling reply. He was sure, he said, that to have spoken out would have ruined his business. Eighty per cent of his work came from city and county establishments and the involvement of the Kennedys, he said, made him fear the worst.

Another consideration was that each ambulance company had to compete with its rivals, and the wrong kind of story circulating could have had a bad effect on business. Schaefer, therefore, would not be anxious to advertise the fact that his ambulance had attended an emergency without providing the maximum possible service, and a dash to the hospital, even though abortive, would tend to recommend the company. On the other hand it would be easy to believe that to convey a corpse back to the place that a live patient had come from would be something of an embarrassment, so that particular service might not have been on offer.

But Hunter, as a mere employee, would not have had the same concern for the reputation of the company, and may have been telling the truth when he said that no trip had been made to the hospital. It is entirely possible, however, that there was indeed a hospital dash and, if Marilyn died on the way, that Hunter was leaned on to return the corpse to Fifth Helena Drive. He would neither wish it to be known that he had not reached hospital in time for Marilyn to be saved – not that it would have been his fault – nor that he had used the ambulance as a hearse and returned the body where it had come from. It was perhaps better for him to play down the fact that a trip to hospital was ever made.

It is most unusual for a hospital to send back home a patient who has died soon after being admitted and while in its care. What is more believable is that Marilyn may have died on the way to hospital and that the hospital was reluctant to admit a dead body. In a competitive society the number of deaths at a hospital must reflect on its record, and Santa Monica might not have wanted to add one more.

It was an extraordinary lapse of memory which prevented Walt Schaefer from remembering that James Hall ever worked for him. However, he was positive enough when identifying Ken Hunter and Murray Liebowitz as the two who went with the ambulance that night, and there is no real reason to doubt this. Additionally, since neither man is forthcoming on the subject, this might well be construed as behaviour consistent with the two who actually took the ambulance to Marilyn's home. To researchers, Liebowitz would never even acknowledge that he was there, and now Hunter has joined the ranks of the silent. James Hall tells an interesting story about a call to a radio chat show which he heard. The call was another colleague of Liebowitz's who spoke of him stopping at as many as six car washes, explaining that he owned them. He bought them, he was quoted as saying, with money paid to him to keep quiet. 'The only reason I'm still working at Schaefer's is to keep up appearances,' he is quoted as saying. If the story is true, one is left wondering how many other people may have been paid hush money.

I believe Walt Shaefer when he says his ambulance took Marilyn to Santa Monica Hospital the night she died. It was important to those who were conspiring in the cover-up that she should be brought back home where they had full control over the image they were presenting to the world. Had the body remained at the hospital, they would have lost that control. The ambulance story is extremely important if only because it sheds light on the conspiracy of silence. For twenty years after Marilyn's death not a word of this story was breathed by any of those involved, and it demonstrates how well the secrets of that night have been kept.

As recently as 1985 there was a further investigation into Marilyn's death by the LA County District Attorney. However, in spite of the well-grounded information relating to the presence – and significance – of the ambulance which was called to the Monroe house, and the testimony of Ken Hunter and Walt Schaefer, that investigation dismissed the attendance of the ambulance as mere rumour and declined to waste time considering it.

Even Eunice Murray, Marilyn's housekeeper and the scourge of researchers with her ever-changing stories, admitted that the ambulance had come when she finally spoke up in 1985 at the time when *Say Goodbye to the President* was made for the BBC. But while she was forthcoming on some issues, Mrs Murray remained silent on the subject of what had really happened to Marilyn Monroe.

The people who would have been able to shed instant light on doubts about the presence of an ambulance at Marilyn's house were her neighbours. They saw it there in the early hours of the Sunday morning, but then next day they heard that she had died. So the fact that an ambulance had stood in her driveway – so commonplace, even expected, in the case of someone dying from an overdose – did not merit much discussion, much less drawing to anyone's attention. Though anxious not to divulge their names at the time, Abe Landau and his wife answered questions from journalists on what they saw, but questions were never asked by the police.

The Landaus had seen the ambulance at about one in the morning, a time which would grossly contradict James Hall's story but which would accommodate the Ken Hunter time, quoted variously as 'the early morning hours' and about 1.30 a.m. It is interesting that the Landaus speak of seeing a police car and several other cars with the ambulance, and Hunter spoke of seeing the police arrive as the ambulance crew left, though he later denied this. A police presence, let alone a police involvement, as early as 1 a.m. would give the Los Angeles Police Department a great many questions to answer.

# 7

# WHAT THE EYE
# DOESN'T SEE . . .

It appears that, from the moment Marilyn died, the wheels of authority were set in motion to prevent the truth of her death being exposed. This is not to say that information was not sought and collected. A huge file soon built up in the LAPD, but most of it quietly disappeared. It was not long before the only official record on the death of Marilyn Monroe to be found in the Police Department files consisted of little more than a few sheets of paper.

On the face of it there was likely to have been only one reason for this: the association between the Attorney General and Marilyn at the time of her death. Any whisper of involvement would have damaged the reputation of Robert Kennedy and, by association, that of his brother, the President. Any brush with the law over her death, no matter how slight, would have been likely to cause them political damage beyond repair. Fortunately for them both, they had an instant ally in the Los Angeles Chief of Police, William H. Parker.

In a long conversation that I had with the retired Chief of Police Tom Reddin, who succeeded Parker and was one of his assistants at the time Marilyn died, he described the relationship between his chief and Robert Kennedy. 'There he was in a room full of chiefs of police being addressed by the Attorney General. Kennedy indicated Chief Parker saying, "And here is the finest of them all sitting in the front row," or something to that effect. Parker would have killed to get attention like that. Despite the attention he had already been given, here was the chief law enforcement officer of the United States saying that he was the best police chief in the country or in history, or whatever the grand terms were. This would indicate to me,' said Tom Reddin, tactfully, 'he might be prone to do something that might be of assistance to the Kennedy family.' He continued, 'Parker loved being close to those in power, and he was rumoured for some years as a possible successor to J. Edgar Hoover. He loved national attention and it makes one wonder could he, perhaps, have the motivation or the inclination to get rid of that report.'

Tom Reddin had put his finger right on it. As Jack Clemmons, the first policeman at the scene of the crime, told me, there was only one man who had the power and authority to carry out the kind of cover-up which took place there, and that was Chief William Parker. 'And no one would dare challenge his orders, such was the authority he commanded.'

I talked further with Tom Reddin on the question of whether the file might still survive somewhere. He said it was hard to

Chief of Police Tom Reddin (right) with Chief of Detectives Thad Brown.
*Tom Reddin.*

tell whether it lay in someone's garage or whether it had been destroyed, perhaps shredded. Pressed to render an opinion on who might have it if it had escaped destruction, he named the man who was Chief of Detectives at the time Marilyn died, Thad Brown. 'Thad was an avid collector of documents – he had a garageful – and it is the kind of thing he might acquire,' he said. Unhappily, I discovered that I was not the first to be led to Thad Brown, and documents which Thad most certainly acquired had been reacquired after his death by the Police Department. Thad's son, Wayne, sorted through his mountain of papers – in his garage, as Tom Reddin had suggested – and found documents which constitute some of the surviving items which now lie in the file at Police Headquarters. The bulk of the documents which made up the Marilyn file were not found in Thad Brown's garage, however. They are still missing.

If Chief Parker confiscated the file to control the reports, that was not the only paperwork of which he took possession. Probably within hours of Marilyn's death, two men in smart suits took from the files of the General Telephone Company the records which showed which numbers Marilyn had been calling during the period before she died. The toll sheets would have provided the skeleton around which the story of her relationship with Robert Kennedy could have been built. It would have shown that recently Marilyn had called the Washington number which Robert Kennedy had given her without getting any answer, for he had had the number changed. The records would have told the complete story of how she had then tried the Justice Department number without reaching him, and had next transferred her attempts to the hotel in San Francisco. It would have been clear that he was not receiving or returning her calls.

These records had almost certainly been taken by FBI men, but it seems that they quickly found their way into Chief Parker's possession. To reporters, he boasted of having them: Florabel Muir, a crime reporter for the Hearst Corporation, spoke of him waving them in front of her. James A. Hudson, news editor for United Press International, said Parker told him that 'at least six phone calls were made by Marilyn to the Justice Department'. To newscaster George Putnam he said, 'Marilyn was trying to reach Mr Kennedy. She called the Justice Department in Washington, DC – not his private number but through the switchboard. Marilyn tried to reach Bobby Kennedy on eight different occasions the week before she died but was unsuccessful.'

It would at first seem curious that, after confiscating the toll records, Parker was announcing what was on them. Two reasons for doing so stand out immediately. First, he was defusing the clamour for reporters to see them, and secondly, he was only telling them what he was prepared to let them know. The reporters did not learn from Chief Parker of the relationship between Marilyn and Robert Kennedy, which the toll sheets would have told them. They did not find out from him about Marilyn being dumped, nor that afterwards RFK refused even to speak to her. Chief Parker spoke only of a number of unsuccessful attempts on Marilyn's part to reach the Attorney General. After all, the Attorney General is, technically, a public servant available for anyone to contact.

Parts of the toll records were found after twenty years by Anthony Summers in research which he concluded in the mid-eighties. These sheets showed that Marilyn had telephoned RE7-8200, a Justice Department number, eight times between 25 June and 30 July. They showed only one call having been made on the day Marilyn died, however, and it was not to Robert Kennedy. Also among the missing records were those relating to the period between Marilyn's death and its being reported to the police.

It was probably Chief Parker who was instrumental again in the decision not to conduct a coroner's inquest. There were sufficient peculiarities in the autopsy report alone to warrant the holding of an inquest, but it would have involved witnesses giving evidence under oath and enabled anyone to ask questions. This, of course, would have diluted Chief Parker's power to control events and would have demanded answers from those who had so far failed to tell what they knew. Peter Lawford, for instance, volunteered superficial answers at the time of Marilyn's death, but otherwise answered no questions from the authorities for about thirteen years. In fact he went off promptly to the East Coast, to the Kennedy compound at Hyannis Port, while both Eunice Murray and Pat Newcomb took off on trips to Europe, well away from any questions that they might have been asked.

Chief Parker took advantage of the fact that the Los Angeles health authorities had recently created an investigatory team whose function it was to enquire into the circumstances of suicide victims. He promptly passed the matter to them, precluding further police enquiries. Headed by psychologist Dr Norman Farberow, the team included Dr Robert E. Litman, a psychiatrist, and Dr Norman Tabachnik. Dr Farberow wrote to me, 'As a psychologist my activities were directed to attempting to learn what the psychological status of Ms Monroe was at the time of her death.'

When I interviewed Robert Litman in his offices in Los Angeles, he pointed out that any investigation into the physical circumstances of her death would have been the job of the police. In the event there was, overtly at any rate, little more than a token investigation by the Los Angeles Police Department. This was carried out by Sergeant Robert E. Byron, and both his preliminary report (see pp. 155–6) and follow-up report demonstrate what a superficial affair it was. Retired Chief of Police Tom Reddin spoke highly of Byron and his abilities, which, he said, were not reflected in the scant enquiries he made into Marilyn's death. Reddin had no quarrel with my suggestion that the sergeant appeared under specific orders to carry out only a minimal investigation which added up to nothing. He also agreed that those instructions would probably have come down directly from Parker. Byron himself will not discuss his investigation.

While Byron's investigation was intended for public consumption, secretly, as has been stated, a massive file was built up at Police Headquarters. Much of what went into it would come from covert enquiries conducted by officers of the LAPD's Organized Crime Intelligence Division (OCID), whose activities were recently exposed in a book by a former OCID detective, Michael J. Rothmiller. It is more than likely that Rothmiller's book was the cause of the closing down of OCID operations in 1992. The Marilyn file appeared to be under the specific control of Chief Parker, who, it is rumoured, took it on a trip to Washington and did not bring it back. There was no suggestion that he also took the telephone toll records, however. These he may have kept as 'insurance'.

Whatever was the case, the file disappeared. After Parker's death, when Tom Reddin was Chief, Mayor Sam Yorty, who was Reddin's boss and had been Parker's also, decided he wanted to see any records they had on Marilyn's death. He had, it seems, previously been kept in the dark on the subject by Chief Parker. Reddin told Yorty that the file did not exist, which by then was true – it had long since disappeared. Robert Slatzer quotes a conversation with Mayor Yorty in which he said, 'Later I found out they did have records. And that surprised me. Because I had a very good relationship with them, and I really thought they didn't have any.' Then he added, 'They must have had a secret they didn't want to come out.' By the time the LAPD admitted the records existed, what in ex-Chief Tom Reddin's opinion should have been a file at least an inch thick had become little more than fifty pages of routine documents.

The team of doctors given the task of examining the psychological circumstances of Marilyn's death was variously known as 'The Suicide Investigation Team', 'The Suicide Team' and, oddly, 'The Suicide Prevention Team'. The picture they drew of Marilyn's state of mind – and their reasons for drawing it – raises many questions. Dr Farberow summed up the doctors' position for me as follows: 'The factors that emerged were of a person who was markedly depressed, under considerable emotional strain (problems with the studio), in poor physical health, and under both psychiatric and medical care. These, along with information that she had had similar episodes in the past, some accompanied by hospitalization and with prior suicide attempts, were enough to indicate further suicidal behaviour.'

If the doctors had been aware of the many other factors which would have pointed away from suicide, they did not mention them. This was in spite of Farberow asserting that their enquiries would have no limitations. They appeared oblivious to the fact that Marilyn had, for instance, just purchased a complete new wardrobe, which was hardly the behaviour of someone contemplating suicide. They seemed unaware that her past upheavals with the studio had been resolved in a brilliant new contract with a salary larger than she had ever had in her life before.

As for any depression, this might well have been explained by the fact that she had recently had gynaecological problems and had been seeing a specialist. It was the belief of some of her friends that she had, in fact, just had another abortion. (Her autopsy revealed that she had had several.) Whatever the case, there were indications that she was steadily recovering, however, and her friends commented on how well she looked. She had turned her mind to matters such as furnishing her new house, negotiating new film deals and, shortly before her death, stopping off at a nursery to buy plants for her garden.

It appears that Marilyn's general health was not as bad as had been painted by the Suicide Team. She was suffering only minor ailments, and her long-term sleeping problems were abating in the weeks before her death. She was being weaned off her sleeping pills, and Dr Litman told me he was aware of the changes in her drug intake. He believed she had been drug-free for seven weeks before her death, yet he still saw her as being in poor health.

The team's evaluation of her previous 'suicide' attempts was also puzzling. They had agreed that on several previous occasions there had been an observable pattern of behaviour which added up to her 'planning to take her life' with such timing that she was bound to be rescued and receive attention and sympathy from those around her – the ploy acknowledged by psychologists as a cry for help rather than a real wish to die. Dr Litman told me that the Suicide Team was aware of this situation and considered that she might have died because her cry for help was not answered quickly enough. In the circumstances this idea is altogether odd. Marilyn had had people around her all day and Mrs Murray was staying the night. She spoke on the telephone to her friends until about ten o'clock that night, which was probably very shortly before she died, without raising the alarm.

It seems to me that the doctors ought not to have drawn their conclusion in such a matter-of-fact way. There were many strong reasons for believing that had she planned another cry for help – which would have been curious in the circumstances – she would not have miscalculated her timing. People who do that sort of thing don't; people who actually kill themselves usually intend to kill themselves. That Peter Lawford spoke of her saying on the telephone that she planned to commit suicide is, in my opinion, better disregarded. It must be remembered that he was substituting this account of the conversation for one he had given earlier, in which he had said, 'Marilyn said she was happy and was going to bed.' In the overall context of events that day it would seem extremely doubtful that such a 'suicide' conversation ever took place. Had she really been alerting him she would have left no doubt that she required him to take action, and it is unbelievable that Lawford would deliberately have let her die knowing that suicide was her intention. Besides, Marilyn did not talk in such terms to the other people she spoke to on the telephone that evening. Though she sounded depressed to one or two of them she did not take advantage of the ample opportunity she had to enlist help if she felt she needed it. To see Peter Lawford's statement in a proper context we would do well to remind ourselves that he had a very good reason for wanting Marilyn's death to be thought of as suicide.

The Suicide Team, therefore, made a great deal of their theory that Marilyn's death may have been a cry for help which went wrong. They did not appear to give due attention to the various indications of her wellbeing. Had they properly considered the evidence of her sleeping better, taking an interest in her house and garden, shopping for clothes and entering into contract negotiations with gusto, they could hardly have thought that there was any cry for help in the offing. Other indications seemed to be ignored, also. The fact that she was found dead in a naked condition should have raised questions. It is an unusual thing for a woman to commit suicide in the nude. And the fact that she was found lying face down, head pointing to one corner of the bed and feet to the diagonally opposite corner, with her legs together and her arms roughly by her sides, ought to have set up at least minor worries about the possibility of something going on. Sergeant Jack Clemmons, the policeman first at the scene, described it as a 'soldier' position. 'There were often convulsions which left the body contorted,' he said.

At bedtime, Marilyn's routine was to slip on a bra and place earplugs in her ears and eyeshades on her eyes to help her sleep. All of these were absent when she was found, and it is strange that the Suicide Team did not find it necessary to enquire into the reasons for their absence. There was sufficient reason to suspect that she had died elsewhere and been placed on the bed on which she was supposedly discovered. Had they asked Jack Clemmons he would have told them that there was no drinking glass in the bedroom in which she was found, and that he and the others present searched for it without success. This would have strengthened a belief that she had been moved. Moving a body would not necessarily have involved criminal actions, but if this had happened the actual scene of death should have been established and examined.

The comment made by Guy Hockett, the coroner's man, about Marilyn's body being in an advanced stage of rigor mortis would surely have been as available to the doctors in the Suicide Team as it was to others around at the time, and this might have inspired questions about *when* she really died. Dr Hyman Engelberg might then have been questioned on the state of the body when he signed the death certificate, and doubts as to what really happened might have emerged from the timescale involved. The Suicide Team, whose leader, Dr Norman Farberow, went on record as saying, 'We are interviewing anybody and everybody . . . ' did not, apparently, get as far as interviewing the housekeeper Eunice Murray, who was in the house when Marilyn died. They took only one week to reach their conclusions, and appeared to go in one direction only, that of suicide. They appeared simply not to notice the indications that something was wrong with this verdict.

They did not, apparently, see anything odd in the autopsy finding that Marilyn's stomach was empty: no sign of the drugs in the stomach – neither the gelatine capsules nor the dye from them. It appears that Marilyn's house was not sealed off quickly enough, so there must have been limited value in any investigations they carried out there. Inez Melson, Marilyn's business manager, said that she gained entry to the house early on the Sunday morning, just hours after the body had been removed. She also said she discovered numerous pill bottles at Marilyn's bedside which the police had not taken. They contained Nembutal and Seconal capsules, all of which she flushed away, she said. One has to wonder first what Mrs Melson was doing in the house when it should have been sealed, and secondly whether the Suicide Team ever questioned her about what she did. In what the Suicide Team seem to rate an orgy of pill-taking, it would have been extremely pertinent to ask why there were so many pills left.

The autopsy had accounted for a probable forty-seven Nembutal capsules taken by Marilyn when she died. This was based on her being known to have taken three from a bottle which they said contained fifty. The fifty Nembutals were supposedly from a repeat prescription which Dr Engelberg said he had given her the day before she died. The facts appeared to be, however, that no repeat prescription was made up by the Vincente Pharmacy, which Marilyn used. They made up only a new prescription for twenty-five from Dr Greenson; deducting the three she was known to have taken previously, the remaining twenty-two would not have produced the enormous volume of drugs found in her bloodstream.

The Suicide Team appeared to get into something of a muddle when attempting to increase the number of Nembutal pills at

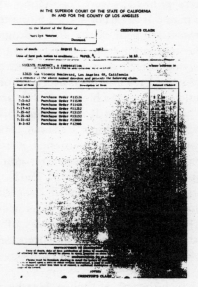

The last bill from the Vincente Pharmacy showed exactly what had been dispensed for Marilyn.

Marilyn's disposal. They credited a Dr Lou Siegel with having prescribed further drugs for her, leaving the indignant doctor to point out that in fact Ms Monroe was not his patient at all. They were probably thinking of the studio doctor, Dr Lee Siegel, but here they got it wrong again. Dr Lee Siegel had not treated Marilyn for several weeks before her death.

Inez Melson spoke of others who were also at the house that Sunday morning, 5 August. Twentieth Century-Fox publicists Frank Neill and Johnny Campbell were among them, and all were busily engaged in sorting out documents, contracts, letters and other papers which were removed in bulk. Evelyn Moriarity, who was Marilyn's stand-in, told me that Hazel Washington, Marilyn's studio maid, who had gone to the house to retrieve some small leather-topped tables which she had loaned Marilyn, saw documents being burnt. A filing cabinet which had recently had a new lock fitted to it was broken open by some interested party.

Censorship of a different kind took place in 1985, when Anthony Summers' publishers were negotiating with ABC News for his *Goddess* material to be condensed into a television news story to go out as a segment of the *20/20* programme. Sylvia Chase had been appointed reporter and put a great deal of effort into satisfying herself on points of research. It was felt that the material was so sensitive that decisions on what should be included should be taken at a high level. The programme was shown to ABC News President Roone Arledge, Vice-President Richard Wald and Arledge's senior assistant, David Burke. On transmission day the *Daily News* carried a column by Liz Smith which began, 'I just hope ABC isn't going to let itself be a party to suppressing the history of 1962 . . .' At 6 p.m. that day the programme was cancelled altogether, dismissed as 'gossip-column stuff'. Since Arledge was a close friend of Ethel Kennedy, Robert's wife, and Burke was a former member of the Kennedy staff, suspicions that it had been axed for political rather than professional reasons might be forgiven.

The cover-up which began at Police Headquarters on the day Marilyn died was very successful. The anomalies in the investigation were not to be challenged and information received was to be kept secret: reporters were to be kept at bay. After the 'Probable Suicide' decision from the Suicide Team most journalistic interest melted away. Otherwise even the most tenacious of crime reporters yielded to the defences they could not penetrate. When he became Chief, Tom Reddin had no axe to grind. He knew that the cause of the LAPD cover-up was Marilyn's relationship with Robert Kennedy. 'The Kennedy connection – and I mean both Kennedys – was common knowledge at the Police Department,' he said. 'We heard that one of Marilyn's last calls was to Robert Kennedy.'

# 8

# EXPERT MEDICAL OPINION

I felt it would be highly desirable to seek the opinion of a leading pathologist who would give me the benefit of his expertise concerning the findings of Marilyn's autopsy. Dr Cyril Wecht, who agreed to assist me, is coroner of Allegheny County in Pennsylvania, and a former President of the American Academy of Forensic Sciences. I sent him all the published documents on the autopsy and a number of additional papers which included the statement issued by the Los Angeles coroner, Dr Theodore Curphey. Over a period of time I asked Dr Wecht a series of questions which were based either on the documentation he had been sent, or on relevant issues. Some questions he answered straightaway, while in respect of others he asked for more information, which I supplied as soon as I was able. Here are Dr Wecht's answers.

*Q*: Having examined the autopsy data, how would you regard the conclusion [quoted as stated by LA coroner Dr Theodore Curphey] that Marilyn ingested a large number of capsules orally 'within a short period of time', or with 'one gulp within – let's say – a period of seconds'?

*A*: It is quite unlikely that these levels [of barbiturates] were attained following a one-time, quick ingestion of all the pills and capsules which would have been required to reach the levels found at autopsy. A large amount of barbiturates will slow gastric motility; therefore if all the drugs had been ingested at once, there would not have been enough time for her stomach to have emptied almost completely before death.

Q: Would you have expected to find traces of the dye from the large number of Nembutal capsules she was said to take?

A: Pentobarbital capsules would most likely have produced yellowish streaking in the small intestine in the proximal portion.

Q: If she did not ingest the large amount of pills and capsules she was said to have taken by mouth, could she, for instance, have been injected with the drugs?

A: Injection was possible though no site was noted. I cannot be sure that all possible sites were carefully checked inasmuch as such a probability was not being seriously considered.

Q: The purple discoloration of the sigmoid colon is said by some to indicate, at once, the presence of barbiturates in the large intestine. What do you think about this?

A: I do not agree that purplish discoloration definitely indicates the presence of drugs in the large intestine. Post mortem discoloration of the bowel is not an uncommon finding of a non-specific nature.

Q: Would you consider a suppository a means by which the drugs may have been administered to Marilyn?

A: I do not think you could get the levels of drugs found in the blood and liver from suppositories.

Q: What about enema?

A: The presence of faecal contents in her body at first suggests the drugs were not introduced by enema.

Q: But if the drugs in liquid form were administered by enema, a plug device of some sort would be necessary to prevent the liquid from running out. If this were used the faecal contents would be retained, then, wouldn't they?

A: Let me say at once that I know of no such plug, neither what you might call a legitimate use for such, but assuming this were an improvised device, that would make it possible.

Q: You pointed out to me in another context that if Marilyn was a chronic abuser of drugs, she must have built up an increased tolerance to them. Does this mean it would have taken a greater volume of drugs to kill her than it would someone who had no increased tolerance?

A: Oh, yes. Very much so.

Q: Did the autopsy reveal all it might have been expected to reveal?

A: Segmental intenstinal testing should have been done. I am certain that if Dr Noguchi, whom I hold in the highest regard, were to 'do this over', he would undertake such a detailed approach.

Q: Dr Noguchi could not carry out further work on Marilyn's body because the specimens he preserved were thrown out. Was this a normal procedure?

A: The various body tissues, fluid and excreta taken at autopsy by Dr Noguchi should not have been disposed of within a short time by a toxicologist or anyone else at the LA Medical Examiner-Coroner's Office. Those materials should have been retained for repeat testing and more detailed analysis, especially in light of the apparent inconsistencies and unanswered questions.

From this point, where views are given they are my own and

not those of Dr Wecht. This should not be taken to mean that he does not agree with me, however.

Dr Wecht agrees that the cause of death is not in dispute. Marilyn died of barbiturate poisoning. This is one of the few things we can be certain about in this case. It is interesting to note, however, that Dr Wecht effectively rules out the possibility of Marilyn having taken a huge volume of capsules and pills by mouth in a short period of time, though he is of the opinion that, if she had taken them over an extended period, this could be consistent with the autopsy findings. This was assuming that she survived long enough to take them all.

Dr Wecht told me that if Marilyn had ingested pills for some hours before finally dying she would have acted in a 'toxic' fashion, and from what we know this was not the case. She made a number of telephone calls from which the worst which was apparent was that she sounded drowsy – consistent with someone who had had difficulty getting to sleep the previous night. None of those who heard her speaking in this fashion thought any more of it. They did not find it in any way alarming. Her drowsiness did not last very long, in any case. By ten o'clock, when she telephoned her friend Jeanne Carmen, other than sounding a bit 'uptight' she sounded fine.

Dr Wecht gave what consideration he could to the possibility that Marilyn had been injected with the barbiturates. This would have represented an injection of some size and it was likely that, even with the most carefully administered hypodermic, at least a small tell-tale mark would indicate the spot where it had been inserted. Dr Wecht could only note that the autopsy pathologist, Dr Noguchi, and the District Attorney's observer, John Miner, had carefully examined the body and found no such mark. Dr Wecht rightly reminds us, however, that neither Noguchi nor Miner was giving serious consideration to injection as the means of death.

But the drugs had to get there somehow, and if she did not take them by mouth and was not injected, there are few alternatives left. A suppository was considered by Dr Wecht but dismissed on the grounds that the volume of barbiturates was too great to have been contained in one. The possibility of several suppositories being used is not realistic.

The large volume of drugs found in Marilyn's blood and liver – there was sufficient to kill several people – suggests to me that whoever administered them was aware of her tolerance to drugs and intended to do the job properly. Overkill was the keynote. But just how was this large volume of pentobarbital and chloral hydrate introduced into her system?

I had several conversations with Dr Wecht on the subject of enema being the means of death. Broadly, his immediate objection was based on the presence of faecal contents in Marilyn's body at the time of her autopsy. I pointed out that if drug-containing liquid was injected by enema, a plug would be required to prevent it running out, in which case the faecal contents too would be contained. While Dr Wecht accepted the theory, he reminded me that no such surgical plug existed. But I believe it would have been an improvised device, made on the spot.

When the plug was eventually removed the remains of the liquid together with some of the faecal content would have soiled the bedlinen. This would account for Eunice Murray using the washing machine in the middle of the night. I cannot believe that Mrs Murray was so fastidious that she was doing a routine wash while still traumatised by her employer's death. She was cleaning up what she saw as an embarrassing mess where Marilyn had died, and that would fit the enema scenario well.

Dr Noguchi decided to carry out further work, but when he asked for the samples he had supplied to the toxicologist, Raymond Abernathy, he was told they had been disposed of because a verdict had been reached in the case. Dr Wecht points out that this was quite irregular, and that Dr Noguchi had a right to expect the samples to be available when he wanted them. Dr Noguchi was trying to correct what he felt was an omission on his part. As he said in his book *Coroner*:

> I had forwarded certain organs, including the stomach and its contents, and the intestine, for 'further toxicological study'. Now I instantly noted that the lab technicians had not tested the other organs I had sent them. They had examined only the blood and liver.

Why this failure to perform all the tests, which is a routine procedure in the department today? The evidence found . . . pointed so overwhelmingly to suicide that the head toxicologist, Raymond J. Abernathy, apparently felt there was no need to test any further . . .

Still, I should have insisted that all the organs, including the contents of the stomach and the segments of the intestine, be analyzed. But I didn't follow through as I should have. As a junior member of the staff, I didn't feel I could challenge the department heads on procedures, and the evidence had persuaded me as well as the toxicologists that Marilyn Monroe had ingested a sufficient amount of drugs to cause her death.

Dr Noguchi here admits that he at first allowed himself to be dominated by the Chief Toxicologist, and one wonders why Abernathy felt he could make decisions over his colleague's head. Dr Noguchi was not unassertive on the matter, however, but found his guns spiked when Abernathy had disposed of the vital samples. Altogether this was a most undesirable sequence of events, which indicated at least incompetence within the coroner's office or possibly much worse.

I asked Dr Wecht if he thought an inquest should have been ordered into Marilyn's death and he replied, 'Yes. I do believe that the Los Angeles County Medical Examiner-Coroner, Theodore Curphey, should have conducted an inquest into this case.' Dr Wecht thought that ' . . . the inconsistency of the toxicology findings, coupled with all the other unanswered questions, should have mandated an open inquest'.

Had an inquest been held and questions freely asked, the mystery would have been dispelled at the very beginning. People who declined to say what they knew about the affair would have been compelled to speak out, and those like Pat Newcomb who have never answered questions from the authorities since the day of the event, would have found themselves testifying under oath. Testifying under oath would also have had a salutary effect on those who changed their stories, such as Peter Lawford and Mrs Murray. The doctors could have been asked to explain why the police were not called for hours after Marilyn had died, and the Los Angeles Police Department itself would have been pressured to carry out the workmanlike investigation into the circumstances of her death which it never did.

But then, an open inquest would have set hares running in every possible direction.

The coroner's case report. The question mark next to the word 'suicide' is interesting.

MORTUARY DEATH REPORT

FILE NO. _81178_

DATE _8/5/2_

PLEASE OBTAIN THESE FACTS CONCERNING THIS PERSONS DEATH

NAME OF DECEASED _Marilyn Monroe_ SEX _____ AGE _36_

STREET _____ CITY _____ STATE _____ RACE _Cauc._

DOCTOR (YES) (NO) DOCTORS NAME _____ TEL. NO. _____ COLOR EYES _Br._ HAIR _Blnd._

DOCTORS DIAGNOSIS _Overdose of ___ @ 3:30 A.M._ HEIGHT _5-4_ WEIGHT _115_

HOSP. DIAGNOSIS _by Dr Engelberg_ AT WORK WHEN ILL OR DIED (YES) (NO)

PLACE OF DEATH — STREET _____ CITY _____ STATE _____ DATE _____ TIME _____ (A.M.) (P.M.)

SYMPTOMS PRECEDING DEATH _____

DURATION OF SYMPTOMS _____

PAIN? (YES) (NO)  LOCATION OF PAIN _____ VOMITING (YES) (NO)

CONVULSIONS OR OBSERVATIONS _____ UNCONSCIOUS (YES) (NO)

ACCIDENT (YES) (NO)  PLACE OF ACCIDENT — STREET _____ CITY _____

ACCIDENT DATE _____ TIME _____ A.M. P.M. NATURE _____

INSURANCE? (YES) (LIFE) (NO) (ACCIDENT)  POSSIBLE (YES) SUICIDE? (NO)  GIVE DETAILS _____

NAMES AND ADDRESSES

OF PERSONS PRESENT AT DEATH _____

ADDITIONAL INFORMATION _Dr. Hyman Engelberg - 9730 Wilshire Blvd._
YOU THINK _had given refill on Nembutal day before yesterday_
IS OF VALUE

**IF NON-POLICE ACCIDENT**

DATE OF INJURY _____ TIME _____ (A.M.) (P.M.)  PLACE _____

DETAILED REPORT OF ACCIDENT, INJURY OR ADDITIONAL INFORMATION OF VALUE IN DETERMINING CAUSES OF DEATH:

_Gladys Baker - mother in Lawndale_
_Mrs Eunice Murray 937 Ocean Ave S.M. 395 775-2_
_Housekeeper_ _Gr 6 1890_

_Gall bladder operation 1½ yr ago_
_Psychiatrist talked to her yesterday, very despondent_

INFORMANTS SIGNATURE _____ MORTUARY _Westwood Village_

STREET _____ STREET _1218 Glendon Ave._

CITY/STATE _____ CITY/STATE _L.A. 24_

RELATIONSHIP TO DECEASED _____ REPRESENTATIVE _Guy R. Hockett_

A specimen of blood must be taken on every body before embalming and the bottle must be labeled immediately and carefully.  Use only bottles furnished by the Coroner.

75M20--- CAP L-6

The mortuary death report compiled by Guy Hockett.

# 9

# THE PURPLE COLON

John Miner is a distinguished Los Angeles lawyer who specialises in medical and psychiatric law, frequently handling medical malpractice suits. A graduate in psychology, he has lectured as an Associate Clinical Professor at the University of Southern California, and at the Institute of Psychiatry. In 1962 he was Deputy to the Los Angeles District Attorney whom he represented at many autopsies, including that of Marilyn Monroe which he observed in its entirety.

The examination of Marilyn's body has been described by John Miner in detail. First, he and Dr Noguchi used magnifying glasses to carry out an inch-by-inch search of her whole body, between the toes and in the orifices, for needle marks which would have indicated that she had been injected. There were no such marks.

Much has been written on this subject, since it is difficult to understand why no marks were found for the injection that Marilyn was known to have received from Dr Engelberg on the Thursday before she died. This was believed to have been a vitamin B-12 shot, an injection made with a short, very small-gauge needle and usually administered in the buttock. If this kind of injection is given properly and the site is massaged with a sterile pad, spreading the substance around, it does not become sore and the needle mark disappears quickly. Two days afterwards it is unlikely that such a mark would be detectable.

But when it came to an injection large enough to administer a lethal dose of drugs, that was a different situation. If the volume of drugs found in Marilyn's body had been injected, she would have died within minutes. There would not have been enough time for the body to absorb this quantity before death, and a large swelling containing unabsorbed drugs would have remained under the surface of the skin. No such swelling was found on Marilyn's body, so it can be said with confidence that injection was not the means of death.

Several bruises were noted, the largest of which was on her hip. These were examined and given consideration, but there was no indication that they were connected with her death. They were the kind of marks that come from bumping into furniture.

The first part to be removed when the body was opened was the ribcage. During one of several interviews given to me by John Miner, the question of the validity of James Hall's statement was discussed. Hall, it will be recalled, claimed to have been the driver of the ambulance which went to the house, and to have seen Marilyn being murdered by Dr Greenson injecting her with a large hypodermic needle, crunching what sounded like a rib to achieve the right position. The absurdity of his claim has already been demonstrated; the search for needle marks mentioned above rules out such an injection completely. I also asked Mr Miner whether the removal of the ribcage revealed

John Miner, a man of enormous integrity. The opinions he expressed in the context of this book are nothing short of momentous. He has also now released information that he has guarded in complete secrecy for thirty-four years. *Robert F. Slatzer Collection.*

any damage to the ribs, and was assured that there was no evidence of such damage.

Next the chest organs and those in the abdomen and throat were weighed and examined, with samples being taken and stored for further examination. The liver was completely removed; since it is the body's detoxifier, in cases of barbiturate overdose it plays an all-important role in helping to pinpoint the time of death, and in providing evidence of the time it took for the victim to die and information on the volume and type of drugs involved.

When the stomach was opened the expected evidence of drugs was completely missing. A little fluid was present but nothing else. There was no sign of the gelatine capsules which might have contained the drugs, and no staining from the yellow dye in the gelatine. The search for the pills was continued into the duodenum but, again, with a negative result. After this the large intestine was inspected and then the rectum. There was no sign of suppositories having been used, but the sigmoid colon showed a purplish discoloration. 'I had observed many autopsies of overdose deaths but I had never seen a purple discoloration of the colon before,' said John Miner. 'I asked Noguchi to take an anal smear but for some reason this was not done. I now wish I had pursued it further at the time. I didn't, however.'

Raymond Abernathy, the chief toxicologist, received samples of blood, organs and tissues, and conducted a whole series of tests on them. He discovered in Marilyn's blood 4.5 milligrams per cent of barbiturates and 8 milligrams per cent of chloral hydrate, enough to kill several people. He also found that her liver contained an incredible 13 milligrams per cent of barbiturates.

But John Miner, of course, was not the only one with regrets after the completion of the autopsy. Dr Noguchi noted that the laboratory technicians had not tested all of the organ samples he had sent them – only the blood and liver. And when he decided to pursue the matter a few days later he was told by Abernathy that the other samples were no longer available: 'I'm sorry but I disposed of them because we had closed the case.'

The coroner wanted Marilyn's psychiatrist, Ralph Greenson,

questioned, a task which John Miner was asked to undertake
– no doubt because of his background and qualifications. The
meeting lasted about four hours. Greenson, Miner told me,
spoke freely about Marilyn's tragic death. 'We discussed many
aspects of his patient which I undertook not to speak about
to anybody. He played me forty minutes of sound tape of
Marilyn. These were not tapes made during therapy; Marilyn
had made the recordings herself.' Marilyn had recently acquired
a tape recorder and it would appear that she was experimenting
with using it in conjunction with her therapy. 'The contents of
the tapes convinced me it was highly improbable that Marilyn
deliberately took her own life. She had plans and expectations
for her immediate future.'

Shortly before this book went to press, John Miner decided he
would tell more of what he had learnt at his meeting with Ralph
Greenson. Maybe he was influenced by our discussions on the
way so many people had suffered from the lack of information.
Marilyn Monroe suffered the ignominy of being declared a
suicide, Ralph Greenson was regarded by some as being her
killer, and many people held Robert Kennedy responsible for
whatever happened. In an interview with Charles Lawrence,
published in the London *Daily Telegraph* on 31 May 1996,
Miner said that the tapes she had made offered 'conclusive'
proof that Marilyn did not commit suicide. He confirms mention
of both John F. Kennedy and Robert Kennedy. 'She says this,
and I quote, "As long as I have memory I have John Fitzgerald
Kennedy." '

Her relationship with Robert Kennedy was confirmed, but
the tapes indicated she had ended the relationship. According
to Miner the tapes 'specifically say that he could not fit into her
future plans'. He continued, 'She explained and analysed why
he felt the love for her that he did, and expressed tremendous
concern that in breaking off their relationship she would
hurt him.'

Robert Kennedy stopped seeing Marilyn or even speaking to
her some weeks before she died; and she was greatly upset
by this and tried hard though unsuccessfully to make further
contact with him. Then there was a reversal of roles, and
when Kennedy decided he wanted to speak to Marilyn she had

changed her mind: she was not interested. *This suggests that the tapes could only have been made a day or two before Marilyn died.* The evidence that they contain of her planning her future and displaying no hint of feeling suicidal was therefore highly relevant to any consideration of what happened to her.

John Miner told me that Ralph Greenson was deeply distressed by Marilyn's death, and particularly by the idea that she had committed suicide. 'I can tell you without doubt,' said John Miner, 'Greenson did not believe that. He did not believe she had committed suicide.' This raises the question of why the man who had announced Marilyn's death as suicide to the first police officer on the scene, and who had supported that notion throughout the initial enquiries made by Sergeant Jack Clemmons and the later investigation by other police officers, should within the space of four days have changed his mind completely. Was Greenson drawn into some kind of conspiracy to promote the idea of suicide when he was at Marilyn's house shortly after she died? He was a man of considerable integrity and it would be logical, when he later realised what he had been party to, that he became anxious to withdraw from such collusion.

This was undoubtedly a major development at a time when Arthur Jacobs' publicity machine was blasting worldwide the news that Marilyn had taken her own life. Miner was not forthcoming when it came to giving an opinion on whether Greenson was saying he believed Marilyn had been the victim of an accident or whether he believed she had been murdered. 'I simply do not know,' he said. But for Ralph Greenson, who had adamantly presented Marilyn's death as suicide on the previous Sunday morning, now to make a particular point of going on record officially that he believed she was *not* a suicide merited the closest official attention.

It was John Miner's responsibility to make sure this new turn of events was promptly reported to the appropriate authorities. After his meeting with Greenson, which took place on the Wednesday following Marilyn's death, he wrote a report for submission to the coroner with a copy to go to the District Attorney. He waited, fully expecting his superior to convene a grand jury to reconsider the case in the light of his report, which for him personally would bring nothing but trouble. 'I could not have testified on ethical grounds since Greenson had my word I would not reveal what I had heard,' said Miner. 'Of course I might have been cited for contempt but I could not help that.' He waited and waited, apprehensively, for a response to his report – but nothing happened. He could not explain it. He had dropped a bombshell into the middle of the whole affair and there was no explosion. Time would prove that the Miner report, both copies, had simply disappeared.

John Miner could not forget the purplish discoloration of the sigmoid colon, and finally decided to obtain expert opinion on what he had seen. He contacted the distinguished Dr Milton Halpern, Chief Medical Examiner of the City of New York, sending him the complete Monroe autopsy file and describing what he had seen. In reply, Dr Halpern said that in his opinion the purplish discoloration was a manifestation of an inflammatory response to barbiturates in the large intestine. For another opinion, Miner sent the autopsy records to Dr Leopold Breitenecker, probably the foremost pathologist in Europe. The opinion he received was the same as Dr Halpern's. Miner now knew that the only way he could account for what he had seen was for the drugs to have been absorbed through the large intestine.

The significance of the barbiturates in the large intestine, in the context of the other autopsy data, was that it was consistent with the drugs having been introduced anally. This made sense to Miner. He knew that they had not been injected, and that it was impossible for Marilyn to have ingested such a large volume of pills orally since she would have died long before taking the number of capsules represented by the volume of drugs found in her liver. An examination of the kidneys revealed them to be clear of barbiturates, and this should have provided the clue that the stomach may have been by-passed. Of the two means of introducing the drugs anally, suppository was ruled out. 'In the case of suppository it would not have got far enough to discolour the sigmoid colon,' said Miner. 'Any discoloration and irritation would then have been confined to the rectum.

If the drug was introduced into the large intestine it is most unlikely it was by means of suppository.' This left only one alternative: infusion by enema.

Said John Miner, 'There is no question that what could have been done is – the supply of barbiturates being there – the capsules could have been opened and the powder dissolved in water, and that water administered by enema very slowly could account for her death.' It would have been easier still had Nembutal in liquid form been used. The availability of the surgical equipment to carry out an enema was no problem. Marilyn had it at home and, as part of her beauty, health and fitness treatment, took enemas from time to time. In fact it is known that she had several during the period just before her death.

In my discussions with John Miner it was as though I knew at that point which way my investigation would finally take me: for some reason I pursued the question of the time which would be necessary for a fatal enema of this kind to be administered. 'It might have taken as long as a half hour to two hours . . . How slowly or whether it was in one or two or three or four administrations one doesn't know,' he said, 'but we do know that the absorption must have been over a period of considerable time because of the 13 milligrams per cent in her liver . . . such a high percentage indicates that she was alive and the barbiturates were reaching the liver over a period of time.'

I pressed him on this subject, and he made a suggestion which was of little interest until much later in my research. 'There's this scenario,' he said, ' . . . as it was gradual absorption she lost consciousness, and if she lost consciousness, merely by . . . an anal plug . . . or whatever, the fluid could be kept there and gradually absorbed.'

John Miner wants Marilyn's body to be exhumed for tests on the lining of the lower colon, or large intestine. This will please Dr Noguchi, who will happily collaborate in any new investigation. Miner believes that because she is buried in a crypt there will be sufficient tissue to show that the drugs were administered by way of enema.

Since questioning Dr Greenson and listening to the tapes he played to him John Miner had been convinced that Marilyn did not take her life deliberately, but to researchers and writers he always left the door open to the possibility of her death having been brought about accidentally by her own hand. During the lengthy period that he and I talked about these matters, it was natural that the discussion would turn to this question. This time it seemed that John Miner was finally prepared to go further. With my tape recorder running, by permission, the questions and their answers ran as follows:

*Smith*: 'I have to say I believe unequivocally she did not commit suicide.'
*Miner*: 'Well, you've got good medical evidence to support that.'
*Smith*: 'Furthermore, considering all the facts in this case, I do not believe her death was an accident.'

John Miner looked at me and in his measured, cultured voice surprised me with his response.

*Miner*: '*I go with you there.*'

I did not pause, but pressed home the argument at once.

*Smith*: 'And in that case there is only one alternative.'

Now he said it for the first time.

*Miner*: 'Homicide.'
*Smith*: 'Is there any question of it? *Can* there be any question of it?'
*Miner*: 'I would think the medical evidence strongly supports that.'
*Smith*: 'Could anything contradict it?'

There was an incredibly long pause at this point and I repeated the question. But the answer finally came both strong and clear.

*Miner*: 'No. I don't know of anything.'

# 10

# SPINDEL'S TAPES

Some years after Marilyn Monroe's death, the occupant of her former house on Fifth Helena Drive had a roof leak, and in order to repair it a workman had to climb into the space above the ceiling. He found it strewn with wires and electronic gadgets, and since he had had experience of such devices in his army days he had no difficulty in recognising them as surveillance equipment. Marilyn's house had been well and truly bugged.

Time has revealed that the man who had Marilyn's home wired for sound was Bernard Spindel, at that time probably America's leading exponent of electronic surveillance. His 'front office' business was a detective agency: registered in his wife Barbara's name – she had been born Barbara Fox – the B. R. Fox Company was the public image created by Spindel.

Trained to the highest standards in the US Army Signal Corps, he worked for many clients, including politicians, for whom he bugged premises or debugged their own. Although his operations kept him mainly on the wrong side of the law – and to Spindel keeping out of trouble was something of a fine art – he was public-spirited enough to give lectures to the New York City Anti-Crime Committee. He accepted smaller jobs, in connection with divorce and to support charges of fraud, but it was Jimmy Hoffa, leader of the Teamsters' Union, who became his most important client and represented the big time. Hoffa retained Spindel's services not only to carry out surveillance on others but to keep his own environment free of listening devices.

He commissioned Spindel to carry out surveillance on both the President and more especially Robert Kennedy, on whom he sought embarrassing information. The Attorney General and Hoffa were sworn enemies, and RFK made no secret of his burning ambition to put his adversary behind bars. The running battle had begun in the mid-fifties when Kennedy was on McClellan's Committee on Investigations. Spindel must have been very proud of his achievement in planting a bug in the Justice Department.

When visiting the West Coast the Kennedys stayed at the Lawford beach house at Santa Monica, once owned by Louis B. Mayer. This became another target for Spindel, though since he was based in the East he got others to carry out the work. Detective Fred Otash was sub-contracted by Spindel and gave the job to his employee John Danoff. Danoff has admitted publicly that he bugged the Lawford house and speaks of placing four or five devices. He also monitored the tapes.

When John Kennedy began a relationship with Marilyn Monroe, later to be replaced by Robert, Spindel's activities were extended to Monroe's apartment and later to the house she bought at Brentwood. In the house Spindel's people really went to town. As Milo Speriglio put it: 'Everything that took place within the confines of her walls was tapped, taped, bugged and recorded. Every word she or anyone with her uttered would find itself transposed on to tapes. They even listened in her bathroom. Some of the most advanced bugging apparatus of its time – such as the voice-activated recorder – was operating in her home.'

It had again been Otash who provided the technicians for the clandestine work on Marilyn's home. A man named Arthur James, who knew Marilyn, was asked to participate by luring her away for a few days while the taps and bugs were put in place. Being a friend, he refused, but it seems he was not friend enough to warn her what was happening. The work was simply carried out without James' help. When everything was in place, Fred Otash completed the job by collecting the recorded tapes and sending them back East to Spindel.

Marilyn's meetings with John Kennedy were, therefore, monitored and recorded, and this continued when she later began an affair with his brother Robert. Marilyn eventually began to suspect that her phones were tapped and spoke to her

friend Robert Slatzer about it. It would seem that John Kennedy
had no idea what was going on, and Robert suspected nothing
until the very end of their relationship, when, it was said, he
became extremely agitated and sought furiously to locate one
of the offending bugs, probably believing it was the only one.
Whether he did in fact locate one of those placed in the house
on Fifth Helena Drive is not clear, but it is doubtful.

For years many people did not believe that the Spindel tapes ever
existed, and among those who did believe, argument raged about
what was on the recordings. Verification of the existence of the
tapes has come from various sources, one instance being the
close interest shown by the authorities. In a dawn raid carried
out on 15 December 1966, four years after Marilyn died, a
team of policemen and staff from the District Attorney's office
demanded entry to Spindel's house in upstate New York. At first
Spindel resisted and would not open the door. He faced them

Wiretapper Bernard Spindel (left), in his day the best in the business, was
commissioned to record Robert Kennedy in both the Lawford beach house
and Marilyn's house on Fifth Helena Drive. *Corbis-Bettmann/UPI.*

with a shotgun and yielded only when they produced warrants and held them up to his window to read. Ostensibly the raid was to recover property said to belong to the New York Telephone Company; when Spindel was arraigned he produced receipts for all the disputed items.

Spindel's wife, Barbara, suffered a serious heart attack while this intrusion was taking place. Men were everywhere and, though electronic equipment and other items were taken away, Spindel recognised that this was a subterfuge. They were after the Monroe–Kennedy tapes, which they took along with much of his tape bank. It is the subject of speculation that the raid was carried out at the request of Robert Kennedy, who had become Senator for New York.

In promptly filing suit for the return of the items taken, Spindel virtually went public on the existence of the Monroe tapes and the most startling result obtained from them. Among the items he specified a 'file containing tapes and evidence concerning circumstances surrounding the causes of death of Marilyn Monroe'. And, as though to underline what he had written, the affadavit contained a statement which ran: '[the confiscated tape] strongly suggests that the official reported circumstances of her death are erroneous'. While the case was waiting to be brought to court the tapes and files were 'routinely destroyed'. Bernard Spindel died before the case was heard.

A number of people claim to have heard small extracts from Spindel's tapes and, as might be expected, those which have appeared in print appear at first glance to be quite electrifying. Said to be recorded the night Marilyn died, one snippet ran, 'What do we do with the body now?' In another version of the same quotation this became, 'What do we do with her dead body?', which leaves little to the imagination. Another example was said to be a recording of an incoming telephone call from San Francisco later that night – in those days the operator announced where a long-distance call was coming from. The caller asked, 'Is she dead?' Since the Attorney General, who had been visiting Marilyn, had returned to San Francisco by the time the call was supposed to have been received, the clear implication was that he was the caller and that he was involved in some way with her death. In another version of this quotation it became, 'Is she dead yet?', as though to hammer home the message to anyone slow on the uptake.

Only one or two people have claimed to have heard lengthy sequences from the tapes. What they heard would not have included the long silences when nothing was happening, since Spindel would have edited those out. The vast majority of footage – those hours and minutes which were valuable in establishing a timescale – would in fact already have been discarded. It is this necessity to get rid of the dead wood which introduces the greatest problems with recorded sound. There is no way of knowing if 'unhelpful' parts have been discarded, if sequences have been placed in a different order to suggest a different meaning, or whether sounds have been joined together from different sources. There is no way of guaranteeing that a tape was recorded in a particular place or at a particular time.

The genuineness of what is on a tape depends, therefore, almost entirely on the integrity of the sound recordist. Bernard Spindel was considered by many to be a man of integrity, though he was also acknowledged as a man dedicated to the service of those for whom he worked. Since his main client was Jimmy Hoffa, and through him Sam Giancana and the mob, there is no telling what he did for him. The only certainty is that with bugs he was a genius and with recorded sound he was a magician.

In carrying out the raid on Spindel's home, the New York District Attorney was wasting his time. As any professional recordist will tell you, the first thing to be done with a recording of any importance is to copy it. Copies are normally kept in a different location from the original so that if one is destroyed by accident the other is safe. In some cases more than one copy is made. In the case of the Marilyn Monroe–Robert Kennedy tapes it is hard to say how many copies survive. No inference should be drawn from the show that Spindel put on when he attempted to recover his belongings through the courts. Not to have taken out a suit against the New York District Attorney's office would merely have advertised the fact that a copy or copies existed. Anthony Summers interviewed technician Earl

Jaycox, who was Bernard Spindel's assistant. Jaycox told him that Spindel had given him copies of the early Monroe tapes – 'So you can keep a set,' he had said. There is an implication here that Jaycox would eventually acquire copies of all the tapes, for it would make little sense to keep only part of the set in reserve. It is widely believed that Spindel put a set into his wife's safe keeping also.

It will be recalled from Chapter 4 that soon after the time of the raid on Spindel's house Ralph de Toledano was commissioned by a group of people with cross-party interests to locate and buy taped evidence of Robert Kennedy's affair with Marilyn Monroe. The powerful Washington group had heard of Spindel's tapes and it was clear that they did not believe the copy destroyed as a consequence of the dawn raid was the only one. Ralph de Toledano assured me that he did locate the tapes and a price of $50,000 was being asked for them – a small fortune at the time. He reported the asking price to those who had commissioned his search, but it coincided with the news that Robert Kennedy had been murdered and interest in acquiring the tapes ceased at once.

The big question relating to the tapes is what do they really contain and, therefore, what is their real value? If they contained material which would be damaging to the Attorney General, why did Jimmy Hoffa not use them against him? Of the extracts from the tapes which people claim to have heard, those most bandied about by authors are the two already quoted: 'What shall we do with her body?' and the telephone tap of the incoming call, 'Is she dead?' It should be noted, however, that to have these same extracts quoted by many authors creates the illusion that many people have heard them on the tapes. This is not true. They were originally quoted by Milo Speriglio and have been requoted over and over in various books on the subject. It should also be noted that, in one version or another, 'What shall we do with her body?' acquired both the word 'now' at the end and the word 'dead' before the world 'body', as though to make sure that the listener did not fail to understand the implications. Once again, 'Is she dead?' became 'Is she dead yet?', changing what was, perhaps, a concerned enquiry into a callous question from someone awaiting her death. It would seem clear that those who have requoted the original extracts were determined to drive home the most damaging message. All that was really achieved was that the authenticity of the first-quoted examples was weakened.

The sounds transmitted by bugs are, by general recording standards, very poor. Extraneous buzzes and hisses – often called 'mush' – impair definition. Additionally, even bugs placed in strategic places are not guaranteed to be spoken into directly by the person or persons being bugged, so it is easy for voices to be too faint to be properly heard. Surveillance tapes often need interpretation, and interpretation admits not only the possibility of error but also that of bias. One example of an extract which lends itself to both is that quoted by Milo Speriglio in his book *Marilyn Monroe: Murder Cover-Up*: 'Marilyn was slapped around. You could actually hear her being slapped, even hear her body fall to the floor. You could hear her hit the deck, and all the sounds that took place in her house that night . . .'

One is left to wonder what distinguishes the sound of slapping from many other similar sounds – unless, of course, one is listening to what might be termed 'movie slapping', where such sounds are full-blooded and resounding. It is interesting to note, however, that in making movies such sounds are recorded separately and only used when they are full-blooded and resounding enough. Assuming for a moment that the extract actually did contain the sound of slapping, there still remains the question of who was slapping whom. As for hearing Marilyn fall to the floor, this can hardly be credible in view of the thick carpet she had had laid only a few weeks before. Robert Slatzer visited Marilyn's house soon after she died and confirmed what could also be seen in the police photographs. The pile, he said, 'was so deep, the legs of Marilyn's bed disappear into the nap; the mattress appears to be lying on the floor'.

And as for hearing 'all the sounds that took place in her house that night', this is a generalisation which cannot be taken literally. A great deal of imagination would seem to have been used in interpreting whatever was on this extract from the tape.

The above extract, as quoted, is a far cry from another

version of, presumably, the same extract rendered by an informant who spoke to Anthony Summers of 'thumping, bumping noises, then muffled, calming sounds. It sounded as though she was being put on a bed.' 'Thumping' and 'bumping' are sufficiently indeterminate not to be disputable, and 'muffled, calming sounds', again, is hardly specific. When it comes to sounds of her being put on a bed, however, we get into the realm of sounds impossible to make. Even the most professional sound recordist could not capture sounds which would be recognisable as someone being put on a bed.

As already stated, the trouble with Spindel's tapes is that they require interpretation and this allows misinterpretation and bias. Additionally, it has also been stressed how easy it is to edit tapes, even to shuffle the order of sequences to produce a different meaning. Regardless of all this, however, the recognisable voices of Marilyn and Robert Kennedy would tend to provide a basis for establishing the real worth of the tapes. It is these sounds which are valued most of all, rather than the uncertain 'noises off' which are so frequently quoted.

Anthony Summers' informant had some other interesting things to say when it came to the voices of Marilyn and Kennedy. He speaks of a heated argument on the day she died:

> Their voices grew louder and louder. They were arguing about something that had been promised by Robert Kennedy. Marilyn was demanding an explanation as to why Kennedy was not going to marry her. As they argued their voices got shriller. If I had not recognised RFK's voice already, I am not sure that I would have known it was him at this point. He was screeching, high-pitched like an old lady . . .

It was thought that Robert Kennedy was seeking a bug which he now knew was in Marilyn's house. 'Where is it? Where the —— is it?' he kept demanding. A door slammed and that was the end of the sequence. In this last account of what was purported to be on the tape we were being given yet another kind of second-hand version. We were not hearing that Robert Kennedy said, for instance, 'What am I expected to do?' or that Marilyn said,

'Why won't you marry me?' We were hearing not an account of direct speech, but what someone *said* was being said.

When the tape resumed, Peter Lawford appeared to be with them. They were still looking for something, which might have been a bug or Marilyn's red diary which RFK was very anxious to acquire. 'We have to know. It's important to the family. We can make any arrangements you want, but we must find it,' seemed to be the drift of what was being said. Then there was another sequence in which tempers were raised and Marilyn was ordering them out of the house. Following this was the 'thumping and bumping' from the earlier extract.

According to Summers' source, the tape ended with the telephone ringing and being picked up. This was the supposed 'Is she dead?' call. Spindel is quoted as saying that the purpose of this was to establish that the phone was answered, raising a toll slip for the call and indicating that Marilyn was still alive. Spindel hinted that she was really dead before Kennedy left the house but, like so many things he said about the tapes, that was his opinion. Other evidence supports the idea that he had left the house long before Marilyn died.

One big question is whether Spindel would, to satisfy Hoffa's demands or even his own wishes, edit the tapes. There is always a great temptation with recorded sound to 'improve' on what is on the tape. Also, there is no knowing whether others, into whose hands the tapes fell, did not edit them. It would be interesting to hear what was really on Spindel's tapes. What started out as a boxful of 15-inch spools, recorded at the slow speed of 15/16th of an inch per second, came down to two 7-inch reels after the blank sequences were taken out. I believe that the tapes still exist, but it is puzzling that one copy or another has not surfaced. It could mean that they have been acquired by the Kennedy family or that they have fallen into the hands of enemies of the Kennedys. They would no doubt be pleased to obtain tapes which might be used maliciously. On the other hand, if the tapes proved nothing other than that Robert Kennedy did nothing or said nothing to be ashamed of, they may have fallen into the hands of Kennedy friends, who would never be likely to let them be examined.

*

Bernard Spindel, however, was not the only one listening in to what was happening at the Lawford and Monroe houses. On the grounds that Robert Kennedy was considered a security risk by conducting an affair with Marilyn, the FBI were keeping the couple under surveillance. In fact, she qualified for being kept under surveillance all on her own since, in respect of 'foreign counter-intelligence matters', the FBI had raised what was known as a 105 file on her (see Chapter 12). Marilyn had obtained a reputation for talking to all the wrong people, and the concept of the Attorney General talking to Marilyn was dynamite to the FBI. They had their bugs and taps in place and listened avidly to what was happening. There is little doubt that all the material collected from the Marilyn and Kennedy affair was given the personal attention of J. Edgar Hoover, the FBI Director, and much of it finished up in his notorious files.

And even this was not all. The CIA, for much the same reason as the FBI, had the place wired too. Members of the Agency were sworn enemies of both John and Robert Kennedy, and it is disturbing that even if the agents on the ground were not personally involved in the active hatred campaign the product of the tapes was transmitted upwards, where the risk of it falling into vindictive hands grew. The CIA at this time was a rogue elephant, controlled by no higher authority, and it was quite on the cards that the tape product was quickly made available by CIA personnel to the bitterest enemies of the Kennedy clan.

# 11

# TARGETS

There is no doubt that John and Robert Kennedy made many enemies while in office. It is inevitable, of course, that those holding high office will displease some of the people some of the time and, indeed, even incur their wrath when decisions do not suit them. But in the case of the Kennedys it was more than that. It was a deep hatred laced with venom, which they attracted by their handling of the first crisis encountered by the administration, the President's Achilles heel, if ever he had one: the Bay of Pigs episode.

When John F. Kennedy became President in January 1961, he found a timebomb waiting for him in the Oval Office. It was a plan agreed by his predecessor, Dwight D. Eisenhower, for the invasion of Cuba by Cuban exiles who had already been trained and equipped under the auspices of the CIA, whose inspiration the plan was. The Pentagon stood behind the CIA in this planned operation to oust the unwanted Castro and restore a non-communist government to Cuba. At its closest point that country is only 70 miles from the USA and it was seen as both militant and hostile, its treaties with the USSR only serving to underline the threat it constituted to the United States.

Behind Eisenhower's back, however, the CIA had made one or two changes to the planned operation. Eisenhower had agreed to the recruitment, training and arming of a band of guerrillas, who would return to Cuba as an army of liberation. The CIA had, in fact, recruited a greater number of exiles than had been envisaged, and so the general nature of the operation had changed. Additionally, the recruits had been trained not as guerrillas but as a conventional army, and these changes profoundly altered the agreed plan and intention. All this was taking place at a time when the CIA had illegally assumed so much power and authority that it was virtually a secret, independent government in its own right. It was making unilateral decisions on behalf of the United States without reference to the President or, for that matter, to any other branch of government. Former President Harry S. Truman would later refer to this when he said: 'For some time I have been disturbed by the way the CIA has been diverted from its original assignment. It has become an operational arm and at times a policy-making arm of the government. I never had any thought, when I set up the CIA, that it would be injected into peacetime cloak and dagger operations.'

The invasion plan had been in preparation for about a year and was in the final stages of preparation when John F. Kennedy took office. The new President was put on the spot. He was told that the entire success of the plan depended on the military weakness of Castro's army. Delay would allow the revolutionaries time to strengthen and benefit from MiG fighters and Russian-trained pilots promised by Moscow. In other words Kennedy was being stampeded into accepting the plan. Allen Dulles, head of the CIA, added to the pressure by publicly speaking of 'a group of fine young men who asked nothing other than the opportunity to try to restore a free government to their country . . . [They were] ready to risk their lives . . . Were they to receive . . . no sympathy, no support, no aid from the United States?'

Kennedy was on the horns of a dilemma. He had been landed with a now-or-never situation, and if ever he displayed his youth and inexperience it was over the decision he had to make at this time. Had he jettisoned the plan he would have alienated not only the CIA but those in the Pentagon who had approved it and were waiting for it to be set in motion. To add to this, there were 1400 exiles in the camps who were likely to accuse him of going 'soft' on Cuba. There was little time to debate the issues involved, but certain considerations pushed him in the direction of accepting the proposed plan. Basically this would be Cuban fighting Cuban and the USA would not be directly involved. The fact that the plan had been approved by the chiefs of staff reassured him that it had high prospects of success. Kennedy went with the operation but still had reservations. At a press conference he declared that

> there will not be, under any conditions, any intervention in Cuba by United States armed forces, and this government will do everything it possibly can – and I think it can meet its responsibilities – to make sure there are no Americans involved in any actions inside Cuba . . . the basic issue in Cuba is not one between the United States and Cuba; it is between the Cubans themselves. And I intend to see that we adhere to that principle . . . this administration's attitude is so understood and shared by the anti-Castro exiles from Cuba in this country.

The CIA made its first error two days before the invasion proper, when air attacks to destroy Castro's planes were carried out in advance of the main action. They were singularly unsuccessful and succeeded only in alerting Castro to the fact that an assault was about to be launched, for hitherto he had been in ignorance of the purpose of the camps in Guatemala. The CIA had scored a classic 'own goal'. The advance air attacks smacked of recklessness and the world was due an explanation of this behaviour. The cover story put out – that the attacks were carried out by Castro's own pilots who were revolting against him and defecting – was patent nonsense and did not fool anyone. The world was shocked at America's deception. A second air strike, planned for the day of the invasion, was cancelled by Kennedy.

Ironically, considering that the plan was organised by the CIA, the basic flaw in the operation was lack of accurate intelligence. Since the British were in possession of much superior intelligence on this particular subject, the CIA might have profited from consultation with their country's allies. One significant error was that the CIA had not expected anything like the opposition they received. Castro was able to muster 20,000 troops to repel the 1400 insurgents, and it was clear that he was not dependent on the expected consignment of MiGs from Russia, nor on the newly trained pilots. He had enough fighter planes of his own at the ready. And in addition to all this, perhaps the most fundamental error was in misjudging the reactions of the Cuban people. The CIA-predicted uprising to support the exiles did not happen.

The insurgents were soon fighting a losing battle on the beaches of the Bay of Pigs, their chosen landing point. They found themselves short of ammunition and their prospects took a nasty knock when two of the four supply ships carrying replenishments were sunk and the other two driven off. As to the battle in the air, the exiles fielded a mere sixteen elderly B-26 aircraft which were simply not up to coping with Castro's jets. Additionally, because they had to fly so far before engaging in combat their tanks only contained enough fuel to allow them one hour's activity after they arrived. In short, the invasion at the Bay of Pigs was an unmitigated disaster.

The sting in the tail seems to vary according to who is telling the story. One version is that the President was begged to intervene with airpower which could possibly have rescued many of those on the beaches – including a number of CIA personnel who were participating in the action. The CIA and the exiles asserted that Kennedy had promised this assistance and reneged. In his book *Kennedy* Theodore C. Sorensen, who was close to the President, tells a different story. He recalls that one of the supply ships driven off returned but it was by then approaching daylight.

The Cuban crew threatened to mutiny unless provided with a US Navy destroyer escort and jet cover. With the hard-pressed exiles on the beaches pleading for supplies, the convoy commander requested the CIA in Washington to seek the Navy's help; but CIA headquarters, unable to keep fully abreast of the situation on the beach and apparently unaware of the desperate need for ammunition in particular, instead called off the convoy without consulting the President.

The fact that the President had made his position clear on the issue of the intervention of the armed forces was forgotten. It was also forgotten that the basic problem with the operation was flawed planning based on poor intelligence. The CIA argued that the plan had been allowed to flounder by the President and the Attorney General, and that they personally were responsible for the slaughter on the beaches, including that of many of their colleagues.

Wisely or unwisely, John Kennedy, in statesmanlike fashion, accepted responsibility for the débâcle. From then on the relationship between the CIA and the President went into a steep decline. In short, the CIA hated the Kennedys' guts.

The growing independence of the Agency worried the President too. The Ngo Dinh Diem affair was an example of how wayward and difficult it could be. Ngo Dinh Diem was a powerful ruler in the early days of US involvement in Vietnam. The problem he created was given to the CIA to resolve, but Kennedy made a specific stipulation that murder was ruled out. In the event Diem was overthrown and killed, which a furious Kennedy saw as the defiant hand of the CIA cocking a snook at him.

This was by no means the only example which could be quoted. Another related, again, to relations with Cuba. In the settlement resulting from the eyeball-to-eyeball confrontation with Khrushchev over the Cuban missile crisis, Kennedy gave assurances that there would be no more invasions of Cuba nor attempts on Castro's life. The CIA, disregarding these assurances, set up new camps to train an army for a second invasion. Kennedy sent in the FBI to dismantle the camps and destroy the armaments.

The CIA was no longer to be trusted. When the President decided that the time had arrived to develop peaceful relations with Cuba, he obtained the services of others and kept his plans secret from the CIA. The chips were down: he declared an intention to 'splinter the CIA into a thousand pieces and scatter it to the winds'. It is hardly surprising, then, that many people believed the CIA to be behind John F. Kennedy's assassination. Whatever the truth of such allegations, there is no doubt that the CIA and the Kennedys were sworn enemies.

When both the President and the Attorney General were having affairs with Marilyn, there is no doubt that the CIA and the FBI also knew what was going on. Robert Kennedy's relationship with the FBI was problematical since he did not get on at all with the Director, J. Edgar Hoover, whose boss he was. The Kennedy brothers wanted to fire Hoover and a story circulates that they thought they had enough on him to force his hand. They invited him to lunch to tell him he must accept retirement, but Hoover was an astute man and no doubt knew of their intention. When the meal started the President withdrew an envelope from his pocket and, without a word, placed it on the table by Hoover's plate. The meal continued, and Hoover reached into his pocket to take out a larger envelope which he put by the President's plate. It was Robert Kennedy who took the envelope that Hoover had produced and read its contents. He then went away and vomited. Hoover was the only one to eat dessert, and there was no further talk of his retirement. John Kennedy had learnt that Hoover kept a personal file on him just as he did on many other leading politicians and prominent people. No doubt the reports from FBI agents on the President's womanising went straight to the Director's desk. It is surprising that John Kennedy did not curtail his amours when he discovered how much was known about them, but it seemed to make little difference. When Robert Kennedy began his affair with Marilyn, Hoover undoubtedly had a file on him too.

Robert Kennedy was not previously known as a womaniser, but that did not mean that Hoover had not found dirt of other kinds to dish on him: there was, for instance, the touchy issue of the telephone wire-taps that he approved, which would not have gone down well with the voters. The FBI always had the Attorney General under surveillance, and little happened to him that it did not know about. When he became involved with Marilyn it was a matter of course for them to watch and listen.

The CIA had an interest in Robert Kennedy's activities too, since national security was high on its list of priorities. The argument that it had no mandate for activities within the boundaries of the United States had long since been lost. The CIA did what it wanted, and for the most part no one knew what it was up to anyway.

It is reasonable to assume that the Attorney General could not make a move without the CIA being aware of it. Because of the ill-will between the Agency and the Attorney General the interest that it took in him was unhealthy, even dangerous. Although it was quite unlikely that every agent disliked the Kennedys, there was a right-wing group whose feelings ranged from intense dislike to deep hatred. And there were, no doubt, those who would have celebrated any mischief they witnessed befalling Robert Kennedy. But there were also those who were prepared to create the mischief or something worse. And when it comes to an understanding of 'something worse' I can contribute a strange tale which explains a lot. It was a well-respected Texan gentleman who told me the story, whose validity I then set about investigating. Everything about the story which was checkable proved entirely correct. The story places in sharp perspective the kind of men who were keeping watch on Robert Kennedy, and revealed how deadly the problem was.

Late in the year following the period of the Attorney General's affair with Marilyn Monroe, on Thursday, 21 November 1963, a CIA pilot was speaking to Hank Gordon, an aircraft worker he had befriended while working at Red Bird airfield at Dallas, Texas. Cuban-born, the pilot had flown for Castro before

FBI Director J. Edgar Hoover with the President and Robert Kennedy.

changing sides and enlisting with the CIA. He had been involved in the Bay of Pigs engagement and spoke of the bitterness that his fellow agents harboured for the Kennedys. He then staggered Gordon by telling him of a plan to kill John F. Kennedy when he visited Dallas on the following day, and added that Robert Kennedy would eventually be killed also. On 22 November, the following day, the President was indeed killed in downtown Dallas, and Robert Kennedy was killed at a political meeting in Los Angeles five years later. The Cuban pilot left no doubt that CIA personnel were involved in both murders.

Nor is this the only source for believing that a right-wing group within the CIA felt a special hatred towards John and Robert Kennedy. It became well known after the JFK assassination. Those in the group were identified as Bag of Pigs survivors, and it was one of these whom Hank Gordon had encountered.

The official preoccupation of the Agency was with national security, and Marilyn by herself caused concern because of the views she held and because of her friends and associates. Ralph Greenson, for instance, held left-wing views, and in 1962, at the height of the cold war, left-wing views were tantamount to communist views, which left their holder vulnerable to attention from the security agencies. Eunice Murray, Marilyn's housekeeper, had been married to a man who was proud to acknowledge that he was a union activist. Meetings were held at the Murrays' house, which marked the couple out as having left-wing sympathies.

Marilyn's physician, Hyman Engelberg, had well-documented communist connections. His name appeared on the register of the Communist People's Educational Centre, where he taught late in 1937. As speaker or supporter, Engelberg had political sympathies which were easily identified. At the US House Committee on Un-American Activities hearings in 1954, he was identified as a member of the communist party.

Marilyn's third husband, of course, was a one-time communist, Arthur Miller. During the time that she was married to him, Miller had a hard time from the House Committee on Un-American Activities. The Committee constituted an unvarnished attack by the US government on the communist party and its adherents. They were determined, whatever the cost to individuals and their civil liberties, to expose those who supported the communist party and who, they believed, were threatening to undermine American society. The Committee had been formed in the late forties, though it was not until Senator Joseph McCarthy took control in 1950 that it became involved in the extreme witch-hunts. Of considerable concern to the Committee was the entertainment industry with its tremendous capacity to instruct and influence and, deserved or not, the careers of many talented men and women were destroyed. Some suffered what might be called professional death; others actually committed suicide. Those who survived were glad to eke out a living by performing menial tasks.

Arthur Miller had had connections of some kind with the communist party but for years his life and work had escaped the attention which had been focused on some of his friends and associates by the McCarthy machine. In 1956 this changed and he was called to answer to the House Committee. He admitted signing a form at a gathering almost twenty years previously, but would not admit to having taken out membership of the communist party. He was pressed to give the names of those he had seen at political meetings and his out-and-out refusal to do so earned the wrath of his inquisitors. He was found guilty of contempt of Congress.

Marilyn's support during the period of his Un-American Activities conflict made a huge difference to Miller. The press portrayed him as the tormented husband of popular film star Marilyn Monroe and this modified attitudes. Marilyn was warned to back off as she was risking her own career, but she staunchly stood by her husband until he won the day. After a two-year battle an appeal was finally upheld, and the contempt conviction quashed. Though politics could hardly have been said to be Marilyn's scene, she was interested and held straight views, usually siding with the underdog. It was strange that she should hit it off so well with Robert Kennedy, although she may not have been aware that he was an impassioned McCarthyite and had been at one time on McCarthy's staff.

On a trip to Mexico Marilyn met and befriended Fred

Vanderbilt Field, an American living there. Field, a member of a wealthy family, was well known as a communist in exile, and he and his Mexican wife got on well with Marilyn. Her political leanings, her feelings for the underdog and the rights of blacks, and her views on civil rights in general endeared her to them and the circle in which they moved. A Mexican with whom she became romantically involved, José Bolanos, was also interested in Marilyn's politics, though he did not mix with the Field group who suspected him of insincerity in this sphere.

Her Mexican friendships, together with the company she kept at home and her staunch defence of Arthur Miller, attracted the attentions of the CIA, who looked at Marilyn in a new light. She was seen as a left-winger and, when she formed a relationship with the Attorney General of the United States, one to keep an eye on. Outlandish though this at first appears, it was not without a degree of merit. Marilyn is known to have given Fred Field an account of various political discussions that she had with Robert Kennedy. If Robert Kennedy was regarded as a security risk, so was Marilyn.

In 1962 the Bay of Pigs disaster was still very fresh in the minds of the American people and in the minds of John F. and Robert Kennedy also. It was also very fresh in the minds of Agency personnel. The CIA men who had watched the President sailing against the wind in forming a relationship with Marilyn and who were now observing Robert Kennedy on his trips to Los Angeles to meet the same girl hovered like vultures. They were watching and waiting for him to put a foot wrong, ready to capitalise on any problems which arose in a matter of this kind. Matters of this kind, handled in the right way, sank politicians without trace.

The CIA personnel were no doubt aware that they were not the only ones conducting surveillance on Robert Kennedy and Marilyn. Hoover's men had their bugs in Marilyn's house and, in circumstances where they were working cheek by jowl, the Agency might well have been expected to rationalise and share facilities with the FBI. This was quite unlikely, however, and with the Bernard Spindel bugs and taps also in place it was getting ridiculously crowded in the star's hacienda.

# 12

# KENNEDY AND HOFFA

Robert Kennedy had always been a man with many enemies, and never more so than at the time when he was conducting an affair with Marilyn Monroe. Some of them were attracted by the fact that he was a Kennedy, others because he was the Attorney General. His greatest enemy, however, he had hand-picked for the part. That was Jimmy Hoffa.

Hoffa was President of the Teamsters' Union, which he had worked for since the early thirties when, as a young man, he had fallen under the influence of Trotskyite Farrell Dobbs. When Dobbs moved on to the Socialist Workers' Party in 1939, Hoffa stepped up in rank but his attraction to Dobbs remained. Later he lured Dobbs back to the Teamsters because he valued his work, ideas and dedication so greatly.

A broad-shouldered, stockily built man, Hoffa was intelligent and charming but also possessed of a flaming temper. Although ruthless, aggressive and lacking in moral standards, Jimmy Hoffa knew the trucking business well and was responsible for obtaining higher wages, shorter hours and enhanced working conditions for the union's members. From a membership of only 7500 in 1933 the Teamsters had grown to well over a million strong by 1956. Here was a man with the capacity for achieving a great deal for the workers in the trucking industry. Unhappily, however, Hoffa was not in business exclusively for the benefit of others. He was in it very much for what he got out of it for himself – immense personal wealth, respect from the Mafia to whom he owed allegiance, and enormous power. Known to take bribes from employers for obligingly calling off strikes, he was suspected of corruption of various kinds and even of committing murder.

Charged with bribery and corruption, Hoffa was – unbelievably – acquitted, but was next served with subpoenas by the Rackets Committee, on which Robert Kennedy served. As Arthur M. Schlesinger Jr put it in *Robert Kennedy and His Times*:

> The testimony before the committee had convinced Robert Kennedy that Jimmy Hoffa had stifled democratic procedures within the union, had ordered the beating and very possibly the murder of union rebels, had misused union funds to the amount of at least $9.5 million, had taken money and other favors from employers to promote personal business deals, had brought in gangsters to consolidate his control and had tampered with the judicial process in order to escape prosecution ... He was running not a bona fide trade union but a 'conspiracy of evil', a conspiracy that had seized control of the most powerful institution in the country – aside from the United States Government itself.

There is no doubt that Robert Kennedy's battle with Jimmy Hoffa took on the attributes of a personal vendetta. Those around him recognised this and were dubious of its wisdom, but Kennedy mustered all his energies in the prosecution of a man whom he saw as corrupt and evil. Attorney General Robert H. Jackson, writing in 1940, warned of such a situation,

> The most dangerous power of the prosecutor: that he will pick people that he thinks he should get, rather than pick cases that need to be prosecuted. With the law books filled with a great assortment of crimes, a prosecutor stands a fair chance of pinning at least a technical violation of some act on the part of almost anyone ... It is in this realm – in which the prosecutor picks some person he dislikes or desires to be embarrassed, or selects some group of unpopular persons and then looks for an offense – that the greatest danger of abuse of prosecuting power lies.

But the vendetta was up and running, and Kennedy's 'Get Hoffa' campaign came into being.

Hoffa attracted to himself and to the union gangsters and people with close connections to the mob. Among those were Tony Provenzano of New Jersey, who gained control of Local 360 of the Teamsters, the infamous Barney Baker from New York, Shorty Feldman, Johnny Dio, Joey Gallo, also from New York, and Joey Glimco from Chicago. His close associates numbered Momo Salvatore (Sam) Giancana, described by Robert Kennedy as 'chief gunman for the group that succeeded the Capone mob'.

Sam Giancana became a friend of Frank Sinatra, and through him met Marilyn Monroe when she was Sinatra's guest at the Cal-Neva Lodge, which was jointly owned by the singer and Giancana. Giancana, the boss of organised crime in Chicago, developed a penchant for the playboy life. He ranked high in the Mafia hierarchy and was involved with activities beyond those common to the hoodlum. Perhaps his most noted escapade was when, with Johnny Roselli, he was sub-contracted by the CIA to murder Fidel Castro. When this came to light it revealed a seamy side of the Agency not hitherto seen and the nation was staggered that it had stooped so low. Besides this, it was a case of one government agency carrying on 'business' with these men at the same time as another – headed by Robert Kennedy, as Attorney General – was trying to put them behind bars. Kennedy loathed Giancana in much the same way as he loathed Hoffa.

Kennedy and Hoffa once found themselves facing each other in a New York courthouse elevator.

'Hello, Jimmy.'

'Hello, Bobby.'

Kennedy enquired how the trial was going.

'You can never tell with a jury. Like shooting fish in a barrel.'

Hoffa was acquitted, and an investigation was ordered into juries and jury tampering. A pattern was forming when it came to Hoffa's acquittals. Once Kennedy accused him of threatening to kill a man, to which he replied, 'If I did it no jury would ever convict me. I have a special way with juries.' Hoffa's 'way with juries' was very successful at keeping him out of jail, which frustrated Kennedy.

The hostility between the two men could rarely be seen in a humorous light, though one well-known story recounts that Robert Kennedy was driving home from work one night when, passing the building which contained Hoffa's office, he looked up and saw his light burning. 'If he's still at work, we ought to be,' he snapped to the colleague who was with him, and promptly turned the car around and went back to work for another two hours. Jimmy Hoffa heard about this and, to tantalise Kennedy, left his office lights burning when he left in the evening.

But such humour was highly unusual. As Arthur M. Schlesinger Jr wrote: 'Each represented what the other destested most. Hoffa saw Kennedy as the arrogant rich kid for whom everything in life had been easy. Kennedy saw Hoffa as the cynic who betrayed honest working men and had no object in life beyond money and power for himself.'

Teamsters' Union leader Jimmy Hoffa was the arch-enemy of Attorney General Robert Kennedy, but Kennedy never managed to put him behind bars. *Corbis-Bettmann/UPI.*

In early encounters with Hoffa, Kennedy had learnt he was not a man to be treated disdainfully. Once when he found himself in the same restaurant he decided he would speak to the union leader off the record. But when he clutched the man's arm to gain his attention a whirlwind was let loose. Hoffa turned on him, grabbing him by the lapels. 'Let me tell you something, Buster, I'm gonna tell you this one time. If you ever put your mitts on me again, I'm gonna break you in half.' Kennedy was then ignominiously dismissed by being pushed against the wall. It was real hoodlum stuff.

One broad-fronted attack made by Robert Kennedy was through the book he wrote in the late fifties, called *The Enemy Within*. Ostensibly Kennedy was writing about the work of the Rackets Committee, which was chaired by Senator John L. McClellan and for which he was chief counsel. His brother John also served on that committee, but it was Robert's show. The book described the operation of the Mafia, though it was never mentioned by name, and the Teamsters' Union and Jimmy Hoffa in particular were paid close attention. In Britain the press magnate Lord Beaverbrook spoke of it as 'a detective story which can be put on the same shelf as the best thriller fiction of the day'. He continued, 'I feel rather like one who has been sent an account of the Crusade written by Richard the Lionheart himself.' It was Robert Kennedy's wish that the book should be filmed for consumption by a wider audience, and it was Twentieth Century-Fox who took it aboard. Veteran producer Jerry Wald, who had produced two of Marilyn's films, was designated to produce and Paul Newman was to star.

Within days of the announcement of the making of the film things began to happen. Threatening letters and phone calls were received by the studio and personally by Wald. The mob had read the book and did not want the movie made. Represented by their man in Hollywood, Johnny Roselli, they had for many years been paid protection money by the studios and they regarded this new anti-Mafia film as a dangerous project. It was tantamount to being bitten by the animal they had tamed. As Hollywood detective Fred Otash put it, '. . . the mob doesn't like the spotlight', and they made it quite clear to Hollywood that they would not have it. A Hoffa attorney completed the harassment and Fox decided to abandon the project.

This was a blow to Kennedy, though it revealed only what he already knew: the power wielded by the forces of the underworld was so great that it could reach out and control even what people saw at the movies. The relentless struggle continued, and nobody knew the score better than Robert Kennedy. While his 'Get Hoffa' squad sought justice through the law, Hoffa's attitude was betrayed in a comment he made to one of his henchmen. 'Kennedy has got to go,' he said. 'Somebody needs to bump that sonofabitch off.'

Hoffa was astutely learning how to handle Robert Kennedy, however. He knew it was not always necessary to use physical violence to intimidate people – as when, arrested for bribery and corruption, he found himself in an empty courtroom facing his enemy. 'He stared at me for three minutes with complete hatred in his eyes,' reported Kennedy. But then, it was not only Hoffa who was learning. There was one particular lesson that Robert Kennedy appreciated after the frustration of trying to question Hoffa in the McClellan hearings. 'My biggest problem as counsel,' he admitted, 'is to keep my temper. I think we all feel that when a witness comes before the United States Senate he has an obligation to speak frankly and tell the truth. To see people sit in front of us and lie and evade makes me boil inside. But you can't lose your temper – if you do, the witness has gotten the best of you.'

Kennedy did not know how closely he had hit the mark when it was Hoffa who was the witness. On the receiving end, however, how did Hoffa rate Kennedy's performance? He thought the chief counsel's questioning was 'painfully amateurish'. It was 'ridiculously simple to get him to lose his temper. It was equally easy to get him to wander from the subject he was pursuing and to tie him up in knots of verbiage and dialectics.' What he did not say was that the chief counsel's questioning was so penetrating and forthright that he was even accused by some of being vindictive. And the Teamsters' President would not be privy to an appraisal rendered by fellow lawyer Paul Porter, who wrote to Kennedy saying that the hearings were 'an oustanding example of preparation, presentation and fairness'.

*

In the 'battle of the bugs', it is hard to say whether the victor was Kennedy or Hoffa. Each kept the other under surveillance, and each used state-of-the-art technology. Kennedy had Hoffa's offices bugged; Hoffa, employing ace wiretapper Bernard Spindel, dealt with this by having them 'swept'. Hoffa also went on the offensive by commissioning Spindel to put both Robert and John Kennedy under surveillance; bugs were placed in the Justice Department when Robert Kennedy became Attorney General, in Peter Lawford's Malibu beach house, in Marilyn Monroe's apartment and, when she bought it, her house. Peter Lawford had married the sister of John and Robert Kennedy, so it was natural that they should stay at the Lawfords' house when they visited the West Coast. So frequent were their visits that it was nicknamed the Pacific White House.

Robert Kennedy was anxious to obtain any information from his surveillance of Hoffa which would help to put the Teamsters' leader behind bars, where Kennedy believed he belonged. Hoffa was seeking to discredit the Attorney General and so rid himself of the permanent state of siege under which he now lived. It would have done equally well for Hoffa to discredit the President, for, since the post of Attorney General was one of patronage, if John went so did Robert.

Both Kennedy brothers appeared to be in blissful ignorance of the existence of the bugs in the Lawford mansion and the Monroe house. As for bugs hidden elsewhere, it would be very hard even to guess where Spindel might have planted his tiny 'ears'. In Washington, however, Robert was either aware or suspicious that Spindel had him wired, for he carried a 'debugging' briefcase containing equipment to interfere with transmissions.

The cost of the war between Kennedy and Hoffa must have been considerable. When official budgets and the like were taken into account, however, there had to be limits on what Kennedy had at his disposal. On the other hand, with the financial power of the Teamsters behind him and control over how it was spent, Jimmy Hoffa had virtually unlimited funds to wage hostilities. The United States (Teamsters) Pension and Welfare Fund was known as the Bank of the Mafia, no doubt from the loans it made to racket-connected projects. The cost of fighting Kennedy and the law would be seen as justifiable expense – even legitimate expense – by Hoffa and his henchmen. Whereas Kennedy had sixteen lawyers and thirty investigators in his 'Get Hoffa' squad, Hoffa had the contacts, the means of obtaining the information he wanted, and the legal backing to give him the advantage. This was periodically advertised by his success in beating off Kennedy's attempts to put him behind bars.

Hoffa knew the law and the way it worked. According to a story which Hoffa told, his very first brush with Robert Kennedy was when the chief counsel stormed into his office during a meeting and demanded sight of the files. The astute Hoffa knew his rights and promptly threw Kennedy out, together with aide Pierre Salinger and accountant Carmine Bellino who had accompanied him. The next day Kennedy, Salinger and Bellino turned up with a subpoena, which Hoffa passed to his lawyer to scrutinise. Since a subpoena had to specify what was being looked for and the law further required that individual papers should each be signed, Hoffa's lawyer decided that this one, which did neither, carried no weight and the three were again escorted to the door.

Hoffa and the Teamsters had at their disposal what has been termed the biggest slush fund in history. Through excessive labour charges, the Teamsters affected the price of almost everything found in any shop in the USA. It is, therefore, ironic to consider that while Kennedy and the United States government had taken on Hoffa and the Teamsters in the best interests of the nation, it was – indirectly – the nation which was providing the funds for Hoffa to fight Kennedy and the government.

It is interesting to note a distinct connection between Jimmy Hoffa and the assassination of President Kennedy. The link is Jack Ruby, the man who murdered Lee Harvey Oswald, the suspect in the assassination, in cold blood in the basement of Dallas Police Headquarters.

Between 1937 and 1940 Ruby, then called Jacob Rubenstein, was involved in the running of Local 20467 in Chicago, otherwise known as the Scrap Iron and Junk Handlers' Union. The founder and president of the union, a high-minded man named Leon Cooke, was shot to death in 1939. John Martin, a union official, was said to have murdered Cooke, while Jacob Rubinstein was suspected of complicity and reportedly spent over a year in prison as a consequence. Years later Eva Grant, Rubinstein's sister, would say of the affair that Cooke was 'a highly reputable lawyer. That's why they killed him.'

The Chicago mob took control of Local 20467, drafting it into the Teamsters' Union and causing consternation at higher levels. The union was suspected of being a front for organised crime and the state of Illinois seized its books. At yet another level, a Senate investigation declared that a link had been established between Hoffa and the underworld. Here lay the connection between Jacob Rubinstein and Jimmy Hoffa.

In 1947 Rubenstein changed his name to Jack Ruby and moved to Dallas with other thugs and hoodlums to take over the slot machine business in Texas, Louisiana and Arkansas. He was described as a 'syndicate lieutenant who had been sent to Dallas as a liaison for Chicago mobsters'. It is left for us to wonder whether, in shooting Oswald, he was carrying out the orders of the mob, or even those of Hoffa specifically. He certainly gave the appearance of a man under orders, and he was certainly in close contact with Hoffa henchmen Barney Baker and Red Dorfman until the event occurred.

A fascinating irony of the Kennedy–Hoffa story was the similarity between the two men. Journalist Hal Clancy wrote of RFK that he was 'the coiled spring of a man constitutionally unrelaxed . . . like the impatient discipline of the hungry fighter, completely confident but truly relaxed only in the action he craves'. Journalist and one-time diplomat John Bartlow Martin, writing of Hoffa, said, 'It is as though the core of Hoffa's personality were all a tightly wound steel spring . . . He is always stripped for a fight, for action.' In a direct comparison of Kennedy and Hoffa, Martin later wrote of them as being 'aggressive, competitive, hard-driving, authoritarian, suspicious, temperate, at times congenial and at others curt'. Arthur M. Schlesinger Jr could add a lot to these, however:

Both were blunt, candid and commanding. Both drove

themselves and their staffs relentlessly. Both, in separate ways, had an instinct for the underdog; both had the instinct of underdogs themselves. Both had devoted friends and deadly enemies. Both had strong veins of sardonic humor. Both prided themselves on physical fitness. Neither smoked. Kennedy drank sparingly; Hoffa never. Neither wore hats. Both loved their wives. Both were risk takers . . .

Although it must be remembered that it was the differences between the two that made them what they were, one final, grisly comparison must be made. Robert Kennedy was shot to death at a political meeting at a hotel in Los Angeles after receiving the nomination to run for the presidency, while Jimmy Hoffa suddenly disappeared when trying to obtain reinstatement to the Teamsters after his term in prison. He was never seen again.

During the 'Get Hoffa' campaign, Robert Kennedy was ostensibly in the driving seat and in control. Hoffa, however, always managed to keep himself far enough from the McClellan chief counsel who became the Attorney General not to be hurt by him, while contriving to remain close enough to constitute a constant threat. The surveillance of the affair between Kennedy and Marilyn Monroe is an example of how the activities of the Attorney General were subjected to the scrutiny of the Mafia chief. The mystery is why Hoffa never used the information he gathered on both John and Robert Kennedy. As was indicated in Chapter 10, however, sound recordings are not the most potent weapon in trying to discredit an enemy. A better explanation, however, might be that Hoffa, a very well-informed man, became aware of a group which had come into existence, dedicated to the removal of the President by whatever means it took, and the removal, also, of any other member of the Kennedy family who became a candidate for the presidency. The tapes may have become obsolete.

Robert Kennedy devoted ten years of his life to 'getting Hoffa' and never had the satisfaction of putting him behind bars. It was his successor as Attorney General in the Lyndon B. Johnson administration, Nicholas Katzenbach, who finally achieved it.

# 13

# THE NEARLY INVESTIGATION

In Chapter 7 the shoddy investigation into the death of Marilyn Monroe was identified as a cover-up on the part of the Los Angeles Police Department at the direction of Chief William Parker. Whilst the cover-up was enormously successful, it did not convince everyone, particularly those who knew rather more about the circumstances surrounding Marilyn's death. Outstanding in this group was Robert Slatzer.

Slatzer had been married to Marilyn for only a few days when the studio bosses took steps to have the union dissolved on the grounds that it interfered with the image they were creating for their star. Slatzer, however, remained Marilyn's friend for life and he it was, together with Lionel Grandison who had been coroner's aide in 1962, who led a campaign to expose the cover-up of what they both believed to be her murder. Robert Slatzer wrote two books on the subject which aroused worldwide interest, and engaged private detective Milo Speriglio – who added a further three books promoting his theories – to investigate her death.

But there were more than these few people who believed there had been foul play. Many journalists had expressed in print their doubts about the coroner's verdict. Among Marilyn's friends and acquaintances, too, doubts had led to suspicion of murder. Her close friend Jeanne Carmen, for instance, believed she had been killed and so did Robert Mitchum, her old friend and co-star of *River of No Return*. The first police officer at the scene of her death, Sergeant Jack Clemmons, was also convinced that she had been murdered.

Through the press and publications, and the persistence of Slatzer and Grandison, pressure was brought to bear on the Los Angeles District Attorney, and a situation was created in which the DA felt compelled to reply. Thus in 1982, twenty years after Marilyn's death, the impossible appeared to have been achieved. A review of the case was ordered by District Attorney John K. Van de Kamp, the consequence of which was the publication, on 28 December 1982, of an official report. As will be seen in this chapter, it did not stand up well in critical analysis as an answer to the serious questions which had been placed before it. The report began encouragingly enough, though: 'The DA review into the 1962 death of actress Marilyn Monroe was conducted under my authorization following a series of well-publicized allegations to the effect that she might have died as a result of foul play, at the hands of another or others.' Any satisfaction in reading this, however, quickly evaporated with the next paragraph: 'Our review has produced no substantiation for such a conclusion. Based on the evidence available to us, it

Robert Mitchum still wonders why Marilyn wanted so badly to speak to him shortly before she died. *Robert Mitchum.*

appears that her death could have been a suicide or come as a result of an accidental drug overdose.' It is extremely interesting, however, to examine the outcome of a review conducted, as the report says, 'because it appeared necessary to determine the truth or falsity of the most recent allegations'.

The report stated that no DA investigation or full-scale case review had occurred in 1962. This was of particular interest in view of its statement that

> The first step in the threshold examination was to secure all existing documents from official sources. District Attorney files and archives were examined; all existing files in the possession of the Coroner's Office and the Los Angeles Police Department were requested. In addition, the United States Department of Justice was queried as were the local FBI offices.
>
> Several agencies routinely purge files after a fixed period of time, usually ten years or less, and therefore some difficulty was experienced in attempting to recreate a complete documentation from official sources. Fortunately many individuals who had personal knowledge of the events surrounding the death in 1962 are still alive and were interviewed. Documents reviewed included LAPD reports (some of which were reconstructed); Coroner's reports (including toxicological reports); FBI reports (although heavily censored); news reports and other publications.

Several important points emerge from this passage. It is noted that 'District Attorney files and archives were examined', which implies that there were documents to find under this heading and that they had survived for twenty years. Disappointingly, there are no quotations from them in the report. When it came to the LAPD files, which should have provided a cornerstone in this enquiry, they required 'reconstruction'. There is an implicit acknowledgement here that the cornerstone was really not there, which comes as no surprise since the bulk of the file had by this time well and truly disappeared. The term 'reconstruction', however, could mean many things, including the revision or sanitation of remaining documents. As for the FBI files, we are left wondering what they were concealing in their 'heavily censored' documents. In total, one is not quite sure whether they really just had little luck obtaining documents or whether they had little luck *apart from documentation still not for publication*. Clearly neither the absence of documents nor the censoring of them raised doubts among the investigators about Marilyn's death.

The DA's investigators interviewed, the report states, forty people. In outlining the 'known facts' of the case they managed to acknowledge only one contentious issue, although almost certainly without realising it. They refer to the time of death as being the night of 4 August or the early hours of 5 August. Knowing that they had interviewed Mrs Murray and in view of her earlier statements, it would have been surprising if the investigators really felt any doubt about the time when Marilyn actually died. The official view had always been the small hours of the morning to comply with Mrs Murray's claim that she called Dr Greenson at about 3.30 a.m. In referring to 'the night

District Attorney John K. Van de Kamp made sure he did not muddy the waters in the investigation that nearly was.

of August 4' the DA's team got it right without knowing it, it seems. We now know it is likely that she was dying for some time before midnight and expired shortly after 12 p.m. Had they realised what they were saying, however, the reference would almost certainly have been changed. The inadvertent expression of doubt about the time of death would have had the effect of heaving large bricks into the pool.

When the review moved to the subject of the autopsy report, a special note was made of the fact that samples were retained: 'At 10.30 a.m. on August 5, 1962, Deputy Coroner Examiner, Dr Thomas Noguchi performed the autopsy on Miss Monroe's body. He also took samples of blood and liver materials which he submitted for toxicological study. Other samples were taken and saved for future study on an as-needed basis.'

It did not, however, mention the fact that when Dr Noguchi sent for his retained samples in order to do further work that he deemed necessary they had been disposed of. There was no mention, either, of the disappearance of the smear-slides which should have survived to this day. When it came to the number of capsules ingested, which had been calculated originally at forty-seven, a number which had justifiably been disputed, no attempt was made in the report to reconcile this problem.

An independent expert, Dr Boyd G. Stephens, the Chief Medical Examiner-Coroner of the City and County of San Francisco, was asked to examine the written reports relating to the autopsy. He found no fault with the conduct of the autopsy. Among other things he addressed himself to that aspect of the autopsy which many people had found the most puzzling. This was the absence of remnants of gelatine capsules, since it appeared strange that after ingesting such a huge volume of drugs no trace of them was found in her stomach or digestive tract. Said Dr Stephens: 'These substances dissolve rapidly and their constituents are rapidly absorbed into the body. On an empty stomach the absorption rate and the movement from the stomach to the duodenum is more rapid.' The report also says on this subject: 'Dr Stephens and others with whom we've conferred do not find this fact to be significant. On the contrary, when the overdose victim does not die rapidly, pathologists expect to find total absorption of the capsules and pills into the intestinal tract.'

It is the last sentence which provides an interesting clue. It appears that Dr Stephens' medical opinions were totally based on the assumption that Marilyn ingested the drugs, perhaps over a long period of time, and then took a long time to die. He quotes the difference between the level of pentobarbital in the blood (4.4 mg per cent) and the level of the drug in the liver (13 mg per cent) to support his assumption, but to other experts this meant quite the opposite. The same documents as were available to Dr Stephens were given to another medical examiner, Dr Sidney B. Weinberg of Suffolk County, New York, by Robert Slatzer. He considered the levels of pentobarbital in the blood and in the liver and rendered this opinion:

. . . since numerous capsules and tablets of prescription drugs were found at the scene, all of the type which are ingestible, it is difficult to conceive that some trace of these drugs would not be found in the stomach or intestinal tract. One might explain the lack of these findings in the stomach on the basis of an exceedingly long interval between the time the drugs were ingested and the time she expired, but in view of the levels in the blood and liver this would not seem to be the case.

The coroner, Dr Curphey, rendered the opinion that Marilyn had taken a large volume of the drugs 'within a short period of time'. He also expressed the view that she had taken them 'in one gulp within – let's say – a period of seconds'. In this case she would have been more likely to have been overwhelmed by the drugs and to have died quickly. Additional evidence comes from the fact that Marilyn went on making telephone calls long into the evening, the last one at about 10 p.m., with no mention in her late calls of any emergency. Her last call was made to Jeanne Carmen, who detected no problem. Marilyn wanted her to come over to Fifth Helena Drive, in fact, regardless of the hour. She was patently not steadily ingesting pills.

If Marilyn died quickly, remnants of the gelatine capsules and traces of the yellow dye from the gelatine should both have been present, unless the drugs were administered other than by mouth. Dr Stephens appears to have been looking in one direction only; and other medical opinion, had it been sought, would strongly contradict the assumptions which persuaded him to do so. Dr Weinberg's expert opinion had been obtained by Robert Slatzer in 1973, nine years before the DA's threshold investigation, and Slatzer provided a copy in 1982. But the DA chose to ignore what Dr Weinberg had to say. It would, therefore, appear that he preferred Dr Stephens' version. The fact that the DA would not concede that there might be another opinion worth considering illustrates the narrow thinking in this so-called threshold investigation.

When the DA's team addressed itself to the question of why the gelatine capsules had not left a tell-tale trail of yellow dye in the stomach and digestive tract, an approach was made to Abbott Laboratories, the company which made the capsules, and investigators spoke to their representative, who forthrightly 'surmised that since a coloring agent is placed in Nembutal capsules, there should be a residue of the coloring agent remaining in the body of overdose victims in cases of large toxic quantities'. Since this would not appear to leave any room for doubt, the DA's investigators must have asked different questions in their attempts to find support for the opposite argument. These elicited the following statement: 'The Abbott spokesman acknowledges, however, that no studies or scientific papers of which he is aware have been written supporting this hypothesis.'

This, of course, is relatively meaningless. The absence of studies or scientific papers in no way proves the representative's original statement wrong. It might be said, also, that chemists usually know the effects and properties of common substances like yellow dye. But, determined to press home the argument, the report quotes three autopsy surgeons, including Dr Noguchi who carried out the autopsy on Marilyn Monroe, who assert that 'such a color residue is almost unheard-of in Nembutal deaths'. They speak of the evidence from hundreds of Nembutal overdose victims, but it is noted that they do not specify any details or make specific comparisons with the Monroe case. Also, in spite of such apparently overwhelming evidence to the contrary, Dr

Sidney Weinberg says on this subject, 'The capsules also usually have some dye in them which stains objects which they come into contact with when moist. This is often seen in the stomach and in cases where large amounts are ingested, there are focal areas of corrosion of the lining of the stomach.'

Finally on the subject, the report implies that there has been confusion with the red dye sometimes associated with overdoses of Seconal, which does leave traces.

> Mr Grandison reported that he saw associated with Miss Monroe's property a scrawled note and a red diary. He alleges that both items disappeared from the Coroner's office shortly after the autopsy was performed. Grandison claims to have briefly examined the diary and noted that it contained the names of government figures and perhaps matters relating to sensitive government operations. Our investigation points to the conclusion that Mr Grandison is in error . . .

Lionel Grandison was a coroner's aide, a fairly low-level job in the coroner's office. His role in the Marilyn Monroe case related to two claims he made, first the sighting of the red diary and a scrap of paper, and secondly that he was coerced into signing the death certificate.

As Grandison explained, documents are sometimes removed by the coroner's staff at the time the body is collected in order to obtain the name and address of someone to notify and to whom the official documents may be sent. The red diary, he claimed, was picked up in that context. Grandison said he looked through the book which, he claimed, disappeared and has never been seen since.

The DA's report attempts to establish that the diary never existed, on the one hand, and, effectively, that Lionel Grandison is an inventive liar on the other. Grandison, it argues, had never mentioned the existence of the diary before reading about it in Robert Slater's book *The Life and Curious Death of Marilyn Monroe*. Besides which, it says, it must have been lying handy for it to have been seen and taken from the house, which means that Sergeant Jack Clemmons, the first policeman at the scene, would certainly have seen it. Sergeant Clemmons, of course, did not see it. In fact he commented that there was a curious absence of documents and letters of the sort which are usually found lying around. Grandison's claim was weak in all respects, therefore, and it is small wonder that the DA's investigation dismissed the matter of the disappearing diary. I must, however, profoundly disagree with the DA's next move.

In an attempt to discredit Grandison, the report attacks *all* claims for the existence of the red diary. In identifying Robert Slatzer as the only source for the existence of the diary, there is a subtle hint that he too might be an inventive liar. Thus the credibility of a knowledgeable and reliable man of integrity had an immediate cloud cast upon it. The report quotes Pat Newcomb, Mrs Murray and Marilyn's 'masseuse' as saying they had never seen such a diary: 'Her closest associates seriously doubt that Marilyn Monroe had the emotional strength to maintain any sort of diary during this period.'

It is surprising that Pat Newcomb did not see a diary, for she and Marilyn were close. In the case of Mrs Murray, they must have been as aware as anyone that this lady kept changing her story and a statement on this subject from her was worthless in any case. How a masseuse enters into it is unknown, unless they meant her masseur, Ralph Roberts, who was a close friend. In any case, by the very nature of a diary it is personal, indeed secret, and it should not have come as any surprise to the DA's investigators that those around her did not know of its existence.

In this oblique attack on Robert Slatzer's integrity, the District Attorney sailed close to the wind. It seemed that I was able to achieve what the DA could not. Earlier, reference was made to a statement from Marilyn's close friend, Jeanne Carmen, that Robert Kennedy came across the red diary when visiting Marilyn at a time when Jeanne was also present. She said he became angry when he read its contents and hurled it across the room shouting, 'Get rid of this!' The District Attorney had the same access to Ms Carmen as I did and could easily have identified a second source for the diary. The question must be asked whether he wanted to.

Lionel Grandison's claim that he was coerced into signing

the death certificate against his better judgement was virtually scorned by the investigators. Grandison argued that he saw discrepancies between what was entitled a 'First Call form', which he saw at one point, and the one which was eventually submitted to be enclosed in what was known as the 'Closing Package'. He was responsible for checking that all documents were present, he said. He said he also had to check that the indicated cause of death was appropriate. More than this, Grandison claimed that he saw Marilyn's body which had bruise marks upon it reminiscent of those which occur when injections have been administered.

The DA's report went for the jugular as far as Grandison was concerned, using courtroom tactics to discredit the man and make him out to be an unreliable witness. This does not necessarily mean that what he said was not true, however, but a great deal of doubt has certainly been cast on Grandison's credibility. It was made clear that Grandison's signature implied neither approval nor disapproval of what was in the documents bearing it, and that his status carried no authority. When it came to the bruises seen on Marilyn's body, this claim was promptly dismissed. It should be remembered that Dr Noguchi noted certain bruise marks and was in a better position to judge whether they were from injections than Grandison. Both Noguchi and Miner, the assistant DA who was present at the autopsy, declared that there was no evidence of injection marks.

James Hall, who claimed to have seen Marilyn murdered by Dr Ralph Greenson (see Chapter 6), made contact with the DA's office under the name of Rick Stone, offering to sell the information about the alleged murder. Not surprisingly, the District Attorney declined to buy. Eventually, in a telephone conversation, he offered to give him the story. He supplied an outline and promised to 'get back to him', but never did. The details appeared in a local weekly, the *Globe*, and presumably Hall was paid for that.

Somewhat remarkably, the District Attorney addressed himself to Hall's story on a point-by-point basis. He denounced the claims on the grounds of (a) discrepancies in timing; (b) his claim about the presence of police cars, otherwise unsubstantiated; (c) rigor mortis had set in, so she must have died long before the time Hall said he arrived; (d) lividity showed that she died face down, not on her back as Hall claimed; and (e) lack of evidence regarding the supposed fatal injection.

Also remarkable was the fact that the District Attorney used the other ambulance story (see Chapter 6) to denounce Hall. Ken Hunter's attendance with Liebowitz is supported though, amazingly, further enquiries were not made into this startling new evidence. It was merely stated in order to discredit Hall and left at that.

On the subject of the missing telephone toll charge records, the report freely acknowledges that the Police Department took them: 'Confidential LAPD records supplied to our office support the published media reports that toll records were seized by the Los Angeles Police Department.' The report repeats much of what Chief Parker had announced to journalists, then – as though to make sure readers did not miss the point – expanded upon it to press home the point that Marilyn was not making contact with the Attorney General.

> During this toll period eight calls were placed from Miss Monroe's residence to a Washington DC number. The last such call was made on July 30, 1962, six days before her death.
>
> Utilizing law enforcement resources we were able to determine that the number called, RE 7-8200 in Washington DC, was the published number of the US Department of Justice headquarters in Washington. The number was the general listing for the Justice Department, the main switchboard number, rather than a private line. If Miss Monroe was in fact calling the Attorney General himself, she had to be first transferred via operator assistance to another number. *Incoming* calls to Miss Monroe of course were not recorded on her toll charges, but her charged tolls gave some support to the allegations that she had contact with someone in the Department of Justice.

Better diffuse the picture than attempt to deny what cannot be denied seems to be the message to be drawn from these statements. Better admit Marilyn was speaking to someone at the Justice Department and imply it was someone other than the Attorney General. The report followed this by heading off the obvious claim that, since Robert Kennedy was in San Francisco for some days before Marilyn died, she tried to contact him there. 'Newspaper articles provided to this office place Robert Kennedy in San Francisco the weekend of Miss Monroe's death. A review of the toll records indicates that no phone calls were made to the San Francisco area during the entire time period covered in the records.' The report is now beginning to get out of its depth. Hollywood crime reporter Florabel Muir obtained confirmation that calls from Marilyn had been received at the St Francis Hotel in San Francisco where she expected Robert Kennedy to be staying. If Kennedy was there they were not accepted by him, and he did not respond by returning them. Unless Marilyn made the calls from somewhere other than her house, which is exceedingly unlikely, the calls must have shown in the toll charges.

The District Attorney's report sinks further into the mire when it seeks to deal with the charge that Chief Parker personally obtained the toll charge records. 'The exact motivation for the Police Department's securing of the phone records cannot be determined,' it euphemistically states, and continues in like manner, 'There is no evidence that Chief Parker did or did not ask his investigators to secure the records. There was, however, a clear investigative purpose for securing the records.'

This is quite absurd. The only reason for the exact motivation for the securing of the phone records not being determined is that the authorities would not come out into the open and confirm what we already knew, that Chief Parker, an ambitious man, saw political advantage in being helpful to Robert Kennedy. In trying to extricate Chief Parker from the blame for acquiring the toll charge records they were seeking to close the stable door on a horse which had bolted twenty years previously. In any case, Parker had made no secret of having the phone records in his possession. He discussed them with journalists and showed them to Florabel Muir. The report continues, 'The records were secured approximately 14 or 15 days after the death of Miss Monroe.' This is even more absurd, for when journalists went to enquire about the phone records they were told they had been taken within hours of Marilyn dying. And had the DA's investigators checked the files, they would have found that the police follow-up report on Marilyn's death, completed on 6 August, the very day after her death had been reported, stated, 'Miss Monroe's telephone, which is GR 61890, has been checked and it was found that no calls were made during the hours of this occurrence. The telephone number of 472-4830 [Marilyn's second line] is being checked at the present time.' In order to be able to say this, the police obviously had the toll records.

Page 17 of the report features a hot denial that Ed Davis, a police official who was promoted to Police Chief and later became a senator, ever took a trip to Washington DC to discuss with Robert Kennedy his relationship with Marilyn Monroe. One telephone call from the District Attorney to Senator Davis, during which he flatly denied the trip, was sufficient for the report. It concluded that it did not occur and, to seal off the subject, added that no other official made the trip either.

The remainder of the report is devoted to an attack on the existence of the Spindel tapes and an attempt to negate the claims that wiring from bugging operations was found at Marilyn's house after she died; denials that Robert Kennedy was at the Monroe house the day she died and even that he was in Los Angeles; a rebuttal of a claim that a 723-page file on Marilyn's death ever existed; an attempt to debunk the time discrepancies reported by Sergeant Jack Clemmons; and the provision of so-called answers to other outstanding questions relating to Marilyn's death.

The District Attorney's Report on the Death of Marilyn Monroe was ranked a threshold investigation of the case, carried out in order to determine whether a full-scale investigation was warranted, and observing that there is no Statute of Limitation applicable to murder under California law. In his closing summary, John K. Van de Kamp concludes:

Our threshold examination of documents and reports of personal interviews was approached with an open mind. We examined documents and witness statements without any preconceptions, bias, or prejudice. However, as the various allegations were subjected to detailed examination and as the scenario of Marilyn Monroe's death was fitted into place, we were drawn to the conclusion that the homicide hypothesis must be viewed with extreme skepticism.

Thus he made clear that the disturbing circumstances surrounding the case carried no weight. His conception of an open mind, lack of preconceptions, bias and prejudice, in my opinion, leave a great deal to be desired. The entire report invites criticism for the hope it appears to express that the word of the District Attorney might be final, no matter how flimsy the evidence on which his decisions are based.

Twenty years before this, another District Attorney's investigator, Frank Hronek, had made discoveries which persuaded him that Marilyn Monroe had been murdered. This was never published, neither does his report survive in the files. The District Attorney in 1982 had the opportunity to open up a much needed full-scale investigation into Marilyn's death, but he declined. The lid was screwed down on the Marilyn case once more. Even as a threshold examination of the evidence it was nothing more than a 'nearly investigation': it nearly happened but never did. No cans of worms, it seems, were to be opened here.

# 14

# SERIOUS ABOUT SUICIDE

When Ralph Greenson telephoned the police at 4.25 on the morning of Sunday, 5 April, he made no bones about it: he described Marilyn's death as suicide. During the following critical few days when people read about the tragedy and formed their impressions of events, suicide was predominant in the headlines – so suicide naturally became predominant in their thinking.

It should not be thought that Dr Greenson was on his own in calling her death suicide; his voice spoke for Dr Hyman Engelberg too. When Sergeant Jack Clemmons answered Greenson's call and drove to the house he found no dispute on this subject. Neither had Clemmons himself any predispositions when he arrived: from the phone call he had no reason to doubt what had happened.

As far as the world was concerned, it was Arthur Jacobs who was the architect of the suicide theory. As Marilyn's publicist at Twentieth Century-Fox, he took control of the announcements of her death to the media. He was planning strategies from the night that she died, and his press releases came even before the coroner's verdict. Pat Newcomb, Marilyn's friend and press agent, worked for Jacobs and her grief had to be contained during four solid days working on the official releases to radio, television and the press.

For most people at the time, the coroner's verdict was the last word on the subject. That the verdict was softened to 'probable suicide', which left it open that her death might have been the consequence of an accident on Marilyn's part, made it all so much easier to bear for her millions of fans. It also made it possible for Twentieth Century-Fox to collect millions of dollars in insurance they had on their star and the film, which went a long way to preventing the studio from going under at a time of severe financial strain.

Thomas Noguchi, who was delegated to conduct the autopsy, was a brilliant young pathologist who would one day become coroner. It has to be said, however, without disrespect to Noguchi, that it was surprising for the autopsy of such an important person as Marilyn Monroe to have been left to an assistant, no matter how proficient. Dr Noguchi observed a fresh bruise on Marilyn's lower left back, the nature of which indicated it was

Marilyn's death certificate clearly states: 'Probable Suicide'.

caused by a recent injury. It did not tell Noguchi a great deal. A bruise to the neck or throat would have alerted him to possible foul play, but a mark on her hip was hardly suggestive of this. Perhaps she had stumbled into something. Noguchi noted it.

The autopsy was regarded as having been competently carried out, and the coroner, Dr Curphey, next asked for the services of the newly formed Suicide Team, led by psychologist Dr Norman L. Farberow and including psychiatrist Dr Robert E. Litman and Dr Norman Tabachnik. It was the Suicide Team who, after investigating Marilyn's background and circumstances, reached the conclusion that it was a 'probable suicide' – the recommendation made to Dr Curphey. The report ran:

Marilyn Monroe died on the night of August 4 or the early morning of August 5, 1962. Examination by the toxicology laboratory indicates that death was due to a self-administered overdose of sedative drugs. We have been asked, as consultants, to examine the life situation of the

Dr Robert Litman, seen here in his Los Angeles consulting rooms still maintains that he and the Suicide Team got it right.

deceased and to give an opinion regarding the intent of Miss Monroe when she ingested the sedative drugs which caused her death. From the data obtained, the following points are the most important and relevant:

Miss Monroe had suffered from psychiatric disturbance for a long time. She experienced severe fears and frequent depressions. Mood changes were abrupt and unpredictable. Among symptoms of disorganization, sleep disturbance was prominent, for which she had been taking sedative drugs for many years. She was thus familiar with and experienced in the use of sedative drugs and well aware of their dangers.

Recently, one of the main objectives of her psychiatric treatment had been the reduction of her intake of drugs. This has been partially successful during the last two months. She was reported to be following doctor's orders in her use of the drugs; and the amount of drugs found in her room at the time of her death was not unusual.

In our investigation we have learned that Miss Monroe had often expressed wishes to give up, to withdraw, and even to die. On more than one occasion in the past, when disappointed and depressed, she had made a suicide attempt using sedative drugs. On these occasions, she had called for help and had been rescued.

From the information collected about the events of the evening of August 4, it is our opinion that the same pattern was repeated except for the rescue. It has been our practice with similar information collected in other cases in the past to recommend a certification for such deaths as probable suicide.

Additional clues for suicide provided by the physical evidence are: (1) the high level of barbiturates and chloral hydrate in the blood which, with other evidence from the autopsy, indicates the probable ingestion of a large amount of the drugs within a short period of time; (2) the completely empty bottle of Nembutal, the prescription for which was filled the day before the ingestion of the drugs; and (3) the locked door which was unusual.

On the basis of all the information obtained it is our opinion that the case is a probable suicide.

When interviewed by me, Dr Litman was still convinced that the conclusion they reached was correct. 'My special experience relates to interviewing many thousands of persons who have made suicide attempts and survived,' he said. 'Also I have reviewed many thousands of completed suicides, persons who did not survive. From this viewpoint Monroe's death as a suicide appears pretty typical of a whole class of deaths where the person places himself/herself in jeopardy, but there is a chance of rescue.' Dr Farberow, in correspondence, is equally adamant.

Journalists writing at the time also had the police reports to help them frame their articles and these, while they may have preserved a semblance of keeping an open mind, did not in any way challenge suicide. The Police Death Report stated:

Death was pronounced on 8/5/62 at 3:45 A.M., Possible Accidental, having taken place between the times of 8/4 and 8/5/1962, 3:35 A.M. at residence located at 12305 Fifth Helena Drive, Brentwood, in Rptg. Dist. 814, Report # 62-509 463.

Marilyn Monroe on August 4, 1962 retired to her bedroom at about eight o'clock in the evening; Mrs Eunice Murray of 933 Ocean Ave., Santa Monica, Calif., 395-7752, CR61890, noted a light in Miss Monroe's bedroom. Mrs Murray was not able to arouse Miss Monroe when she went to the door, and when she tried the door again at 3:30 A.M. when she noted the light still on, she found it to be locked. Thereupon Mrs Murray observed Miss Monroe through the bedroom window and found her lying on her stomach in the bed and the appearance seemed unnatural. Mrs Murray then called Miss Monroe's psychiatrist, Dr Ralph R. Greenson of 436 North Roxberry Drive, Beverly Hills, Calif., CR14050. Upon entering after breaking the bedroom window, he found Miss Monroe possibly dead. Then he telephoned Dr Hyman Engelberg of 9730, Wilshire Boulevard, also of Beverly Hills, CR54366, who came over and then pronounced Miss Monroe dead at 3:35 A.M. Miss Monroe was seen by Dr Greenson on August 4, 1962 at 5:15 P.M., at her request, because she was not able to sleep. She was being treated by him for about a year. She was nude when Dr Greenson found her dead with the telephone receiver in one hand and lying on her stomach. The Police Department was called and when they arrived they found Miss Monroe in the condition described above, except for the telephone which was removed by Dr Greenson. There were found to be 15 bottles of medication on the night table and some were prescription. A bottle marked 1½ grains Nembutal, prescription #20853 and prescribed by Dr Engelberg, and referring to this particular bottle, Dr Engelberg made the statement that he prescribed a refill for this about two days ago and he further stated there probably should have been about 50 capsules at the time this was refilled by the pharmacist.

In a footnote the probable cause of death was shown as 'overdose of Nembutal'. The Police Follow-up Report amplified a few of the most important points made in the Death Report but said little else. Those journalists who referred to these documents could hardly be blamed for writing off her death as an open-and-shut case.

The word of those close to Marilyn carried a lot of weight as they were regarded as the people most likely to know. Pat Newcomb was sure that Marilyn had committed suicide and Mrs Murray convincingly took this line also. The doctors gave no hint of any alternative, though Ralph Greenson changed his mind within days; this was never publicised, however, and had little effect. Peter Lawford made a great deal of the call that he said he had made to Marilyn, in which she purportedly said, 'Say goodbye to Pat [Lawford's wife], say goodbye to the President, and say goodbye to yourself, because you're a nice guy.' The account rendered of this last conversation, with Lawford's description of the way she had sounded and the fact that the line had gone dead and he could not reach her after that, went a long way to convincing those enquiring into her death that it was suicide.

Housekeeper Mrs Murray said that on the night she died

Marilyn asked if there was any oxygen in the house. On the face of it this was convincing evidence that she had another suicide attempt in mind – assuming Mrs Murray's word could ever be trusted. Another story which lent credence to the idea of suicide was the locked door and the necessity of breaking a window to gain entry into the bedroom where Dr Greenson said he found Marilyn dead.

Of those to whom she had spoken on the telephone on her last day, wealthy clothes manufacturer Henry Rosenfeld said she sounded 'groggy' when he rang at about 9 p.m.; coiffeur Sydney Guilaroff rang shortly after this and said she told him she was 'very depressed'; and her Mexican friend, José Bolanos, said she simply put down the phone after speaking to him – she did not hang up. Also her good friend and masseur Ralph Roberts said his answering service had reported a lady trying to get him who had spoken with a slurred voice.

Susan Strasberg, daughter of Lee and Paula Strasberg, Marilyn's acting coaches, would write a book, *Marilyn and Me*, in which she left no doubt in her readers' minds as to how she believed Marilyn had died: 'Marilyn, half in love with death, half in love with life . . . another flip of the coin, heads or tails, life or death. All those overdoses, all those near misses; the odds had finally turned against her.'

The months before Marilyn's death were fraught with problems and emotional hazards of one kind and another. She had been given a new movie by Twentieth Century-Fox, *Something's Got to Give*, a remake of a Cary Grant and Irene Dunne comedy about a wife who goes missing and returns to find she has been declared dead and her husband has just married someone else. *My Favourite Wife* had been very successful, and Fox looked forward to even greater success with their new version. Dean Martin had been contracted for the husband and Cyd Charisse for his new wife, while Marilyn had the choice part of the returned wife. But all was not well on the set.

Director George Cukor and Marilyn were at daggers drawn over the script. In fact they were probably at daggers drawn about everything. Marilyn had loved the original script by Nunnally Johnson. Since Johnson was not an American, and therefore could not work in the United States, Cukor had retained another writer on the set for the alterations which he required. Marilyn would then pencil in alterations to his alterations, and so the feuding continued. The blue pages – alterations were printed on blue paper – were increasing all the time, and were aggravating Marilyn. They tried slipping in alterations on white paper, but she saw through the ploy and matters were not improved.

There was an armistice for Marilyn's birthday. George Carpozi Jr wrote:

> She was thirty-six years old. It's a significant age in a woman's life. At the studio . . . the staff had arranged a surprise party . . . At the party there was a huge birthday cake. On top in sugar there was the figure of a bikini-clad girl – supposedly to commemorate the one Marilyn had shed for one of the scenes in the new film. As she left

Despite their hostile relationship on the set of *Something's Got to Give*, Marilyn and director George Cukor occasionally found something to smile at. *Robert F. Slatzer.*

the set that afternoon with the party still in progress, she called goodbye to the scene-shifters and lighting men who had been her friends, telling them that she would see them on Monday.

The producer of the film, Henry Weinstein, discussed the rewriting problem with Walter Bernstein, the seventh writer appointed for 'on set' changes – there had been six even before shooting had begun. Bernstein could not understand Weinstein's problem, since Marilyn's contract did not give her script approval. 'Marilyn does not need script approval,' the producer groaned. 'If she doesn't like something, she doesn't show up.' Weinstein knew who was running the show, and it wasn't him.

It is fair to say that Marilyn and Cukor detested one another. The studio began to talk about dropping Marilyn, while she in turn began to talk about dropping Cukor and bringing in Nunnally Johnson to direct. Johnson thought this was a bad idea. Even had he been able to obtain a work permit he felt it would only be a question of time before Marilyn took exception to him too, and things would be no better. None the less he cabled studio chief Peter Levathes, 'If you're going to take anybody out of this picture, shouldn't you decide first who brings the people in, George Cukor or Marilyn Monroe? You should remove George because they are so antipathetic that that's what's causing Marilyn's disturbance.'

This was not completely true. Marilyn was beset by emotional problems and had also had a number of absences from the set because of physical ailments. She suffered from a sinus infection and could not cope on set with a cold. But more than this, she was said to have developed a fear of performing. Henry Weinstein said he recalled Marilyn throwing up from terror before entering the soundstage. With all these things striking at the roots of studio organisation, it was the last straw when she announced that she intended flying to New York to sing at the President's forty-fifth birthday celebrations. Fox were aghast at the idea of another, completely avoidable, delay of several days and absolutely forbade the trip. Marilyn's attitude did nothing for relationships when she simply ignored the studio bosses and went.

Fox decided they had had enough; Marilyn's frequent absences and bickering with George Cukor over script revisions had already made them go a massive one million dollars over budget, against which they had only about six minutes of screenworthy film in the can. Marilyn was fired. Then word started to get around that she was being blamed by over one hundred studio staff for the loss of their jobs. Though Fox would eventually reinstate Marilyn to the picture, there is little doubt that at the time of her dismissal her life lay in ruins, reason enough for the blackest of depressions. As George Carpozi Jr commented, writing before her death, 'She wasn't seen around. There was her doctor; there was her lawyer, reassuring. A couple of close women friends saw her, and worried. There was the woman who came in to clean. The whispers were becoming audible, and they were saying that as a big star Monroe was finished.'

Although this was not true, there is no doubt that Marilyn's demeanour gave rise to concern. And to make matters worse, there were other, unadvertised reasons for Marilyn's depression. Chief of these was that her love life was in disarray. Her relationship with John F. Kennedy had ended abruptly, while her more recent affair with Robert Kennedy was going wrong. The Attorney General was putting out signals that he had no intention of carrying out his promise to divorce his wife and marry Marilyn. To this must be added the tension which would have accompanied being weaned off the drugs which she had previously relied on to help her sleep. For a time she was in a mess.

As had been pointed out by the Suicide Team, Marilyn had attempted to kill herself before. On at least two occasions she had overdosed, but had communicated her distress signals in time to be rescued – the classic 'cry for help' syndrome. The Suicide Team made it clear that they believed her drug-taking this time was intended to be accompanied by the usual distress signals, which for once did not attract attention. But in view of the telephone calls which Marilyn made until as late as 10 p.m., in which she made no attempt to raise the alarm, the Suicide Team's theory does not stand up in the way those who are convinced she committed suicide would like it to.

During this period of turmoil, a mysterious incident recorded by Peter Harry Brown and Patte B. Barham in their book *Marilyn: The Last Take* is worthy of note. These authors speak of a secret visit that Marilyn made to plastic surgeon Dr Michael Gurdin, to whom she showed a black and blue nose and cheekbone. Dr Ralph Greenson, who accompanied her, assured Gurdin he was looking at the consequences of an accident. She had slipped in the shower and hit her head on the tiles, he explained. As was pointed out by Brown and Barham, she seldom used her shower, and it was not tiled anyway. It proved to be no worse than bruising – bruising which Robert Slatzer believed was caused by a beating-up. While her face healed and the discoloration faded, Marilyn remained on her own, taking sleeping pills and drinking champagne.

The supposed events of the last weekend before Marilyn died have already been described. She was Frank Sinatra's guest at the Cal-Neva Lodge, the hotel and gambling house which he jointly owned with Mafia boss Sam Giancana. In addition to Marilyn, Pat and Peter Lawford were among his guests at what was believed to have been a few days of booze, sex and drugs. Some are convinced that this weekend featured yet another suicide attempt on Marilyn's part, this time accompanied by a successful cry for help. Whatever the truth, she was reportedly suffering the effects of alcohol when flown back to Los Angeles in Sinatra's private plane. A theory has emerged that the weekend was arranged by Pat Kennedy Lawford at her brother Robert's request. He was flying to the West Coast that weekend and wanted Marilyn out of the way.

So much for the so-called 'evidence' that Marilyn took her own life. There are plenty of other examples for those who are prepared to disregard the massive indications to the contrary which, in spite of the authorities' efforts to conceal the truth, have surfaced over the years. Nevertheless it is understandable that some people had no doubts that it was suicide. The cover-up to prevent Robert Kennedy's name being linked with Marilyn's, in order to protect his political career, was engineered on the one

hand to persuade the world that Marilyn and Robert had barely –
and then only socially – met, and that Marilyn had taken her own
life, a 'cry for help' which had gone wrong. For twenty years that
cover-up was almost completely successful, but truth will out.
Thanks to those few who relentlessly pursued their conviction
that she did not kill herself, and to the researchers who followed
them, we have now an understanding of what really took place.
Brown and Barham expressed well in *Marilyn: The Last Take*
why we cannot entertain the idea of suicide.

> The last two weeks of Monroe's life have almost always
> been portrayed as a countdown to tragedy – as if the black
> figure of death cast a shadow over her final days.
>
> Each of her words and all of her actions have been
> weighted with the gloom of fate. Her friends and enemies
> alike have been depicted as larger-than-life heroes and
> villains, playing their roles under the glare of interna-
> tional fame.
>
> Actually, Monroe's death interrupted a life and career
> that was in midpassage. Her last days were a time of
> exhilaration, activity, tears and laughter.
>
> She had million-dollar deals to sign, including an
> $11-million pact with Italian filmmakers for four films
> in Italy; a film to complete; a garden to plant; and a house
> to finish.
>
> She had planned lunches and dinners for the near future,
> as well as a three-day theater trip to New York City. And
> like many a Hollywood celebrity, she maintained a degree
> of mystery and a touch of glamorous subterfuge in her
> life as she tried to keep her distance from an increasingly
> vigilant press.

This was Marilyn.

# 15

# EMPHASIS ON ACCIDENT

Of those who believed that Marilyn Monroe killed herself, a very large number were of the opinion that she died by accident rather than intention. This number would include those who had been convinced by the 'evidence' of suicide, and could not bring themselves to believe she would deliberately do such a thing. It would include those who were benignly seeking to change the act of self-destruction to one to which they could be sympathetic. These were people who could not really understand suicide, could not conceive of Marilyn being 'that kind of person'. This group consisted mainly of her best fans, who could not understand how someone so beautiful, talented and wealthy would ever wish to destroy herself. These admirers were reluctant to let her go on terms of straight suicide, or perhaps unwilling to make up their minds on the subject.

Pat Newcomb would rate as Marilyn's closest friend. In the time since her death she has consistently placed herself in the category of those who believe that her death was an accident. Pat went for a meal with Marilyn on the Friday evening before she died, stayed overnight and spent most of her last day with her. No one knew Marilyn better than Pat. She knew of her periodic moodiness and all about her times of depression. She also knew, however, how happy, lively and gay she could be. Marilyn's last day was not spent broodily contemplating suicide. After another night with little sleep, which was her besetting problem, her morning featured predictable grizzling at Pat, who enjoyed sound sleep, followed by a day busily engaged in one thing and another, sitting out on the patio looking over scripts, and making and answering telephone calls.

Eunice Murray lent support to the idea of Marilyn's death being accidental in a fashion. It is my opinion that when she spoke of Marilyn asking on that last day if there was any oxygen in the house, she was underlining her own determination to present Marilyn's death in the light of a planned overdose which had gone wrong. It is nonsense to think of Marilyn somehow expecting to hear Mrs Murray tell her there was an oxygen cylinder in a cupboard. There was never oxygen around – there is never oxygen around in any normal household. More than likely this was Mrs Murray's inventive way of expressing the notion that Marilyn had planned another 'attempt' from which she would be rescued. But something had gone awry: she had miscalculated.

Ex-Chief of Police Tom Reddin, having considered the many theories about Marilyn's death, believed it was some kind of accident. He believed she died by her own hand without intending to do so – that one of the drugs she ingested interacted with another, causing a fatal mix. This idea is not uncommon among those who do not accept that she meant to kill herself. Author Donald Spoto favours the idea that the interaction of Nembutal with chloral hydrate killed her, the one ingested and the other administered by enema: 'In his haste that evening, Greenson perhaps overlooked one crucial factor, the adverse interaction of the two drugs. Chloral hydrate interferes with the body's production of enzymes that metabolise Nembutal. It was the chloral hydrate that pushed Marilyn over the edge.'

The notion of Marilyn's death being accidental achieves a variety of things. For one thing it relieves the embarrassment that suicide brings – the sense of shame is avoided if the victim did not intend to die. Then, looking in a totally different direction, it does not introduce the complications which accompany murder. Where murder occurs, there must be an investigation dedicated to identifying and apprehending those responsible. Where the death of Marilyn Monroe was concerned, an investigation would have been distinctly unwelcome if it involved questioning a member of a prominent family, for instance. Accidental suicide would be convenient.

For a great many years the public knew nothing about the relationship between Robert Kennedy and Marilyn Monroe. When it became common knowledge, the reasons for the Los Angeles Police Department cover-up were understood, even if not condoned. In 1962 for the Attorney General to be questioned in connection with a murder, particularly that of a beautiful film actress, would have given rise to calls for his resignation. Even if he was totally innocent of any involvement it would have made no difference. And since the appointment of the Attorney General is made by the President, calls would have risen for his resignation as well – especially since he was the Attorney General's brother.

When Chief William Parker stepped in and threw a blanket of secrecy over Marilyn's death his intention was to protect not the guilty but the innocent. A man of considerable integrity, he would not have considered making this move had he believed Robert Kennedy to be implicated in Marilyn's death. The intelligence which he received on the subject convinced him that the Attorney General was not involved in the tragedy and, since mere routine questioning would have been enough to place the reputations of both Robert and John Kennedy in jeopardy, he acted promptly to prevent what he felt would have been a gross miscarriage of justice.

Chief Parker's actions raise all kinds of questions. There is an obvious one relating to the morality of what he did. Police chiefs are there to see that the process of law enforcement is carried out, not to subvert it. Was it not the task of his experts in the police force to sort out the innocent from the guilty? Was Chief Parker also to act as judge and jury? And then the sixty-four thousand dollar question: would he have done the same for a less prominent person?

Chief Parker had a vested interest in jumping to the aid of Robert Kennedy: he had his eye on succeeding J. Edgar Hoover as Director of the FBI. Parker was, after all, America's most outstanding chief of police and it was not immodest to believe he was next in line for this plum job. The Attorney General had already advertised his high opinion of the Chief in public. Parker would probably have made an outstanding Director of the Bureau, but died before the appointment fell vacant. Nevertheless it is unlikely that his timely gesture to the Kennedys went unappreciated.

On close examination, the accidental death theory does not stand up very well. There are incontrovertible shortcomings, particularly in the autopsy report. The notion of one drug interacting with another to cause her death is erroneous. The barbiturates alone were sufficient to kill Marilyn – and several other people too. The chloral hydrate would no doubt interact with the barbiturates simply because they were there, but they might be thought of as quite superfluous. It was not a case of a non-fatal dosage of barbiturates interacting with a non-fatal dosage of chloral hydrate to result in a fatal dosage. And in any case, the volume of either drug was too great to be taken accidentally.

The only real support for the accidental overdose idea is that on the day before her death she displayed no positive indications of feeling suicidal. As to other indications, there are none. No part of the medical evidence supports the notion. Those who wish to hang on to the theory that she died by accident may derive comfort from the opinion of the Suicide Team, who decided that she had set her course for death with every expectation of being rescued, but that the rescue, for whatever reason, did not come. But the Team did not derive this opinion from medical fact: it was a psychological deduction on their part, based on the knowledge that she had made previous attempts which had had satisfactory conclusions.

Those close to her at the time she died went to a great deal of trouble to support a suicide theory of whatever kind. Dr Greenson had pushed the idea from the very first telephone call to the police, and he spoke of her being depressed when he saw her in the late afternoon of her last day. Even though he admitted that she had sounded cheerful when she spoke to him on the telephone during the evening, the damage had been done: Dr Greenson supported suicide. Dr Engelberg tended to melt into the background, but he it was who certified her dead, and he had seen the same as the others in the house that night.

Dr Engelberg certainly went along with the suicide verdict, if only in his failure to say otherwise.

In all Mrs Murray said there appeared to be a distinct intention of pushing the suicide theory. She spoke of the light showing beneath the locked bedroom door, under which the telephone cord snaked. When she became alarmed, she said she used a poker through a small open window to push back the curtains when she saw Marilyn lying face down on the bed. Marilyn was naked when they found her. Mrs Murray never volunteered that that was decidedly odd: her employer normally wore nightdresses and ritually used an eyeshade and earplugs to help her sleep, and never went to bed without putting on a bra. These were deliberate omissions to encourage the idea of suicide.

Pat Newcomb, who had spent so much of Friday and Saturday with her, did not argue with the suicide verdict, though she must have found it strange when she recalled how bright Marilyn had been. Pat had been fighting a touch of bronchitis and had spoken of going into hospital for treatment. On the Friday Marilyn had persuaded her to come over to her house, where the quiet poolside was available for a spot of recuperation. They had dinner together at a local restaurant on the Friday night when, it is said, Marilyn got a little tipsy. The memories of those last hours with Marilyn must be firmly engraved on Pat Newcomb's mind. But Pat, always reluctant to speak of Marilyn's death, is nevertheless anxious when she does do so to promote the idea that she committed suicide.

It was quite the reverse with Peter Lawford. He, too, advanced the suicide theory, particularly by means of the story about the telephone call in which Marilyn gave him farewell messages. For those who believed the story, it put the seal on suicide. This was not all that Lawford contributed to the suicide theory, however. He also told how he had discussed the phone call with his agent and debated what he should do about it. Claiming to be following advice, he contacted Marilyn's lawyer, Milton Rudin, who telephoned Mrs Murray and asked if there was any problem with Marilyn. The reply that all was well was transmitted back to Lawford. The whole episode advertised concern on Lawford's part that Marilyn intended suicide.

If Lawford had really known at that time that she was about to commit suicide, he was, of course, wasting precious time making telephone calls when he could have been saving her. The advice he was supposedly given by Ebbins – and that he said he accepted – was that because he was the President's brother-in-law he could not afford to get enmeshed in anything involving drink or drugs. Could anyone really be callous enough to place such considerations before saving the life of a friend? He said he had tried repeatedly for an hour and a half to get an answer from her phone, which always gave a busy signal. Any normal human being would have jumped into his car – he could have been at her house in minutes to find out for himself how she was. That he may have been too drunk to drive, as has been suggested, is no excuse: Los Angeles is full of taxicabs.

On the face of it the story will simply not stand up. A sequence of telephone calls might easily have been taken advantage of to substantiate Lawford's suicide story through the involvement of others, but the intervals between the calls would seem to have been too

## Lawford Tells Phoning Marilyn

**By HARRISON CARROLL**

Film star Peter Lawford last night revealed that he called Marilyn Monroe at approximately 7 p.m., Saturday night, and may have been the last person to talk to the blonde star before she was found dead in her bed from an overdose of barbiturates.

He has no way of knowing, though, said Lawford, whether his was the final "mystery" call received by the actress after she retired to her bedroom.

The actress' housekeeper, Mrs. Eunice Murray, earlier had reported that Marilyn received such a call.

Lawford relayed his story through a close friend and business associate, Milt Ebbins.

"There certainly was no mystery about Mr. Lawford's call," declared Ebbins. "He was a close friend of Miss Monroe's.

"At approximately 7 p.m., he called to invite her and her friend, Pat Newcomb, to attend a small dinner party at his home.

"He says Miss Monroe told him she would like to come but that she was tired and was going to bed early.

"He says that he noticed nothing unusual except that she did sound tired."

According to Ebbins, he and his wife were among the guests invited to Lawford's small dinner party. Others included TV producer Joe Naar and his wife, and Bullets Durgom.

Never one to attend many Hollywood social affairs, Marilyn often had been a guest at the Lawford home. Recently, she flew to Cal-Neva Lodge at Lake Tahoe in company with the actor and his wife.

The *Los Angeles Herald Examiner* of 8 August, only a few days after Marilyn's death, quoted Peter Lawford before he transformed this telephone call into the 'intended suicide call'. Note the statement: 'He says that he noticed nothing unusual except that she did sound tired.'

great for them to have been genuine enquiries about a woman feared to be about to commit suicide. Since Lawford had previously reported, far more believably, on a phone call from Marilyn about which he said, 'There didn't seem to be anything at all wrong with Marilyn. She sounded fine,' this would broadly accommodate what was probably the true version of the 'Say goodbye to the President' conversation which came from Fred Otash. Lawford's later stories did not make sense. They appear to have been introduced to reinforce the suicide idea.

His subsequent calls to Joe Naarr appear patently to establish that he was not present when she died. It seems that Lawford, well informed on what was happening, was imaginatively embroidering the true events to keep himself at arm's length and his brother-in-law completely out of sight of what was taking place at Marilyn's house the night she died.

Robert Kennedy's wellbeing was Peter Lawford's chief concern. He would have gone to any lengths to prevent the Attorney

Hollywood detective Fred Otash was involved in the bugging operation organised by Bernard Spindel. He later claimed that Marilyn asked him to bug her own telephone. Was it her conversations with Robert Kennedy that she wanted to record? *Corbis-Bettmann/UPI.*

General from being involved in the remotest way with enquiries relating to Marilyn's death. He was said to have gone to Marilyn's house while she was lying there to take a note that she had left, though the truth of this is uncertain. What is confirmed is that he engaged detective Fred Otash's men to 'sweep' her house and remove any trace of her relationship with Kennedy before the police were called.

Similarly, as already noted, it was reported that representatives of the studio sorted through her documents, removing them in armfuls, in order that no breath of undesirable publicity should surface after her death was announced. The publicists, the other group who had homed in on Fifth Helena Drive, had, they thought, sealed off further public interest by promoting the suicide story worldwide.

So with the Los Angeles Police Department, the coroner, the press and those close to her when she died all promoting the idea that she died by her own hand but unintentionally, is it still possible that this was not the way she died? Is it possible that there was a gigantic conspiracy to keep the truth from being known? The answer to both of these questions is yes.

# 16

# THE CASE AGAINST THE MAFIA

Among those who believe Marilyn was murdered, a significant number believe she was killed by the Mafia. Two prime reasons are put forward for the mob wanting to murder her, both apparently inspired by information obtained from Spindel's tapes – commissioned by Jimmy Hoffa and also available to senior Mafia figures such as Sam Giancana and Johnny Roselli.

The first reason is that, in view of the up-to-the-minute information to which they were privy, they decided that the time had arrived to get Robert Kennedy off their backs. The Attorney General's successes against them in the courtroom were spurring law enforcement agencies across the country to prosecute Mafia figures on their own home patch, and an increasing number of mobsters were ending up in jail. Arthur M. Schlesinger Jr wrote:

Under Kennedy's pressure the national government took on organised crime as it had never done before. In New York, Robert Morgenthau, the Federal attorney, successfully prosecuted one syndicate leader after another. The Patriarca gang in Rhode Island and the De Cavalcante gang in New Jersey were smashed. Convictions of racketeers by the Organised Crime Section and the Tax Division steadily increased – 96 in 1961, 101 in 1962, 373 in 1963. So long as John Kennedy sat in the White House, giving his Attorney General absolute backing, the underworld knew that the heat was on.

It would be easy to imagine, therefore, that the listeners despatched 'soldiers' to 'take care' of Marilyn, believing that Robert Kennedy would be implicated – possibly even indicted for murder – and would quickly resign because of the disgrace. Unfortunately this scenario does not stand up to scrutiny. The main reason was that, had the mob killed the Attorney General, his brother the President would have turned up the heat on them even higher. Besides, had the mob decided to kill Robert Kennedy they would far more likely have shot him; this was their way, not the subtle placing of blame for another murder which they had set up to look like suicide. As a means of removing Robert Kennedy, the Marilyn murder was too convoluted to be Mafia-inspired.

From listening to Bernard Spindel's recordings of what was happening inside Lawford's mansion and Marilyn's house at Brentwood, it was clear that Marilyn was coming into possession of classified information. It was the introduction of one particular subject which caused Mafia alarm bells to ring. The Attorney General was enlightening Marilyn on the subject of one of the most recent events in his office, one of the greatest scandals to arise during the Kennedy administration. This may have been the second reason that the Mafia had to kill her.

Robert Kennedy had received a CIA memorandum which revealed the existence of a relationship between the CIA and the Mafia, an unholy alliance in which the mob were, effectively, authorised to murder the Cuban leader, Fidel Castro, on the CIA's behalf. The Mafia had a strong vested interest in disposing of Castro: he had taken control of the lucrative gambling houses they had been running in Havana, and there was no way they would recover them without a change of government. The deal was that they would recover their casinos if they killed Castro. As far as the CIA were concerned, John F. Kennedy had forbidden them to murder to achieve their aims. This was just another example of the Agency going its own way and making its own decisions, regardless of the President's instructions.

The 'arrangement' had been made in the utmost secrecy and had come apart because of Sam Giancana's jealousy. His girl at the time was singer Dorothy McGuire, and, because he suspected that something was going on between her and Dan Rowan of

Rowan and Martin fame, he asked the liaison between the Mafia and the CIA, a man named Robert Mahueu, to have Rowan's hotel bedroom bugged. Mahueu agreed, and a private investigator called Arthur J. Balletti was hired to place the bug. However, Balletti was seen doing it by a maid, who informed the manager. The manager called the sheriff and had Balletti arrested. The FBI was informed by the sheriff and the FBI followed the trail back to the CIA.

Robert Kennedy read the memorandum with amazement and had a copy sent to the President. Giancana's love life had succeeded in blowing the secret alliance formed between the CIA and the Mafia, so secret even the Attorney General and the President did not know about it, and the makings of a scandal of incredible proportions lay at the CIA's door. The Attorney General, who could have blown a hole through the CIA, saw fit not to embarrass the Agency any further and the matter was buried: it did not come to light for more than ten years after the event.

But here was Robert Kennedy telling Marilyn about this highly sensitive situation. All the listeners were, no doubt, simply dumbfounded. The FBI would have had their ears glued to the story while the CIA would have found it hard to believe what they were hearing, for it would be known about by few agents outside a closed circle. When Mafia representatives eventually heard the recordings the shock waves were electric.

This crisis took a sharp turn for the worse just a few weeks later when Robert Kennedy was pulling out of the relationship and Marilyn was threatening to go public on the affairs she had had with both Robert Kennedy and the President, 'to blow the lid off the whole damn thing'. She was furious. What would prevent her telling the world about – among other things – the CIA–Mafia alliance? If the security agencies, the CIA in particular, were worried about this, so was the Mafia. That this may have constituted a strong motive for murdering Marilyn was evidenced by events which took place some years later.

Sam Giancana was murdered on 18 June 1975, shot in the back of the head and his mouth 'stitched' with bullets. He had been executed to prevent him answering Senate Intelligence Committee questions on the CIA–Mafia collaboration which

**CENTRAL INTELLIGENCE AGENCY**
WASHINGTON 25, D. C.

FOI
N B

14 May 1962

MEMORANDUM FOR THE RECORD:

SUBJECT: Arthur James Balletti et al - Unauthorized Publication
or Use of Communications

1. This memorandum for the record is prepared at the
request of the Attorney General of the United States following a
complete oral briefing of him relative to a sensitive CIA operation
conducted during the period approximately August 1960 to May
1961. In August 1960 the undersigned was approached by Mr.
Richard Bissell then Deputy Director for Plans of CIA to explore
the possibility of mounting this sensitive operation against Fidel
Castro. It was thought that certain gambling interests which had
formerly been active in Cuba might be willing and able to assist
and further, might have both intelligence assets in Cuba and
communications between Miami, Florida and Cuba. Accordingly,
Mr. Robert Maheu, a private investigator of the firm of Maheu
and King was approached by the undersigned and asked to establish
contact with a member or members of the gambling syndicate to          FILE
explore their capabilities. Mr. Maheu was known to have accounts        N B
with several prominent business men and organizations in the
United States. Maheu was to make his approach to the syndicate
FILE    as appearing to represent big business organizations which wished
N B     to protect their interests in Cuba. Mr. Maheu accordingly met
and established contact with one John Rosselli of Los Angeles.
Mr. Rosselli showed interest in the possibility and indicated he
had some contacts in Miami that he might use. Maheu reported
that John Rosselli said he was not interested in any remuneration
but would seek to establish capabilities in Cuba to perform the
desired project. Towards the end of September Mr. Maheu and        1960
Mr. Rosselli proceeded to Miami where, as reported, Maheu was
introduced to Sam Giancana of Chicago. Sam Giancana arranged 82-46-
for Maheu and Rosselli to meet with a "courier" who was going back

CIA

Copy No. 1 of

FILE
N B

Page 1 of 3 Page

DEPARTMENT OF JUSTICE

22    JUN 27 1962

RECORDS BRANCH
ATTORNEY GENERAL

The CIA report to Robert Kennedy which detailed their Mafia involvement.

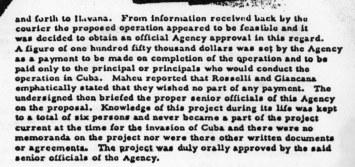

and forth to Havana. From information received back by the
courier the proposed operation appeared to be feasible and it
was decided to obtain an official Agency approval in this regard.
A figure of one hundred fifty thousand dollars was set by the Agency
as a payment to be made on completion of the operation and to be
paid only to the principal or principals who would conduct the
operation in Cuba. Maheu reported that Rosselli and Giancana
emphatically stated that they wished no part of any payment. The
undersigned then briefed the proper senior officials of this Agency
on the proposal. Knowledge of this project during its life was kept
to a total of six persons and never became a part of the project
current at the time for the invasion of Cuba and there were no
memoranda on the project nor were there other written documents
or agreements. The project was duly orally approved by the said
senior officials of the Agency.

    2. Rosselli and Maheu spent considerable time in Miami
talking with the courier. Sam Giancana was present during parts
of these meetings. Several months after this period Maheu told me
that Sam Giancana had asked him to put a listening device in the
room of ████████████████████████████████████████
At that time it was reported to me that Maheu passed the matter
over to one Edward Du Boise, another private investigator. It
appears that Arthur James Balletti was discovered in the act of
installing the listening device and was arrested by the Sheriff in
Las Vegas, Nevada. Maheu reported to me that he had referred
the matter to Edward Du Boise on behalf of Sam Giancana. At the
time of the incident neither this Agency nor the undersigned knew
of the proposed technical installation. Maheu stated that Sam
Giancana thought that ████████████████ might know of the proposed
operation and might pass on the information to █████
████████████████ At the time that Maheu reported this
to the undersigned he reported he was under surveillance by agents
of the Federal Bureau of Investigation, who, he thought, were
exploring his association with John Rosselli and Sam Giancana
incident to the project. I told Maheu that if he was formally approached by the FBI, he could refer them to me to be briefed that
he was engaged in an intelligence operation directed at Cuba.

    3. During the period from September on through April
efforts were continued by Rosselli and Maheu to proceed with the
operation. The first principal in Cuba withdrew and another principal

Page 2 of 3 pages

Copy No. 1 of 2

was selected as has been briefed to The Attorney General. Ten thousand dollars was passed for expenses to the second principal. He was further furnished with approximately one thousand dollars worth of communications equipment to establish communications between his headquarters in Miami and assets in Cuba. No monies were ever paid to Rosselli and Giancana. Maheu was paid part of his expense money during the periods that he was in Miami. After the failure of the invasion of Cuba word was sent through Maheu to Rosselli to call off the operation and Rosselli was told to tell his principal that the proposal to pay one hundred fifty thousand dollars for completion of the operation had been definitely withdrawn.

4. In all this period it has been definitely established from other sources that the Cuban principals involved never discovered or believed that there was other than business and syndicate interest in the project. To the knowledge of the undersigned there were no "leaks" of any information concerning the project in the Cuban community in Miami or in Cuba.

5. I have no proof but it is my conclusion that Rosselli and Giancana guessed or assumed that CIA was behind the project. I never met either of them.

6. Throughout the entire period of the project John Rosselli was the dominant figure in directing action to the Cuban principals. Reasonable monitoring of his activities indicated that he gave his best efforts to carrying out the project without requiring any commitments for himself, financial or otherwise.

7. In view of the extreme sensitivity of the information set forth above, only one additional copy of this memorandum has been made and will be retained by the Agency.

Sheffield Edwards

Copy No. _____

Page 3 of 3 pages

by then had come to light. A year later, in August 1976, Johnny Roselli's body was found floating in an oil drum off the coast of Florida shortly after he had testified in secret session to the Senate Intelligence Committee. Giancana's other hit-man, Charles Nicoletti, was found riddled with bullets in a blazing car.

Jimmy Hoffa, who survived the cut and thrust with Robert Kennedy for so many years, eventually lost the fight under Kennedy's successor. He went to jail, though he did not serve his full sentence. Help came in the form of President Richard Nixon, who intervened on his behalf. Budd Schilberg, writing an introduction to Walter Sheridan's *The Fall and Rise of Jimmy Hoffa*, made the following comment: 'George Jackson rotted in jail for nearly a decade for heisting $70. Jimmy Hoffa cops a million, bribes juries, runs with the most dangerous gangsters in America and, thanks to the intervention of his good friend Dick Nixon, does an easy five. This, after the parole board had rejected Hoffa's appeal three times in a row.'

When Hoffa was released, his influence with the Teamsters' Union had gone and he was distinctly unwanted. He disappeared on 30 July 1975, a few weeks before his friend Sam Giancana was murdered. His body was never recovered. It was later revealed that Hoffa had acted as liaison man when the CIA–Mafia alliance was first mooted, and it appears that he was killed to keep the secrets of those negotiations.

In their book *Double Cross* Sam Giancana's godson and brother, Sam and Chuck Giancana respectively, claim that it was the CIA, 'fearful of exposure by the vengeful, drug-addicted Monroe, [who] requested Mooney [Sam Giancana] have her eliminated'. The Giancanas describe in detail how Needles Gianola and Mugsy Tortorella, with two other professional killers, 'sometime before midnight' entered Marilyn's house, taped her mouth and killed her by introducing a suppository containing a 'massive combination of barbiturates and chloral hydrate'. They speak of the medication being quickly absorbed directly into the bloodstream, and rate a drugged suppository as being just as fast-acting as an injection. The book says that the plot did not succeed in its second objective, that of exposing Robert Kennedy, because of the extraordinary lengths to which he went to cover up the affair.

This account has a number of fatal flaws, however. The first is that a suppository could not have contained the volume of drugs which were found in Marilyn's body. The second is that, in this context, a suppository is not as fast-acting as an injection, and drugs released from a suppository would have taken a long time to kill Marilyn.

Finally, if the murder took place 'sometime before midnight', what would account for Arthur Jacobs being called out of the Hollywood Bowl to an emergency at Marilyn's house at 10.30 p.m. and driving to the house, where he arrived at 11 p.m.? 'Before midnight' simply would not fit the known sequence of events.

The claims of *Double Cross* are further discredited by another story, published in 1993, which also promoted the idea of Marilyn being murdered by the Mafia. In this version the murder – a different murder – is again graphically described, enema being the means of introducing the drugs into her system. The professional killers involved in this account were also named, and the names were different from those quoted in *Double Cross*.

It is not possible for both of these completely different accounts of her being killed by the Mafia to be correct. In my opinion, the likelihood of the Mafia being involved in Marilyn's demise at all is so unlikely that it can be dismissed. In the United States the Mafia sometimes make a convenient garbage bin and are credited with many crimes because they are easy to blame where other answers are not forthcoming.

I spoke to Antoinette Giancana, daughter of Sam, on the subject of *Double Cross*, which purports to be an account of her father's involvement in the murder of Marilyn Monroe and in the assassinations of President Kennedy and his brother Robert. Antoinette denounces the book as scurrilous and says that had her father been alive it would never have been published. The implication was not so much that he would have controlled his godson and brother, but that he would have scorned the book's contents.

Antoinette told me that Sam did not have Marilyn Monroe

killed. She also told me that Chuck Giancana had been disowned by her father. Chuck, prepared to use the name Giancana for the authorship of his book, had, she told me, actually changed his name to Cain, which Sam deplored.

The Giancanas' claim that the CIA asked the Mafia to kill Marilyn as a favour does not stand up well under scrutiny. In the first place the alliance forged between the two organisations for the purpose of killing Castro did not mean they had suddenly become pals. The Mafia would not be likely to do this kind of thing as a favour to anyone, and it is really quite unlikely that, outside the terms of the alliance, they would murder someone to oblige the CIA. Secondly, the CIA had, as the headlines have revealed across the years, all the expertise they needed to carry out their own 'dirty tricks', including murder. They would have found it neither necessary nor desirable to ask the Mafia to do their dirty work.

Taking all things together, the murder of Marilyn Monroe cannot be credited to the Mafia. The idea of framing Robert Kennedy in such an imaginative scenario to get him out of office was hardly the way the Mafia did things. As for killing him, the Mafia were not without intelligence and knew the repercussions that such an action would bring from the President. To those in the know about Spindel's tapes, the Mafia were advertising their real intention loud and clear. They were expertly collecting sound recordings with the intention of eventually using them to *control* the Attorney General. This was a far better proposition. A dead Robert Kennedy might relieve the pressure they were currently suffering, but he was far more useful to them if they could manipulate and control him.

Killing Marilyn because of her knowledge of the alliance between the CIA and the Mafia was another matter, however. It could be argued that, if secrecy was so important to the hierarchy of organised crime that they were prepared to murder three of their own top people to seal their lips, they would have no problems with taking the life of a movie actress. There are a number of objections to this, however.

The first and most important is the mode of death. If the Mafia had simply wanted to silence Marilyn a gun would have been the most likely means. To kill her in a way that even superficially resembled suicide was nonsense: it achieved nothing that a swift bullet would not have achieved, and it represented an illogical, roundabout way of going about things. The mob was not illogical. and it did not take roundabout routes unless it had a reason. The idea of the Mafia using an enema and liquid drugs to kill a troublesome girl is quite ludicrous.

The mob also knew a great deal about Marilyn, which provided a strong reason for them not taking her too seriously. Had she gone ahead with her press conference she would only have been keeping her normal schedule. She held press conferences every month, so there was nothing unusual about that. If, in the middle of this one, she had announced that she had had a relationship with both the President and the Attorney General and given details of some classified information, the reporters present would have tended to ignore it. They would be well aware of the difficulties of getting past their editors with any news items likely to embarrass the President or his administration. Also, it had to be accepted that bombshells of this kind might simply have discredited Marilyn.

Marilyn had threatened a press conference when she was in a furious temper and was trying to get Robert Kennedy's attention. She had now achieved her aim, and it is doubtful that she would ever have got round to an exposé, especially with those who knew of her threat advising against it.

There was an even stronger reason for Marilyn not being on the mob's hit list, however. The killing of their own people some years later indicated that their main preoccupation was preventing information about their liaison with the CIA coming from *inside*. Marilyn could not have revealed the particular secrets they were anxious to keep, whatever they were.

# 17

# THE CASE AGAINST KENNEDY

Among those writers who believe Marilyn was murdered, an increasing number think that Robert Kennedy was the likely killer. Their argument runs that, in view of Marilyn's threat to reveal at her monthly press conference the relationships she had had with both him and his brother, he felt he had to silence her at all costs. Some believe that Kennedy killed her himself; others that he sent one of his faithful underlings to do the job; yet others that one of his men, seeing what a fix his boss was in, did it without being sent. The notion that Robert's father, Joe Kennedy, had someone kill her has also been put forward.

These would all make good scenarios for a thriller, but are less appealing in the light of logic and fact. Perhaps the most crucial point is that Marilyn was probably not the threat she was made out to be. To begin with, there was every likelihood that she would have changed her mind about going public in view of the damage she was likely to do to her own career. Moviegoers in the early sixties were not keen on their screen idols being caught up in scandals, and a national scandal involving the Kennedys might have made her untouchable to any studio afterwards. To speak candidly to journalists was to throw caution to the winds and to risk all she had achieved. Marilyn was being advised by those to whom she confided her intentions to drop the idea.

When Marilyn threatened to tell all about her affairs with John and Robert Kennedy she was seething. Robert Kennedy was ending the relationship without discussing it with her, and that was what had made her so angry. But by the Saturday everything had changed. It was Robert Kennedy who was anxious to talk to

Marilyn and she who was unwilling to see him. Kennedy wanted Marilyn to accept Peter Lawford's invitation for dinner that night so that he would have had the chance to discuss things with her, but she refused. She told Lawford she was too tired and would not be coming. If Spindel's tapes are to be believed, Kennedy himself phoned her some time on the Saturday, but she was adamant. 'Stop bothering me. Stay away from me,' she said. 'She was acting like a betrayed woman,' commented one man who listened to the tapes. In an eleventh-hour change of heart, she was now quitting the relationship on her terms. As far as her press conference was concerned, it was now likely that her friends' advice had been accepted.

There was no doubt that Robert Kennedy visited Marilyn's house that fatal Saturday. In fact there are witnesses to him being there in the afternoon and again during the evening. He had been there before, however, so that by itself was not significant. It was the stories about the contents of Spindel's tapes which roused suspicions, but, as mentioned in Chapter 10, tapes made from surveillance bugs are notoriously unreliable. Subject to editing and other malpractices, the recordings are often fuzzy and incomplete. In the case of Spindel's tapes, most of those who claim to have heard them have in fact heard only extracts, and often the sounds that they contain have had to be interpreted.

One claim made was that there were the sounds of 'bangs or thumps, as if someone was falling heavily'. This is an apt example of the tape's unreliability; a thousand different things could account for the noises said to have been heard, and the 'as if' is a typical example of interpretation. In one version this was followed by Robert Kennedy giving instructions to someone to calm a hysterical Marilyn, or to give her something to calm her. The somewhat sinister suggestion arises that he had taken a doctor with him for this purpose, with the inference that the doctor gave her an injection which proved too much and killed her. There was a distinct claim that Robert Kennedy was present in the house when Marilyn died.

Many strands are confused here, combined with an absence of logic and a total ignorance of what killed Marilyn. To begin with, one does not take a doctor to administer injections to friends who may become excited, and it is nonsense to think that Robert Kennedy would do such a thing. First, there was no way he could predict that Marilyn would become hysterical; and even had he known, it would have been crazy to think he would have brought with him a medico complete with hypodermic. In the second place, Marilyn did not die as the consequence of a small overdose. She died from a massive volume of barbiturates, and there could be no doubt that they were intended to kill. There was no question of them being administered by accident. It may well have been that, if Kennedy really did ask someone to calm her, this was maliciously extended to become incriminating. There was, after all, no love lost between Kennedy and Bernard Spindel, who interpreted the tapes, and the function of Spindel's bugs was to provide Jimmy Hoffa with blackmail material.

On the tape, the calming of Marilyn was said to be followed by the sound of something – or someone – being lowered on to a bed. This provocative claim was probably the most impossible to justify – any sound recordist, even with the finest equipment, would have difficulty in making such a recording recognisable for what it was. It is hard to believe that Spindel's electronic bugs could produce any kind of sound from a person being put on a bed, let alone something recognisable as such. It goes without saying that this was another sequence which required interpretation.

One person who heard the tapes said that a fierce argument took place between Marilyn and Robert Kennedy, and in view of the state of their relationship at that time this is not hard to believe. It is one of the sequences which persuades researchers that Spindel really did make sound recordings from bug transmissions. Marilyn was asking Kennedy why he was not going to marry her, while he became angry that he could not find something he was looking for. Some people believe he was looking for a bug whose existence he had become aware of, though it is far more likely that he was trying to find Marilyn's red diary which contained the notes she had made of their conversations on political issues. There is little doubt that Marilyn angered him by simply refusing to tell him where it was.

The likelihood of it being the diary is supported by other 'dialogue' which reputedly came from the tape. 'We have to know: it's important to the family,' Kennedy is claimed to have said. 'We can make any arrangements you want, but we must find it.' Now Peter Lawford is heard trying to soothe the feuding pair: 'Calm down, calm down,' he said. This suggests that it was Lawford who was asked to do the calming in the earlier extract, which further erodes claims that a doctor was present. Lawford had little success in quieting Marilyn, it seems: she ordered them both out of the house.

Before the sequence ended, some kind of cover-up arrangement was said to have been made between Lawford and Kennedy. Kennedy would telephone Marilyn's number when he got back to San Francisco. This was apparently designed to produce an alibi which would be supported by telephone company records. Before the tape finished it reportedly recorded the phone being answered, the operator identifying that the call came from the Bay area, and Kennedy asking, 'Is she dead?' In another version the question has become, 'Is she dead yet?' which indicates that the embroiderers have been busy again.

Even assuming that this quotation is genuine, it should be pointed out that the conversation in which it occurs is hardly complete. A telephone conversation does not usually consist of one three-word sentence. The likely explanation is that the Attorney General had made an arrangement with Peter Lawford to call him when he returned to San Francisco, by which time Lawford had to tell him that Marilyn had been attacked. In this context the question, 'Is she dead?' would not in any way be unnatural.

But if this is what happened, Spindel was not likely to tell it that way. A couple of snips with the scissors and he would have the most incriminating piece of tape. As for the background story relating to making a phone call as a cover-up, it would be easy to believe that the innocent arrangement described above became the inspiration for such a claim.

There is an example in all this of one extract from the tapes contradicting another. The notion that Robert Kennedy was present in Marilyn's house when she died, as claimed by Bernard Spindel, makes no sense in the light of the last recording on the tape, the one in which he is said to have asked, 'Is she dead?' It is an unlikely question if he knew she was already dead. Besides that, Kennedy's evening visit to Marilyn's house took place at about 7 p.m. or a little before; while he was still there Marilyn would not embark on making the series of phone calls we know she made, so it was impossible for him to have been in the house when she died. According to Mrs Murray she went to bed at about 8 p.m. and took the telephone with her so that she could make the calls from her bed. The last known call was made at 10 p.m., and Kennedy had left the house hours before.

If the extracts we have heard about are any indication, Spindel's tapes are full of improbabilities and as hard evidence leave much to be desired. As reported by those who have listened to extracts, complete with interpretations, they are extremely mischievous. At best they are a sophisticated variety of attack by hearsay; at worst pernicious victimisation. It would be tragic if, because of them, the memory of an able and worthy politician were to be for ever tarnished with doubts that he may have been responsible for the death of Marilyn Monroe.

Robert Kennedy was normally a very moral man. It was an incredible departure from his usual behaviour for him to enter into an illicit relationship with Marilyn. Though human enough to lose his temper at times, he was an astute man who kept both feet firmly on the ground. Seen as a decent, compassionate and fair-minded man, he found his political support among the blacks and disadvantaged. It would have been totally out of character for him to have become involved in murder.

Additionally, the very strongest reason for disregarding such damaging accusations is that Robert Kennedy was no gambler. He would not have been likely to risk his own political future, that of his brother, the President, and his younger brother Edward, together with the reputation of the entire Kennedy family, on one roll of the dice. He was not likely to kill Marilyn or to have her killed and risk all on not being found out. As far as Robert Kennedy was concerned there was little, if anything, to lose by ending the relationship and simply walking away from Marilyn, and everything to lose by killing her. It would have made no sense.

The notion of one of his men killing Marilyn to help his boss does not stand up very well, either. In the first place, apart from the enormous personal risk, if the perpetrator were unmasked the murder would have been laid at Kennedy's door just as though he had done it himself; no loyal member of his team would have put him at such risk. Besides, had it become known to the Attorney General that one of his staff had done such a thing, Kennedy would have dropped him instantly. He would not have been able to stand up for his employee even if he had wanted to, and indeed would have been appalled at such an act being carried out in the belief that it would please him. In fact the greatest reason that such a scenario was so unlikely was that his people would know him too well to believe he would ever wish such a thing to take place.

Robert Kennedy has been the victim of the Spindel tapes. It is interesting to note that the only other 'reason' for suspecting him is the extremely effective cover-up which took place – and that tends to recoil, supporting his innocence. The cover-up was arranged with care and precision by Police Chief William Parker, who realised that the political futures of both Robert and John Kennedy would be in jeopardy if a murder investigation even remotely involved the Attorney General.

Parker, however, was a man of great integrity, and there was no suggestion that he would have set such a cover-up in place had he believed there was the remotest chance that Kennedy was involved in Marilyn's death. Had Kennedy been guilty, the high-flying Chief Parker, the most distinguished law enforcement officer in the United States, would have been an accessory after the fact. The fact that Parker was willing to help Robert Kennedy speaks reams for his innocence, therefore.

In the long run, apart from Spindel's tapes there is nothing to point a finger at Robert Kennedy as being responsible for Marilyn's death. It cannot be argued that because he was in the house the day before Marilyn died he must be guilty. Ralph Greenson, Pat Newcomb, Eunice Murray and hairdresser Agnes Flanagan were all at the house that day, and none of them was accused. It is remarkable that none of those who have inferred he was the guilty party appear to have heard Spindel's tapes for themselves, but have based their suppositions on the word of the very few people who claim to have heard excerpts. And then, the excerpts in question are riddled with holes; the worst they reveal with any substance is that he and Marilyn had a row.

Those who genuinely want to see the stigma of suicide removed from the memory of Marilyn Monroe rightly argue the case for murder, but it is not good enough to set the memory of one person right by damaging the memory of another, innocent, person. Robert Kennedy was not responsible for the death of Marilyn Monroe. His friends were not responsible for the death of Marilyn Monroe. But his enemies . . . That is a different matter, which will be picked up again in Chapter 20.

# 18

# ENTER MR JACOBS

In a book about the death of Marilyn Monroe the reader does not expect to find the story of her life. Had this been a life story, a great many 'feature players' would have been introduced into these pages and Arthur Jacobs, who at first glance plays only a bit part in the story of Marilyn's death, would have been elevated to major role status. To dismiss as only minor the contribution he made to the circumstances of Marilyn's death is to miss the important point of what was sparked off.

Apjac, as he was affectionately called, was more than a storyteller; he was a weaver of dreams. He took the sometimes quite mundane lives of the stars and created an image – a mythology – for them. Arthur Jacobs transformed them into the exciting people they wanted to be, the glamorous people their studios wanted them to be, the captivating people their fans wanted them to be. This was Hollywood in its golden days, Tinseltown, the home of fantasy and make-believe. But he had not reached his own place at the top of the publicity tree through magic: for him nothing had taken the place of effort and hard work.

Coming from a privileged background, Jacobs went to the University of Southern California, graduated in business studies and then fought in the Second World War. Afterwards he returned to Los Angeles with two special friends he had made. The three became runners at the Warner Brothers studios, and when they were all fired on the same day they went their separate ways. Dick Carroll made his way in the haberdashery trade and to this day is well known in this connection in Los Angeles.

Harry Lewis went into the fast food business, and his Hamburger Hamlets are to be found all over the area. Arthur made his way into publicity and rose to represent many famous stars, including Marlene Dietrich, Grace Kelly and Marilyn Monroe.

One day when on the set of a Marlene Dietrich film, *Monte Carlo Story*, he saw an attractive fourteen-year-old actress, Natalie Trundy, who set his heart racing. 'I'm going to marry you when you grow up,' he told her. And he did. In the summer of 1962 they were engaged, and on Saturday, 4 August, he and Natalie, in the company of producer Mervyn LeRoy and his wife, were listening to the music of Henry Mancini at the Hollywood Bowl. It was Natalie's birthday, and as they listened they drank champagne beneath the stars on this lovely warm night. The concert was to be followed by a party at Chasen's, Los Angeles' most famous restaurant.

The magic was rudely disturbed, however, by an attendant who tripped down the steps to inform Arthur of an urgent telephone call for him. The publicist excused himself, returning

Twentieth Century-Fox publicist Arthur P. Jacobs, shown here with his wife Natalie, fed the world the suicide story. *Natalie Jacobs.*

moments later to tell Natalie that there was an emergency involving Marilyn Monroe and that he would have to go to her house at once. Natalie did not see him for the next two days. Arthur Jacobs died in 1973, but in extensive conversations with me his widow places the time of the call at roughly 10.30 p.m., perhaps a little later. Arthur raced across town to Fifth Helena Drive and arrived at about 11 p.m., according to a later comment to one of his employees.

Jacobs had a talented staff which included John Springer, Lois Weber, Rupert Allan and Pat Newcomb. Pat had been attached to Marilyn by Jacobs, though she had known Marilyn for some years already. They had met on the set of *Bus Stop* and had become friendly. This friendship quickly evaporated, however, when Marilyn suspected Pat of becoming involved with a man whom the actress had in her own sights. Marilyn was mistaken about Pat's intentions, but the friendship was left on the touchline for four years. When it came to having a personal press aide attached to her, however, Marilyn insisted it should be Newcomb. Through many ups and downs, the relationship developed into a close personal friendship. Robert Slatzer pulled no punches when he described the aide's function: 'Newcomb was an early "spin doctor": her duty was to keep as many of the mercurial star's indiscretions out of the papers as she could, and to put as positive a spin as possible on the rest.'

It should not be thought that Arthur Jacobs was in and out of Marilyn's life; he was a very permanent part of it. He and his fiancée, Natalie, knew her socially and they both knew about her relationship with John F. Kennedy and, later, his brother Robert. Marilyn leaned on her brilliant publicist. 'I love Arthur,' she murmured to Natalie in her whispered tones. 'He'll take care of me. He'll always be here when I need him.' But when she needed him on that dreadful Saturday night Arthur was too late.

By the time he arrived at Marilyn's house she was comatose, but probably Arthur did not grasp the seriousness of the situation and believed he was there to front for a new illness. He knew what his job was in these circumstances: to protect Marilyn's image both with her public and with the studio, who would be dismayed if their star, reappointed to *Something's Got to Give* and on three times her former salary, were not able to carry out her obligations. From Arthur Jacobs' viewpoint, even the possibility of Marilyn getting fired from her picture a second time would be enough to concentrate his mind on finding some way of resolving this new and alarming situation. But risks would have to be taken, for through the studio Jacobs knew he could obtain the best possible attention for Marilyn, quickly and discreetly. He would then prepare a story for release to the media playing down her illness and, if possible, explaining it away.

But Marilyn died, and Arthur Jacobs' role changed radically. In addition to explaining what had happened to the studio and protecting his client's image, he was immediately aware that the political fate of the Attorney General, and through him the President, might depend on the story he put out to the media and his handling of it.

The first meeting he held was probably with Mrs Murray, Dr Engelberg, Dr Greenson, Peter Lawford – who appears to have been in on events from a very early stage – and perhaps others who have never been identified. It would be remarkable if he did not send for Pat Newcomb, but she denies being at the house before 4 a.m. This meeting would, no doubt, be for the purpose of putting a story together for the police and keeping them at arm's length. It is likely that Chief William Parker was informed of events very early, however, and long before the police were officially called. The officers sent to investigate were not inquisitive: they went through the motions of conducting an enquiry and left it at that. But other meetings were urgently required, for there were gaps which needed plugging and Arthur Jacobs was well aware of their existence.

One gap related to the record of telephone calls made from the house over past weeks, which would quickly alert a sharp-witted reporter to the fact that a liaison had been conducted between Marilyn Monroe and the Attorney General. Lawrence Schiller, who had been one of the photographers to take pictures of the nude swim which had taken place in the pool on the set of *Something's Got to Give*, was in Arthur Jacobs' office while a later meeting was being held. Jacobs was talking to Pat Newcomb about 'what the telephone logs would reveal'. He was right to be concerned, for it was not many days before reporters were trying to obtain sight of the records. They had no luck. The records had been acquired by the authorities within hours of Marilyn dying – taken, it appears, by FBI agents, but by all accounts soon in the hands of Chief Parker.

The meetings which took place in Arthur Jacobs' office were aimed at preventing Robert Kennedy from coming under the scrutiny of reporters covering Marilyn's death in depth – they would quickly recognise a major scandal in the making. It was difficult, because Kennedy had been seen many times with Marilyn and appeared to have exercised little discretion. But in the words of Natalie Jacobs, 'Arthur fudged everything.' He was a past master at manipulating the media. He could put out fictions supported by nothing and they would be seized upon by a hungry press. But this was probably the biggest challenge of his career because he had never played for such stakes before. As one of his staff expressed it to Robert Slatzer, Arthur was the 'architect of the cover-up'.

The story about Marilyn's death put out by Arthur Jacobs was generally accepted as fact by the world and, indeed, is believed by many to this day to be the authentic version. He achieved what he set out to: he kept both Robert and John F. Kennedy out of the affair. It was not until nearly twenty years had elapsed, and long after both brothers were dead at the hands of assassins – John in 1963 and Robert in 1968 – that stories of their relationships began to emerge. Said Rupert Allan, a member of Jacobs' staff, 'It was carefully done and beautifully executed.'

When Arthur Jacobs was at Marilyn's house on the night she died, he had other chores to carry out. Probably assisted by Henry Rogers, a trusted member of his staff, and, one would have guessed, Pat Newcomb – though she denies it – he apparently went through Marilyn's files with the further assistance of two studio men, who were probably sent when Arthur telephoned the news to Fox executives. Their task, no doubt, was to 'sweep' her house of documents which, in the hands of reporters, could have embarrassed the studio or the memory of Marilyn. They were probably not the only ones removing documents: all Marilyn's personal papers seem to have disappeared.

When the dust had settled and Marilyn had been officially

declared a 'probable suicide', which can be interpreted as 'accidental suicide', Twentieth-Century Fox were mightily pleased with the outcome. The inclusion of that word 'probable' in the coroner's verdict made a huge difference, for they could collect on an insurance policy which would have been void if her death had been straightforward suicide. During a period when the fortunes of the studio were at a low ebb, the coffers suffering badly and the shadow of bankruptcy lingering, the money from the insurance cover, quoted by some as one million dollars – an enormous sum in 1962 – and by others as three million dollars, was a real consideration in view of the fact that *Something's Got to Give* had been finally blown. There was also a second insurance policy payable if any of the stars contracted for the movie died during the making of the film.

Fox were also highly pleased with Arthur Jacobs, and it may have been no coincidence that the studio launched him as a producer. He went on to make *What a Way to Go*, which had been planned as a vehicle for Marilyn, *Doctor Doolittle*, *Goodbye Mr Chips* and the lucrative *Planet of the Apes* movies. His wife, Natalie, had a part in all except the first of these.

Like any efficient publicity man, Arthur Jacobs had a talent for melting away before the limelight he had obtained for his star revealed his presence. It was so at the time of Marilyn's death, when he quietly slipped out of sight. In spite of his major role in orchestrating the events surrounding Marilyn's death and pulling all the strings which animated the world's media, he was never questioned by the police. This, of course, may simply have been evidence of their ineptitude, or it might have been a result of their policy not to rock the boat. Or else it might have been further testimony to the magic of the master manipulator.

# 19

# SEQUENCE OF EVENTS

The research which has gone into the writing of Chapters 1–18 has been invaluable for obtaining an understanding of the sequence of events which led up to Marilyn's death. Perhaps the most convenient starting point would be Friday, 4 August.

Bear in mind that Marilyn was on a 'high'. She had been reinstated to *Something's Got to Give* on roughly three times her previous salary, more than she had ever earned in her life before. The one fly in the ointment was that her relationship with Robert Kennedy had recently gone sadly wrong. He had cut himself off from her and she had been unable to reach him. He would not accept her phone calls and had offered no explanation for his behaviour. It appears that her attempts to contact him extended until Friday morning, when she had a sudden change of heart. She later told Robert Slatzer she was considering calling a press conference at which she would make public the relationships that both brothers had had with her.

*Friday p.m.*  Marilyn telephones Robert Slatzer at his home in Ohio. She tells him she has been trying to contact Robert Kennedy in Washington, without success. She tells him she is considering calling a press conference to tell the world about the relationships she has had with both Robert and John F. Kennedy. Slatzer tells her it is in the news that RFK is flying to the West Coast to address a convention at San Francisco and she might have better luck reaching him there. She decides to ring Pat Lawford, RFK's sister, at Hyannis Port to obtain a number where she can reach him. She asks Peter Lawford for her number at Hyannis Port and he gives it to her.

*Friday 7 p.m.* Briggs Delicatessen delivers food to Marilyn's house for a meal for two. Could Robert Kennedy be expected?

*Friday p.m.* If Kennedy was expected for dinner, it seems Marilyn has changed her mind. Dinner is off.

*Friday p.m.* Marilyn decides she will go out for dinner and she and Pat Newcomb go over to a restaurant on Sunset Strip. They are joined by Peter Lawford, and later on Marilyn is seen to be the worse for drink. Newcomb stays at Marilyn's house.

*Friday night* Marilyn's sleep is disturbed periodically by a woman calling her on her private line. The message is always the same: 'Leave Bobby alone, you tramp.' The calls continue all night until about 5.30 on Saturday morning.

*Saturday 6 a.m.* Marilyn cannot now get back to sleep and calls Jeanne Carmen to tell her about the telephone calls. She does not think it was Bobby's wife, Ethel Kennedy, herself but someone calling for her. It is sleepy Jeanne's birthday and she thanks Marilyn for the gold-coloured golf clubs she had sent as a birthday gift. Marilyn confirms she will be playing golf with Jeanne on Monday.

*Saturday a.m.* Marilyn speaks to journalist Sidney Skolsky on the telephone. She talks about his family and then tells him she is seeing Bobby Kennedy that night at dinner over at the Lawford house.

*Saturday a.m.* Marilyn makes telephone calls to her friend, Arthur James, and Isadore Miller, her ex-husband Arthur's father, of whom she is very fond.

*Saturday 10 a.m.* Mrs Murray arrives. Marilyn is still on the phone.

*Saturday a.m.* Agnes Flanagan arrives to do Marilyn's hair. While she is at the house a messenger arrives with a package. It contains a soft toy tiger. Marilyn becomes depressed by this. It is not clear whether a note bearing a message is with the tiger or whether the tiger itself is the message. Marilyn is unhappy. It seems Kennedy now wants to see her and she does not want to see him. He wants her to go for dinner at Lawford's. It is probably now that she calls Ralph Roberts, her masseur and friend, and makes a tentative arrangement to have dinner with him on her patio. He is to call back later in the day to confirm.

*Saturday a.m.*    Pat Newcomb rises late. Marilyn envies Pat's ability to sleep well and long. She grizzles and is ill-tempered, but the reason is probably more to do with Robert Kennedy and his new anxiety to see her than with Newcomb. She later becomes more relaxed, sunbathing beside the pool and looking over new scripts.

*Saturday p.m.*    Robert Kennedy arrives unexpectedly with two of his aides. He has not come for discussion. He has come to recover the red diary containing the notes Marilyn made of the subjects they discussed at their meetings, and though he and his aides turn the place over they cannot find it. Marilyn refuses to help him. She berates him for going back on his word to divorce Ethel and marry her. He is anxious and irritated, and Marilyn is in no mood for an unrepentant Kennedy. It is not long before a blazing row breaks out. But this was never intended as a social visit and Kennedy and his companions are not long in leaving.

Marilyn talks to one of the film crew on the set of *Something's Got to Give*. In the foreground is studio photographer Jimmy Mitchell. *The Robert F. Slatzer Collection.*

*Saturday p.m.* Marilyn makes a number of attempts to ring the White House. It seems she wants to tell JFK how angry and disillusioned she is with Robert and to ask him to tell his brother she does not want to see him or speak to him ever again. She is eventually told the President is not there. He is at his home in Hyannis Port.

*Saturday p.m.* Marilyn rings Jeanne Carmen again. 'Come over and bring a bag of pills with you,' she says. Jeanne told me pharmaceutical drugs were easy to get hold of and she had shared with Marilyn before. But this time she cries off. It is Jeanne's birthday and she has a busy round of engagements. Jeanne thanks her again for her birthday gift and for the greetings card which has been delivered.

*Saturday 4.30 p.m.* By now the strain of the day coupled with her sleepless night is telling on her and she begins to feel low. Mrs Murray telephones Dr Greenson and he arranges to come over.

*Saturday 5 p.m.* Peter Lawford telephones to tell Marilyn he wants her to come for dinner. Robert Kennedy will be there and he wants to see her. Detective Fred Otash rendered an account of this call given to him by Peter Lawford only a few hours after Marilyn died. Otash said:

> According to Lawford, he had called her and she had said to him that she was passed around like a piece of meat. She had had it. She didn't want Bobby to use her any more. She called the White House and there was no response from the President. She was told he [John Kennedy] was in Hyannis Port and she didn't connect with him. She kept trying to get him. He [Lawford] had tried to reason with her to quiet down and come to the [Lawford's] beach house and relax. She said 'No, I'm tired. There's nothing more for me to respond to. Just do me a favor. Tell the President I tried to get him. Tell him goodbye for me. I think my purpose has been served.'

*Saturday p.m.* Dr Greenson arrives. In spite of having plans to take his wife out to dinner, he spends over two hours with Marilyn. He asks Mrs Murray to stay over with Marilyn tonight,

perhaps because he will be unavailable until very late. At about
6.30 p.m. Pat Newcomb leaves. Also at about 6.30 p.m. Ralph
Roberts rings to see if the dinner engagement is on, and Dr
Greenson curtly tells him Marilyn is out. Greenson leaves within
the next half-hour.

*Saturday 6.45 p.m.*    Robert Kennedy returns unannounced
with, probably, Peter Lawford. The likely reason for his presence
is that he is worried about Marilyn's attitude as revealed in her
phone call to Lawford in relation to her threat to hold a press
conference. It is more important than ever that he gets the red
diary. Marilyn becomes hysterical during this visit and orders
them out.

*Saturday 7.30 p.m.*    Joe DiMaggio Jr telephones. Marilyn is
pleased to get the call because she has a great affection for her
ex-husband's son. Whatever variety of hysteria she had suffered
from during Kennedy's visit has quickly evaporated. Joe Jr tells
Marilyn that his engagement is off and knows this will please
her, for she had thought the intended match quite unsuitable. In
fact she thought it would have been a disaster. Marilyn is elated.
She and Joe chatter happily for a while and Joe remembers her
being 'gay, happy and alert' while talking to him. Later Mrs
Murray says she heard Marilyn speaking on the telephone to
Joe Jr. She says she heard her laughing and caught the words,
'Oh, that's wonderful.'

*Saturday 7.45 p.m.*    Marilyn telephones Dr Greenson before
he leaves for dinner. She tells him about Kennedy's second visit
and that her momentary fury had quickly dissipated. Greenson
later said of this call that she assured him she was feeling better.
He spoke of her sounding 'more cheerful' than she had been
earlier in the day, and that he did not feel any further crisis
was likely to arise while he was out to dinner.

*Saturday 8 p.m.*    Marilyn tells Mrs Murray she is going to
bed and retires to her bedroom.

*Saturday 9 p.m.*    Marilyn makes a phone call to dress
manufacturer Henry Rosenfeld in New York from her bed.
Rosenfeld said later he thought she sounded 'groggy'. It may
simply have been that she was just sleepy.

*Saturday 9.20 p.m. (approximately)*    Marilyn rings famous
hairdresser Sydney Guilaroff, who was afterwards reported as

saying that she said to him, 'I'm very depressed.' He said she hung up without saying goodbye.

*Saturday 9.30 p.m.* (*approximately*) Her Mexican friend, José Bolanos, calls her from a local restaurant where he is having a meal. Bolanos will not talk about their discussion but says she did not hang up when they had finished talking. She just put the phone down. Bolanos said there was nothing unusual in this: she had done it before.

*Saturday 9.45 p.m.* (*approximately*) Marilyn rings Ralph Roberts but obtains only his answering service. If Dr Greenson had not told her that Roberts had rung at 6.30 p.m., she would be wanting to ask him why he had not called. Perhaps she still wants him to come across for dinner. If the doctor *had* told her he had put Roberts off she would, no doubt, want to explain and apologise to her friend. The answering service operator tells Marilyn that Roberts has by then gone out to dinner with friends.

*Saturday 10 p.m.* Marilyn telephones Jeanne Carmen once more. She still wants Jeanne to come over to see her, but her friend says she is too tired. Carmen later said that Marilyn had sounded a bit nervous and uptight but otherwise normal.

*Saturday 10.30 p.m.* Publicist Arthur Jacobs is called away from a concert at the Hollywood Bowl. The message said there was something seriously wrong with Marilyn. Jacobs would arrive at Fifth Helena Drive at approximately 11 p.m.

*Saturday 11 p.m.* (*approximately*) It would appear that someone from the house telephones Hyman Engelberg, Marilyn's physician. He would appear to have been difficult to contact and it is uncertain what time he actually arrived.

*Saturday 11.45 p.m.* (*approximately*) Someone at the house calls for an ambulance.

*Saturday midnight* (*approximately*) The ambulance arrives, by which time Marilyn is comatose.

*Sunday 12.10 a.m.* (*approximately*) Mrs Murray telephones Dr Greenson. Greenson has just got back from taking his wife to dinner. He drives over immediately, and since his home is only about a mile from Marilyn's he arrives quickly.

*Sunday early a.m.* Milton Rudin arrives, time unknown, but it is claimed that he called Pat Newcomb from Marilyn's house before 4 a.m. and Milt Ebbins, also, at about 4 a.m.

*Sunday 3.50 a.m.* Hyman Engelberg signs the death certificate.

*Sunday 4 a.m.* Marilyn's press secretary, Pat Newcomb, arrives at the house.

*Sunday 4.25 a.m.* Dr Greenson telephones the police. Sergeant Jack Clemmons takes the call and decides to drive out to the house in case it is a hoax.

*Sunday 4.35 a.m.* Clemmons arrives at the house. He finds Marilyn lying face down across her bed, corner to corner. She is covered only by a sheet which Dr Greenson says he pulled across her. Greenson says that when he himself arrived she was clutching the phone, which he put back on the hook. Clemmons questions Dr Greenson, Mrs Murray and Dr Engelberg. Greenson says the reason for the long delay in contacting the police was that permission had to be obtained from the studio. The washing machine is heard operating in the

Marilyn's bedroom shortly after her body was removed. *Corbis-Bettmann/UPI.*

background. The story told by Mrs Murray is that she went to bed at 10 p.m. and woke at midnight to use the bathroom, when she saw a light under Marilyn's bedroom door, which was locked. The telephone cord stretched beneath it. Because she could not rouse Marilyn she took a poker outside and, through a small window which was open, pulled the curtain back to see Marilyn lying naked and face down. She then telephoned Dr Greenson who came across and broke a window to gain entry into the bedroom. He emerged two minutes later to say, 'We have lost her.' She says he then phoned Dr Engelberg, who came to the house and certified Marilyn dead. It is probable that while this questioning was going on others not interviewed by Clemmons were hiding in a bedroom.

*Sunday 5.30 a.m.* Guy Hockett comes from the Coroner's Department to collect the body. The body is first taken to a mortuary and then taken to the County Morgue for autopsy. Hockett later said the body was so affected by rigor mortis that he had to bend her arms to get her

Guy Hockett takes away Marilyn's body in the coroner's hearse. *AP Wide World.*

on the gurney. He estimated she had been dead for several hours.

*Sunday 5.45 a.m.* Detective Sergeant Robert E. Byron arrives to conduct an investigation. He finds Dr Engelberg, lawyer Milton Rudin and Mrs Murray there. Greenson has left. Engelberg and Rudin are reticent. Murray gives a different timescale for events. She now says it was 3.30 a.m. when she found Marilyn and called Dr Greenson.

*Sunday 10.30 a.m.* Dr Thomas Noguchi begins the autopsy. Deputy DA John Miner observes.

The timetable of events given above needs a combination of commentary and explanation, especially in regard to the more controversial assertions.

The sequence opens with a substantiated statement. Robert Slatzer confirms that Marilyn telephoned him in Ohio on Friday afternoon, the day before she died, to learn from him that Robert Kennedy was speaking at San Francisco and would be on the West Coast the whole weekend. 'I advised her to forget about

Marilyn with one-time husband Robert Slatzer. *Robert F. Slatzer.*

talking with Bobby and to concentrate on preparing for her role in *Something's Got to Give*, the film she was scheduled to finish with Dean Martin when production resumed in October,' he said. 'But Marilyn was determined to talk to Bobby one last time . . .'

It is interesting that Marilyn called Slatzer from a call box, complaining that her phones were tapped. She discovered that Robert Kennedy was bringing Ethel and some of the children and that after the convention they would go further north to Washington state for a holiday. She tried repeatedly to reach him at the hotel she knew he always stayed at in San Francisco, but met with no success.

If at the outset it was Robert Kennedy who Marilyn was hoping would come for dinner on the Friday night before she died – and this would be the most likely explanation for the delivery of such expensive food – it would seem she later went completely cold on the idea. *She* now decided she would drop *him*. It is likely she cancelled any arrangement she had with Kennedy by calling Peter Lawford, who would pass on a message. Kennedy was booked into the Beverly Hilton Hotel for the Friday night, but it appears he changed his arrangements and did not arrive until the next day. We are quite sure he did not come to Marilyn's for dinner that night because she and Pat Newcomb went out for dinner together to a restaurant on Sunset Strip. This being an unplanned meal, it was odd that they were joined by Peter Lawford, but it would seem he had come to ask Marilyn to dinner the following night when Robert Kennedy, who was now anxious to speak to her, would be there. Marilyn was not interested, and that evening she got tipsy.

When Marilyn went to bed that night she took the telephone into her bedroom, and kept it there. If she used the phone in bed she normally placed it later outside the door covered by a pillow so that she would not be disturbed if it rang. But she kept it in her room both this night and Saturday night. She wanted the comfort of calling her friends, it seems, until she dropped off to sleep. Marilyn had two telephones, a pink one for business calls and a white one, the number of which was known only to her close friends. It was the white one which she took into her room, and it was this one by which the night was shattered over and over again by a woman caller who each time said, 'Leave Bobby alone, you tramp,' or something similar.

The fact that the calls came to Marilyn's private line indicated that the number had been obtained from someone close to her. Whoever the caller was, she certainly had Ethel Kennedy's best interests at heart, and it raised the question of whether Ethel had come across Marilyn's number in Robert's belongings. It is unlikely he would give it to anyone, though if Ethel had acquired it by some means it appears that she enlisted the help of a friend to make the calls. The entire episode would be unwelcome to anyone, but to Marilyn, an insomniac, it was disastrous. It was small wonder she was in a bad temper next day.

Marilyn's early morning call to Jeanne Carmen speaks reams for their friendship. It had to be someone close to accept with any degree of cheerfulness a call which had wakened her at six o'clock in the morning. But Marilyn was obviously bursting to tell someone about the calls she had received during the night. It was Jeanne's birthday and Marilyn, who was good about such things, had not forgotten it. She had sent a card and, because Jeanne was a professional-standard golfer, had bought her some attractive golf clubs. Jeanne Carmen had been Marilyn's neighbour when she lived in an apartment before buying the house on Fifth Helena Drive. It is interesting that she confirmed her golfing date with her friend for the following Monday on the night before she supposedly took her own life.

The important thing to observe about the call that Marilyn made to Sidney Skolsky later that morning is that she told him she was going to see Bobby Kennedy that night at the Lawfords' beach house. Some communication had, then, definitely taken place, possibly later on the Friday night, probably via Peter Lawford. It would at first seem that she was weakening in her resolve not to speak to Robert Kennedy.

Jeanne Carmen talked to me about 'taking bags of pills' when she went over to see Marilyn. She told me they shared pharmaceutical drugs from time to time. 'They were easy to get in those days,' she said, 'and we didn't know much about the consequences of such things.' She spoke also about that particular day. 'I'm glad I didn't take pills over to Marilyn's place that day,' she said. 'It was my birthday and I had a lot of things to do. I was seeing Marilyn on the following Monday, anyway. We played golf together.'

When Mrs Murray arrived for work that morning, her employer was still using the telephone. Hairdresser Agnes Flanagan came to do Marilyn's hair, and it was presumably after she had finished that a package arrived. It contained a soft toy, a tiger, and it was either receipt of the tiger itself or a note which came with it which caused Marilyn to become very depressed. Noticing her mood, Agnes Flanagan put on her coat and quietly slipped away. We know that Robert Kennedy wanted to see Marilyn at the Lawfords' house that night and that she had wavered about going. It seems that she now set her face against ever seeing Kennedy again. It was probably at this point that she made a tentative arrangement – to be confirmed later – with Ralph Roberts to have dinner together on her patio that night. It would appear to have been something to do with the toy tiger – probably a note which accompanied it – which set Marilyn thinking and which brought her to a firm decision. Decision or no decision, however, the arrival of the tiger upset Marilyn deeply.

Pat Newcomb seemed to get the rough edge of Marilyn's temper that morning. She slept late, which always maddened Marilyn because of her problems in getting even the basic sleep she needed, never mind the luxury of a lie-in. Her ill-temper did not last, however. Pat Newcomb speaks of the time they spent at the poolside that day, while Marilyn read over possible future scripts.

It seems it was during the afternoon that Robert Kennedy unexpectedly called at Marilyn's house. The account rendered here is constructed from various sources, though the time he called is not certain. The proceedings of the hectic and relatively brief meeting are deduced from the various accounts of what is said to be on the Spindel tapes, which in turn were derived from bugs placed in the house.

According to the accounts of different people of what they heard on the tape, Kennedy conducted a search, and this appeared to be for one of two reasons. Some thought he was looking for Marilyn's red 'bombshell' diary, whilst others drew the conclusion that he was seeking the bug which he had become aware was transmitting from the house. To me the idea of him tearing the place apart to find a bug is unrealistic. In the first place, had he known the house was bugged he would not have come and risked being listened in to any more. He would be aware that any listening device had been placed there because of his visits, and that when he stopped calling whoever had had the bugs put in was not likely to continue to monitor Marilyn's movements. For this reason there was little point in stripping the house to find something which would soon become redundant. Additionally, if he had known that a bug had been planted and he had still felt it important to come personally, he would simply have been extremely careful about what he said and did on what he planned to be his last visit. If the accounts of the meeting are to be believed, they ranted and screamed at each other while the place was being turned over by Kennedy and his aides, and it would therefore seem quite unlikely that he knew the house was bugged.

It is far more logical that he was looking for the politically sensitive red diary, which in the wrong hands could have constituted a risk to national security. It was, indeed, dynamite, and well worth the effort for Kennedy to remove. The trouble was he did not know where it was and Marilyn, being angry with him, would not say.

On the whole the meeting was not on Marilyn's terms. Kennedy appeared to dictate the pace, though Marilyn did not fail to thrust home her chief complaint: that he was going back on his word to divorce Ethel and marry her. In the cold light of day, anyone knowing Robert Kennedy's Catholic background, his passion for politics, his family-man lifestyle and his deep loyalty to the Kennedy family would never have considered such a thing possible. Marilyn, a very smart lady in spite of her screen image, had her feet well off the ground if she believed he would abandon all this to marry her.

Kennedy and his aides left the house without the diary. He would, no doubt, have someone negotiate for it when everyone's emotions had subsided.

Once Marilyn had simmered down, the phone calls went on into the afternoon. According to the Fred Otash interview, Lawford said Marilyn later told him she made several attempts to get John F. Kennedy at the White House, but was unsuccessful. It would seem reasonable to assume that she wanted to tell him what she thought about his brother and his treatment of her. After several attempts the White House operator told her that the President had gone to his home in Hyannis Port for the weekend. Her efforts stopped at this point: she knew she could not reach him there. As the afternoon drew on, the strain of the events of the day, combined with Marilyn's lack of sleep, was no doubt catching up on her. Not surprisingly she felt low, which was taken by Mrs Murray as a signal to call Dr Greenson. Greenson decided to make a house visit.

Peter Lawford's call at 5 p.m. would do nothing for Marilyn because, from what she said in response to the actor's continued pressure for her to have dinner at his house, everything she had no doubt been trying to subdue in her heart and mind since Robert Kennedy's visit was stirred up again. She displayed considerable strength of character, however, declining the invitation and telling Lawford exactly what she thought of his brother-in-law. There was more than a hint in what she said that she felt just the same way about Jack Kennedy too. She had had enough. She told Lawford she had tried without success to reach the President, almost certainly to deliver the same message and to be just as blunt with him, too. That she now had control over her emotions was advertised by the fact that she would apparently not be making a call to the President on Monday, when he returned from Hyannis Port. It seemed she did not feel sufficiently moved to carry her anger over the weekend. Instead she passed a brief message to Lawford to give John F. Kennedy: 'Tell the President I tried to get him. Tell him goodbye for me. I think my purpose has been served.' No temper tantrums, no weeping, not even a suggestion of feeling low, depressed or suicidal. Her attitude was one of determination. She clearly had a grip on things now.

If Fred Otash's account of what Peter Lawford told him can be trusted – and there is no obvious reason why it should not – there was an interesting footnote to his telephone conversation with Marilyn. Robert Kennedy was, it seems, right there beside the actor as he spoke to her, and, after she had hung up and he could not get her back because of the phone being off the hook, according to Lawford, 'Bobby got panicky. "What's going on?" he asked.' Lawford said, 'Nothing. That's the way she is.' That Kennedy was panicky suggests that Marilyn's attitude was unexpected. Perhaps he thought she would run to Peter Lawford and beg him to intercede with Robert. There was none of it. She was her own woman.

Looking at all that Fred Otash had to say about what Peter Lawford told him barely four or five hours after Marilyn died, we have an account which, in my opinion, carries the ring of truth. Otash did not volunteer this information: it was elicited by journalists twenty-three years after Marilyn's death. When he was asked why he had remained silent for so long, he replied, 'I didn't see any purpose of getting involved . . . I'm not being paid. I'm not writing a book. I'm not making a point. If I wanted to capitalise on my relationship in this matter, I would have written my own book.' It is, of course, of enormous value to know what Lawford was saying immediately after Marilyn died. The account that Otash gives of his telephone conversation with Marilyn reveals what is, by all accounts, the true version of what she really said. It is the origin of the 'Say goodbye to the President' story that Lawford invented to persuade the world that Marilyn had committed suicide. The real version bears only a superficial resemblance to his embroidered yarn. And to know the truth has the effect of strengthening the belief that she did not take her own life. Had she committed suicide, it would have been unnecessary to weave such fabrications around what was really said. In my opinion Peter Lawford could have answered all the questions about what really happened to Marilyn.

Dr Greenson was taking his wife out to dinner that night, and it is unlikely that he wanted to pay a home visit that particular afternoon. The reason he did was almost certainly because Mrs Murray told him about Robert Kennedy calling and the terrible row she had overheard. She probably told him what happened, chapter and verse, and added that Marilyn had been depressed by receiving the toy tiger to begin with.

There is no doubt that Dr Greenson saw it as necessary and urgent to rush to the side of his patient in the circumstances. Almost certainly he expected to find her a wreck, and he was probably amazed at the way she was standing up to it all. It seems that Greenson played for safety when, for instance, he brusquely told Ralph Roberts that Marilyn was out when he telephoned. If he knew she planned to eat with him that evening, he was probably asserting that he did not think it wise. It took Joe DiMaggio Jr three attempt to speak to Marilyn on the telephone that night. On the first two occasions he was fobbed off. It was said that Dr Greenson told Pat Newcomb to leave that evening, and if this were true it would have fitted the same pattern of thrusting a protective layer of insulation between his patient and those who tried to get near her. As it happens, Pat Newcomb asserts that this did not happen and that when she went she left of her own volition, leaving a cheerful Marilyn behind. Dr Greenson was no doubt concerned in case Marilyn needed attention of some kind while he was out at dinner that night. He resolved this situation by asking Mrs Murray to stay overnight, but by all indications left no word of where he could be found.

Robert Kennedy's arrival on his second visit to Marilyn was observed by Marilyn's neighbours, and Robert Slatzer interviewed them and recorded their answers to his questions on the subject. They said he arrived at about 7 p.m., but we have pulled this time back to about 6.45 p.m. on the grounds that, allowing for even a short, hectic visit, Marilyn appeared to be so bright and happy when Joe DiMaggio Jr called at about 7.30 p.m. that it seemed reasonable to allow a slightly longer interval between Kennedy leaving and the telephone call. Further confirmation that Robert Kennedy visited Marilyn was obtained when the BBC were interviewing Mrs Murray for their programme *Say Goodbye to the President* in 1985. Murray surprised the producers by admitting that she had lied on the subject for twenty-three years, and now told them that Robert Kennedy was indeed at the house that day.

This second call was, most likely, the consequence of Robert Kennedy receiving a blow-by-blow account from Peter Lawford of the telephone conversation he had had with Marilyn at five o'clock. She was far too calculating and self-assured for Kennedy's liking, given that she was threatening to make exposures at her press conference the following Monday. Her one piece of physical evidence which would support her claims in public was the red diary, and he had failed to remove it. He perhaps regarded it as imperative to pay another visit to her house, probably this time with Peter Lawford, who might have more success in prising the book from her than he had had. The second meeting seemed just as rumbustious as the first but much briefer.

The lurid stories of Kennedy's aide being a doctor who injected Marilyn with something to calm her down may have been inspired by notions which belong just a little further down the line: that Robert Kennedy left her dying. This is extremely far-fetched and smacks of an attempt to smear the Attorney General and involve him in murder. It is unbelievable for all the reasons cited in Chapter 18.

Kennedy left Fifth Helena Drive without the red diary once more. It would require a skilled negotiator to take that away from Marilyn. In the meanwhile he would have to hope that she changed her mind over what she would say at the press conference. There would be much advice for her to do so, if only for her own sake. The public would not take kindly to reading of her exploits with the Kennedy brothers and the whole thing was likely to backfire on her. And all that was supposing she could ever persuade the press to take up the story and, in turn, obtain the cooperation of their editors in running it.

There was no trace of upset or hysteria when Joe DiMaggio Jr spoke to Marilyn on the telephone at about 7.30 p.m. This was Joe's third attempt to reach her, giving a clear indication that he was anxious to speak to her that night. The call has been very well documented in interviews which Joe has given to researchers and writers. He was calling to tell Marilyn that his engagement was off and, because she thought it would have been a disastrous match, she was quite delighted to hear about it. She chatted away to Joe and he spoke of her being 'gay, happy and alert'. There was no depression and nothing amiss. Mrs Murray caught snatches of Marilyn's end of the conversation and recalls one point at which she said, 'Oh, that's wonderful.'

Mrs Murray reported that Marilyn went to bed at about 8 p.m. The early hour would be consistent with her having lost so much sleep the night before. Marilyn, comfortably ensconced in her bed where she could drop off when she was drowsy, made several more telephone calls. One was to Henry Rosenfeld, who recalled her sounding 'groggy', another was to Sydney Guilaroff, who said she told him she was feeling very depressed, and a third was to Ralph Roberts, her masseur and close personal friend, who had faithfully called back hoping to confirm their dinner date that evening, though the call had been intercepted by Dr Greenson. Roberts was not there to take her call; instead she got his answering service, which later told him he had had a call from a lady who spoke in a slurred voice. One incoming call at this time was from her Mexican friend José Bolanos, who said she did not hang up when their conversation ended. She simply put the phone down, but he did not find this unusual: she had done it before.

The interesting thing about this group of calls is that they all fit a pattern. They all present a picture of a sleepy person – or groggy, or depressed, or speaking with a slurred voice – getting more drowsy, perhaps lonely and even a little melancholy. Then, consistent with her difficulty in actually dropping off to sleep, she suddenly – at about 10 p.m. – called Jeanne Carmen once more. Now no longer depressed or groggy or speaking in a slurred voice, she was just a bit 'nervous' and 'uptight', which would easily fit the pattern of the insomniac who, unable to sleep, sought conversation with her friend. In fact she was still trying to persuade Jeanne to come across to see her at this late hour.

Publicist Arthur Jacobs, his wife-to-be, Natalie, and their friends were at the Hollywood Bowl while Marilyn was making her phone calls. At about 10.30 p.m., when the concert was nearly over, an usher told Arthur Jacobs that there was an urgent phone call for him. He took the call and, after stopping to tell Natalie that there was an emergency involving Marilyn Monroe, made off with considerable haste. At that time of night there would still be plenty of traffic about and it would take him until shortly before eleven o'clock to reach Fifth Helena Drive.

Whatever the problem was with Marilyn, it is obvious from the various moves made that she was in deep trouble. A doctor was needed and, though Mrs Murray knew Dr Greenson was out to dinner, she probably rang his number first. Receiving no reply, it is likely that she then rang Dr Engelberg, Marilyn's physician, who, it appears, could not respond at once. Dr Engelberg has said very little about Marilyn's death, but usefully contributed the information that the alarm was raised between eleven o'clock and midnight. Taken in context, this is strong evidence for believing that he was called out to her. It would be hard to believe, however, that he heard there was an emergency involving Marilyn without hurrying to her house as soon as he was able.

It was possibly on Engelberg's instructions that an ambulance was called to take Marilyn to hospital. A call was made to Walt Schaefer's company, which made swift radio contact with one of his fleet of ambulances which happened to be in the vicinity. Accounts vary of what happened next, but it seems that driver Ken Hunter with assistant Murray Liebowitz reached the house close to midnight. Hunter said Marilyn was dead when he arrived and they left, but this was challenged by Walt Schaefer, who claimed that Marilyn was alive and was rushed to Santa Monica Hospital. If this was accurate, however, it appears that she was dead by the time the ambulance reached the hospital, and it turned straight round and took her body back home.

On the other hand, Schaefer denies that his ambulance took Marilyn's body home, but there may have been strong reasons for his unwillingness to admit to this part in the proceedings. An ambulance company which conveyed corpses, for instance, would not be very popular with those such as corporate organisations and civic authorities who regularly used his vehicles. Similarly, if it appeared that Ken Hunter had not made it to hospital in time with an emergency case, he might be unwilling to admit he ever tried. In this case it might not have been too difficult to lean on a hapless driver to take the body home, even though it was strictly against company rules.

It is likely that, while the ambulance was taking Marilyn to hospital, Mrs Murray tried Ralph Greenson's number again. It was just after midnight and he and his wife had not long since arrived home. He hastily drove across to Fifth Helena Drive.

The preliminary investigation undertaken by Sergeant Jack Clemmons was described fully at the beginning of this book.

It was useful for a number of reasons. It exposed the attempt made to falsify the timing of events, and alerted researchers to the probability that other statements were false also, even though his colleagues, in their later investigations, were prepared to let vagueness slide. His perception of the strange atmosphere in the house that night has coloured our understanding that there was nothing straightforward about his visit, and his hunch that there were others in the house who did not reveal their presence may well have been correct. His observation of the sound of the washing machine operating at 4.30 a.m. was extremely important, for it might indicate that there was soiled linen which the occupants of the house were determined not to allow others to know about.

By contrast, the investigation headed by Sergeant Byron told us very little. Byron and his colleagues appear to have been satisfied to treat the investigation as a routine exercise. The fact that those whom he interviewed were unhelpful did not

The rear of Marilyn's house during the time of the investigation. Two stuffed toy animals are prominent, but neither seems to be the tiger she received on the Saturday morning. *Corbis-Bettmann/UPI.*

persuade him to take them to headquarters for more thorough questioning. He might have been expected, however, to have recognised discrepancies such as Mrs Murray telling him she could see light underneath a door beneath which a thick new carpet had been laid, completely filling the gap. There was also the matter of the broken bedroom window, the glass from which was lying outside the house, indicating that it had been broken from the inside.

It would have been normal procedure for the house to be sealed when Byron and his colleagues left. This, apparently, was not done for some time afterwards, given the testimony of Inez Melson that she obtained access in the small hours of the morning. Others were there at the same time, also.

The whereabouts of certain key players at the time of the Marilyn Monroe tragedy have never been resolved. Natalie Jacobs, for instance, believes Pat Newcomb was at Marilyn's home when her husband was called away from the Hollywood Bowl. In fact she thinks it was Pat Newcomb who made the call to him. Newcomb staunchly denies this and says she knew nothing until shortly before 4 a.m. when she was called by lawyer Milton Rudin from Marilyn's house. What time Rudin was called to the house and by whom is a mystery. What is certain is that Rudin was still at the house, answering questions, when Detective Sergeant Byron was there conducting his investigation.

Dr Hyman Engelberg obviously played a much bigger role in the matter of Marilyn's death than he generally advertises. He was on the scene very early in the proceedings and was there right through to the time when Byron was asking his questions, which did not begun until 5.45 a.m. In the meantime, at 3.50 a.m., he signed the death certificate; why he waited until that particular time, when Marilyn had died hours before, is another mystery. It is curious that, though Engelberg was probably one of the first on the scene, when it came to the first round of questioning, which was conducted by Sergeant Jack Clemmons, he stood back and let Ralph Greenson do the talking. Later on, too, when Byron was asking the questions, Engelberg had little to say. In fact, according to author Anthony Summers, Byron had a bad time with both Engelberg and Rudin; '. . . as far as those two were concerned it was a negative result . . . They were telling me what they wanted me to know. That was my feeling at the time. I was thrown by their attitude.' Both Engelberg and Rudin have had precious little to say since that time, too.

When it comes to tracking down the whereabouts of people, it comes as no surprise for Peter Lawford to be at the centre of this kind of mystery also. When he was interviewed by the District Attorney's investigator in 1982, he claimed he was telephoned with the news of Marilyn's death at 1.30 a.m. He was positive about the time, he said, because he looked at a bedside clock after receiving the phone call from his manager, Milt Ebbins. This statement was patently false if Fred Otash can be believed, and Otash had no axe to grind. He said that Lawford first contacted him to conduct a 'sweeping' of the house at shortly after midnight, and by 2 a.m. the actor was in his Laurel Avenue office. Milt Ebbins, in turn, claims he was not contacted until 4 a.m. when Milton Rudin called him from Marilyn's house. But to complete the circle, Ebbins asserts that it was then – at 4 a.m. – that he tried to telephone Lawford. He got no answer.

Lawford knew a lot about what happened to Marilyn, but said little. When it comes to what he did say, he appears to have been trying to lead investigators as far as possible from what really did happen. He is not the only one, of course. When the timing of events was being established, Mrs Murray told one story to Sergeant Clemmons and another to Sergeant Byron just an hour or so later, which typified her contribution to our understanding of what happened. It seemed she changed her story every time she told it. One example of how inventive she could be was discovered in what she told Marilyn's neighbours. Marilyn had woken from sleep and taken pills, she said, slept for a while and had taken more pills having forgotten she had taken them earlier, and so on and so on until she died. This was absolute nonsense, of course, but her stories and Peter Lawford's influenced the way millions of people regarded Marilyn's death, and it has taken many years to overcome the influence of them.

Having now, as an important feature of the sequence of events, sorted out a timescale for the occurrences of that fateful night, we are able to identify the three most critical questions in this investigation. What happened during the short period between Marilyn chatting on the telephone to Jeanne Carmen at 10 p.m. and Arthur Jacobs being called away from the Hollywood Bowl about 10.30 p.m.? Why did those close to Marilyn combine with the authorities to promote a patently false version of how she died? Both of these issues will be addressed in Chapter 20, along with the final question: who were the men who murdered Marilyn?

# 20

# END RESULTS

In Chapters 14–17 important conclusions were reached regarding the death of Marilyn Monroe. I dismissed suicide and accidental suicide, leaving only one alternative: murder. I also eliminated two parties who have been accused of killing the actress, the Mafia and Robert F. Kennedy; earlier I disposed of the claim that Dr Ralph Greenson had administered a fatal dose of some drug while purporting to be rescuing Marilyn.

I can logically argue that we know Marilyn was murdered because she did not commit suicide and did not accidentally take her own life. For many people this would be sufficient, but there is an onus to specify what convinces me that she was the victim of a plot to kill her.

The first and most obvious clue to murder must be the absence of drugs in Marilyn's stomach when the autopsy was carried out. The authorities can explain this away as they wish, but even they have to admit that it is unusual, while others would be more forthright and support the contention that it is a clear indication of a suspicious death.

The second indication of murder was the huge volume of drugs found in Marilyn's body. There was enough to kill several people and taken by mouth, as the coroner stated was the case, she would have been dead long before she had taken enough capsules to account for the entire drug content of her body. I considered this volume of drugs being injected, which would of course have indicated murder since Marilyn did not have in the house the liquid version of the two drugs she took. The evidence, however, is that this did not happen. The strongest indication is that the fatal drugs were injected by enema, and again this could only be murder.

Another strong influence is the fact that Marilyn displayed no suicidal tendencies during the period immediately before she died. She was said to be happy – and she had cause to be when her staggering new contract was considered. The salary, at roughly three times what she had been getting before, was a triumph. Marilyn's response was to go out and buy a new wardrobe – the purposeful act of a successful and positive young woman, not remotely one considering taking her own life.

A number of strange goings on cast doubts on the validity of a suicide verdict. The position of the body was curious and suggested that it had been moved; the curious atmosphere in the house experienced by Sergeant Jack Clemmons did not belong to a straightforward suicide scenario; the changing testimony of Dr Greenson and Dr Engelberg and the times of their arrivals at the house, and the ever-changing testimony of Mrs Murray, raised suspicions; the odd tale told by Dr Greenson that a delay of over four hours had been caused by the need to have clearance from the studio; and the laundry which was being done at about five in the morning – these were all strange occurrences which could not, by ordinary standards, be explained.

The rehearsed answers also gave rise to suspicion, since the normal circumstances of a death by suicide would not create a need for 'pat' answers to straightforward questions. One can understand why Sergeant Byron was 'thrown' by people supposedly answering routine questions about a case of suicide who kept answering the questions they wanted to answer. Why would they do such a thing if this was a simple suicide? Of those being questioned, one was a doctor and another a psychiatrist. One would have expected these professionals to deal easily with a few questions as a standard element of routine proceedings. Instead they gave the officer conducting a brief enquiry a bad time; one would expect behaviour of this kind to have a cause.

The behaviour of Marilyn's friends after her death gave rise to a great deal of concern. These were not a group of people who slowly resumed a normal pattern of life after the death of a loved one. Three of the principals jetted off to faraway places immediately afterwards, which formed a curious pattern.

When they returned, their answers to questions about Marilyn – which they should have been expecting – left a lot to be desired. Some did not make sense, and others were quite misleading. Indeed, some of the friends refused to answer questions about Marilyn's death altogether. The problems appeared not to apply to questions relating to Marilyn's life; it was the answers – or the absence of them – to questions about her death which suggested that something was deeply wrong somewhere.

Taking all these things together, it would be extremely difficult to accept that Marilyn Monroe went to bed and killed herself, even accidentally. In my opinion, only murder would make sense of all the anomalies mentioned above.

It would appear that immediately after hanging up the phone from speaking to Jeanne Carmen at roughly ten o'clock, Marilyn was attacked in her bedroom. Mrs Murray had gone off to bed shortly before the telephone call and was probably sound asleep by the time the crime was carried out. She was undoubtedly disturbed and made her way to her employer's bedroom door. Seeing the telephone wire still stretching beneath the door, it was reasonable for her to assume that Marilyn was still awake and making calls. Mrs Murray no doubt went back to bed, but it is doubtful that she slept any more that night.

Marilyn's assailants needed to remain undisturbed for about ten minutes. A quick whiff of some kind of anaesthetic would reduce resistance to a minimum while the star was picked up and carried to the guest room, furthest away from the other rooms in the house, and possibly the one room which was not bugged. She was stripped of her nightdress and bra, and it was probably while being turned over to take off these garments that she acquired bruises to her arm and hip. The drugs which killed her were then, it appears, administered in liquid form by enema while she was unconscious. The whole proceedings would have taken no more than about fifteen minutes.

There is substantial support in one form or another for this entire argument. The appearance of the body when found in her bedroom suggested that she had not died there. There was no mess, and whether she was murdered or had killed herself there was less likely to be mess of one kind or another to be cleaned up. If she had died elsewhere it would seem logical for it to have been the room furthest away from the living rooms and Mrs Murray's bedroom. There is little doubt that the killers knew every detail of the house and what was happening in it that night. They were aware that Marilyn used enemas occasionally as part of her beauty treatment, and that her own equipment would be in the house. They knew, also, which drugs Marilyn was being prescribed and brought them in liquid form.

Mrs Murray was probably disturbed again by the sound of the killers leaving and this time, somewhat unnerved, she no doubt went into Marilyn's bedroom. The story of the door being locked was not true, which Mrs Murray later admitted: it was part of a subterfuge which belongs to a later part of our account of the proceedings. Unable to find Marilyn, she no doubt experienced a degree of panic as she searched the rooms in the house one by one. She may well have feared that her employer had been abducted. It was probably with a mixture of relief and deep fear that she found Marilyn in the guest

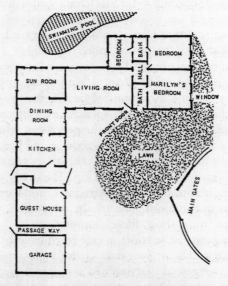

Plan of Marilyn's house, showing how far the guest quarters were from the rest of the accommodation.

room in a comatose state. Her first reaction might reasonably have been that she thought her employer was dead, though her nursing experience would soon make her take Marilyn's pulse and feel the temperature of her body.

There is little doubt that her first thought was to telephone Dr Greenson, but as it was barely 10.20 p.m. and the doctor was out having dinner with his wife that night, she would receive no response. Her next call would be to Dr Engelberg, who, it seems, was difficult to reach for some reason. This could have had something to do with his new domestic arrangements, for he had separated from his wife only the day before. Whatever the cause, the indications are that there was something of a delay before the doctor arrived – he later spoke of the alarm being raised between 11 p.m. and midnight, and it is probable that he reached the house around midnight.

At 10.30 p.m. Arthur Jacobs was requested to take an urgent telephone call at the Hollywood Bowl. The caller, whose identity remains a mystery, told him there was an emergency involving Marilyn Monroe and asked him to go at once to her house. Whoever it was knew he would be at the concert, and this was unlikely to be Mrs Murray; she would, in any case, have more to do than calling the publicity man. Pat Newcomb would be the logical person to know where her boss was and to make a call to him, but she claims she was not at the house at that time and knew nothing about what had happened until shortly before four o'clock when Milton Rudin called her. Rudin was another possibility, but though we know he was at the house during the night we do not know what time he arrived there. And for that matter, we do not know who called him in the first place.

We know that an ambulance was called to take Marilyn to hospital but, again, we do not know who called it. It may have been Arthur Jacobs who put the call through to the Schafer company and, though we know they responded quickly since they radioed to an ambulance in the locality, it did not arrive until about midnight. It would appear that any chance Marilyn had of survival disappeared between 10.20 p.m. and shortly after midnight, for it seems she passed away on the way to Santa Monica Hospital. Nothing is known of what happened when she reached hospital, though it seems likely that she would be seen in the ambulance by a doctor who declared her dead, and she was then returned to Fifth Helena Drive without being taken out of the vehicle.

It would seem that neither of Marilyn's doctors was available when she desperately needed them, and none of those around her knew how to handle the situation. Marilyn was dead before Dr Greenson arrived shortly after midnight. Though Pat Newcomb denies it, she was reported by Mrs Murray to have said, 'If I'd been here, this wouldn't have happened.'

Arthur Jacobs was soon hard at work. Releases had to be prepared for press, radio and television to explain a sick Marilyn. A story had to be put together and stuck to. In the days of the big studios, it was more important to preserve the image of the star and the integrity of the studio than to tell the truth. The truth could be tailored as the scenario demanded. The public would only be told what the publicity people wanted them to know.

But when Marilyn died everything changed. The publicity team were joined by others later on that Sunday to form what was nearer to a council of war, for high stakes were now involved. It could be recognised at this stage that the target in killing Marilyn was Attorney General Robert Kennedy. He had exposed himself to his enemies in his misguided fling with the actress, and they had homed in to make him pay the price. This was 1962, and to be tainted with involvement in a scandal involving sex and murder in those days would have dire effects. If he were questioned about Marilyn's death his political enemies would take up where the killers had left off and he would be hounded out of office. His brother would then be asked to resign the presidency. And worse still: this was the kind of event which caused newspaper editors to remember previously binned stories of romantic liaisons between both Robert Kennedy and Marilyn and John F. Kennedy and various women, including Marilyn, and open season could be declared on the Kennedys.

Although meetings took place throughout the day, the first meeting that Arthur Jacobs held – one of the most important – was early on the Sunday morning, soon after Marilyn died. It is ridiculous to believe that the only people who put their heads together were Arthur Jacobs, Ralph Greenson and Mrs

Murray, however. If Dr Engelberg arrived some time after 2.30 a.m., as some have reported, it has to be wondered whether he was not roped in, but the situation suggests that others were soon there and controlling events. Decisions were apparently taken that the best protection for Robert Kennedy must involve developing the superficial suicide scenario created by the killers. This was thoroughly discussed and plans laid for presenting to the police. When Sergeant Clemmons spoke of those he questioned sounding as though they had rehearsed their answers, he was no doubt absolutely correct. Long before Clemmons was informed of Marilyn's death, however, it was almost certain that Chief William Parker had been called in to take control of the inevitable investigation. It was at the early discussions that decisions were made to carry Marilyn's body from the guest room to her own bedroom, to agree a story in which the bedroom door was locked and the window broken for access, for the ambulance to be forgotten about, and for Mrs Murray to clean up the guest room and wash the bedlinen.

On Sunday night hard-and-fast plans were laid to contain the situation and provide for the protection of Robert Kennedy. A 'strategy meeting', as Rupert Allan called it, was held in Jacobs' offices. They were meeting with someone who had been sent from the Kennedy family, and involved in the discussions with him were Arthur Jacobs and two of his staff, Michael Selsman and Rupert Allan. It is likely that Peter Lawford was there at some time or other during the day. Discussing and debating in a sometimes noisy atmosphere, their task was to devise ways and means of keeping the Kennedy name from being besmirched in the aftermath of Marilyn's death.

The decision to promote the idea of accidental suicide provided the key to covering the killers' tracks. This gave Chief Parker the opening to play the tragedy down, conducting, overtly, a routine enquiry into a straightforward suicide, and effectively disallowing the in-depth investigation which would have been necessary had any suggestion of homicide been raised. In turn, Dr Noguchi would be given no inkling that anything other than suicide was to be considered before the autopsy was carried out. Chief Parker's department did, it seems, carry out a careful investigation quietly and secretly. But it seems that what went into the files was either eventually destroyed or presented to Robert Kennedy.

In the meantime Mrs Murray told her version of events, changing details from time to time and putting around the story about Marilyn asking if there was any oxygen in the house. This was given only faint support by Dr Greenson, but it no doubt impressed those who were prepared to be impressed by such inventive story-telling. Greenson soon backed off from actively promoting the suicide verdict. On the whole he kept quiet on the subject.

A small army of people was either watching Robert Kennedy and Marilyn Monroe or listening to what was happening at the house in Fifth Helena Drive. There has already been much to say about the commission given to Bernard Spindel to record events for the benefit of Jimmy Hoffa, Sam Giancana and other mobsters. Their objective was blackmail. On the face of it, the FBI conducted surveillance because of the risks that the liaison carried for national security, though there could be no guarantees that it was not at the specific behest of J. Edgar Hoover, for whatever reasons he had. It has been claimed that a branch of the Los Angeles Police Department also had the two shadowed and bugged. And not surprisingly, also on the grounds of risk to national security, there were watchers and listeners from the CIA.

By all indication the men who murdered Marilyn knew that she was in her bedroom and that Mrs Murray had just gone to bed; they knew the layout of the house, what drugs Marilyn took, that she used enemas, and generally everything that happened in the house. They also knew that if an attempt was to be made to implicate the Attorney General, tonight was their last opportunity: he would not be visiting the house any more. It was also their best opportunity because of the heated argument in which he had been involved. In view of all this it would seem reasonable to assume that the assailants came from the ranks of one of those groups carrying out surveillance.

In Chapter 16 the idea that the Mafia was behind the murder was dismissed, which narrows the field somewhat. It was unlikely that Hoover would issue instructions for Marilyn to be killed: his malicious penchant for file-keeping would be more than satisfied by the reports of Robert Kennedy's indiscretions, though this did not preclude FBI personnel committing the murder off their own bat – the Attorney General, their ultimate boss, was greatly disliked. But this is probably ruled out on the grounds that should they be unmasked it would undoubtedly elicit the wrath of the Director on them for bringing the Bureau into disrepute. And he would not want to be associated with their defence.

In spite of Chief William Parker's feelings towards the Kennedys, these feelings could not be said to apply to the LAPD in general – far from it. There was considerable anti-Kennedy animosity in the Department, and for this reason it cannot be said with absolute certainty that the watchers they had sent should be completely exonerated. It is true, however, that not the slightest indication of that organisation's involvement has come to light since Marilyn's death, and there is little encouragement to pursue this idea.

On the other hand, there is every encouragement to examine the position of the CIA: did their people send the killers? The background of enmity between the CIA and the Kennedy brothers has been described fully in Chapter 11. Though CIA personnel in general had no love for the President and his Attorney General, the group associated with the Bay of Pigs débâcle hated them. It was believed that at least as much blame attached to Robert Kennedy as to his brother, because the President, who had to accept the ultimate responsibility, was out of action due to his back problems on the crucial day of the Bay of Pigs assault, and it was Robert, they thought, who made the decisions which they considered the direct cause of the bloodbath. The venomous hatred of Bay of Pigs survivors watching the Monroe house or being kept informed by those on the ground could very easily have given rise to an act of murder calculated to result in the downfall of their enemies. Norman Mailer placed it in perspective when he wrote:

But when one remembers the ease with which dirty assignments were taken up by the Plumbers and the cadre of Watergate, there is room to wonder. Marilyn's case, of course, is worse, indeed presents a potential which is so much filthier that analysis must shiver. Watergate, after all, did not seek to murder a woman, merely to sink a party. But then the ante was higher in the late fifties and early sixties. Passionate men, patriots, hoodlums and goons believed equally that Communism was the seed of this country's destruction. . . . In those days, Communism to right-wing minds seemed but a step beyond the Kennedys.

It should not, however, be thought that the theory of a right-wing group of malcontents in the CIA providing the 'mechanics' to murder Marilyn was originated by me. I believed it was an original theory until I embarked on research into the work of others on this subject. Clear indications emerged of one or two others having followed roughly similar paths and reaching broadly similar conclusions but without developing their ideas. This, of course, only serves to give strength to the theory. Norman Mailer, as can be seen above, was one who came close, and the celebrated broadcaster and journalist Dorothy Kilgallen was another. Perhaps the one who came closest, identifying the CIA, was the Los Angeles District Attorney's investigator Frank Hronek, who investigated Marilyn's murder and reached this conclusion. Needless to say, any reports filed by Hronek have long since disappeared.

It is appropriate here to remind readers that I uncovered evidence of the CIA renegades being involved in the conspiracy to assassinate both President Kennedy and Robert Kennedy. This story, detailed in Chapter 11, came from a most reliable informant in Dallas, Texas – Hank Gordon, who during the few days prior to the assassination of the President, was unaware that he was working with a CIA man who was a member of the renegade group. In conversation, the CIA agent told Gordon the day before the President's visit that he would be killed when he came.

But Gordon did not believe the man and ignored what had been said. He was later flabbergasted when he heard about the assassination of President Kennedy, and could not get the agent's words out of his mind. He remembered being told also that Robert Kennedy would be killed 'and any other Kennedy that gets into that position' (becoming a candidate for the White House). Robert Kennedy was killed five years later when he received the Democratic nomination, and the following year his brother Edward, an up-and-coming candidate for the presidency, was disgraced in the mysterious affair at Chappaquiddick.

Gordon remained silent for over thirty years about what he had learned from the CIA agent. He told me he feared for his life and his family, especially when he discovered what had happened to many other witnesses. Hank Gordon is not, of course, his real name: he told me his story on condition that his name was never mentioned. After validating many points in his story and before accepting it, however, I got him to agree to tell the whole story to the distinguished Kennedy researcher and archivist Mary Ferrell, who agreed that both he and his story were quite genuine.

*

Marilyn with top journalist Dorothy Kilgallen, who suspected murder. *Jean Bach Collection.*

Marilyn Monroe had played a dangerous game when she formed relationships with John and Robert Kennedy. The status which she appeared to be seeking was elusive, as it always is in such affairs, and the happiness she thought she had found was short-lived. And when the whole thing exploded in her face, the girl from the orphanage who had been made to take second place so often in her childhood, and who had fought all her short life to achieve first place and stardom in her profession as an actress, was once again made to take second place when it came to her death. It could be believed that in their anxiety to protect Robert Kennedy from his enemies, those who were around her when she died forgot Marilyn. It did not seem to matter that she was tarred with the stigma of suicide. Marilyn Monroe was murdered – she did not take her own life. Let history correct the fiction circulated about the world by Arthur Jacobs and the studio: she was not a suicide. She was the victim of cruel men seeking to use her for political gain.

In the light of the John Miner statements there cannot be any doubt now for those who were previously unsure that Marilyn Monroe was murdered. In identifying the group which sent the killers we have highlighted a plot designed to discredit the Kennedy brothers, which was carried out with the intention of driving them from power. The men who murdered Marilyn failed in their ultimate objective, but the renegade group which sent them was fanatical, and such people do not give up after one failed attempt. It would be logical to assume that they went on to combine with those who were successful in getting rid of the Kennedys by other, more direct but equally bloody, means.

# 21

# AN AFTERWORD

It is interesting to observe what later happened to those who might be regarded as the dramatis personae in the drama of Marilyn's death.

On the Sunday morning, the day Marilyn died, it was said that *Pat Newcomb* virtually had to be put out of Marilyn's house. This was several hours after the police had taken control, and presumably it was when they wanted to close the house. As she left, Newcomb had a run-in with press photographers, screaming at them, 'Keep shooting, vultures.' During the following days she was approached by Dr Norman Farberow, leader of the Suicide Team appointed to look into the circumstances surrounding Marilyn's death, and refused to answer his questions. 'She stonewalled me,' he said. She has not, to date, answered any official questions relating to Marilyn's death.

Newcomb flew to Hyannis Port at the invitation of Robert Kennedy, and immediately embarked on a six-month vacation in Europe. She visited Holland, Germany, France, Italy, Denmark and Switzerland, returning to the United States in February 1963. During this time she was fired by Arthur Jacobs, ostensibly for impeding photographers and preventing reporters from getting stories. Natalie Jacobs told me a different story, however. She told me that they had had a spat and that Arthur had fired her for being insulting to his wife.

When she returned from Europe, she was given a job in Washington as an Information Specialist on Motion Pictures at the US Information Agency. Some time later, however, she went back to work as a publicity agent, numbering among her clients Barbra Streisand and Jane Fonda.

*Peter Lawford* and his wife, *Pat Kennedy Lawford*, flew to Hyannis Port also, and it was several months before they returned to Los Angeles. Lawford was another who avoided official questioning. It was not until 1975 – thirteen years after Marilyn's death – that he was finally questioned by the LA authorities. Lawford's accounts of his supposed phone conversations with Marilyn on the day she died continued to harden the belief of the public that she had committed suicide.

Lawford's third wife, Deborah Gould, said he told her he had removed a note when he went to Marilyn's house to conduct the 'sweeping' operation – the inference being that it was a suicide note. I place little store by the recollections of Deborah Gould, and Peter Lawford himself denied much of what she said before he died. If the unreliable Lawford moved any note, which in my opinion is highly doubtful, it was more likely to be a note that Robert Kennedy had written to her. Lawford died in 1984.

After Marilyn died, *Mrs Eunice Murray* took a trip to Europe also, and when she returned to the United States she continued to tell her varying and unreliable stories to the media. Her incredible 'change of heart' when questioned by the BBC for *Say Goodbye to the President* in 1985, when she appeared no longer willing to continue the cover-up, did not last: she afterwards retreated to her former position. Mrs Murray died early in 1995.

*Ralph Greenson*, Marilyn's psychiatrist, was never the same man again after she died. When details of the methods he had used with Marilyn became known, he was criticised – even ridiculed – by his colleagues. This was sad, for Greenson had had a long and distinguished career in psychiatry and was respected throughout his profession. His book *The Technique and Practice of Psychoanlysis* became a standard text, and in 1978 he also published *Explorations in Psychoanalysis*. Anthony Summers quotes one of Greenson's colleagues who referred to him as 'the backbone of psychoanalysis in the western US'.

An analysis of Greenson's role in the matter of Marilyn's death indicates to me that he was drawn into concealing certain features of Marilyn's death by others who had the strong motive of wishing to protect the best interests of Robert Kennedy. I believe Greenson regretted his involvement and, as soon as he could, withdrew from it, attempting to set the record straight by telling Assistant District Attorney John Miner, his friend, that he did not believe Marilyn had committed suicide. Greenson is quoted as telling a reporter, during an interview some time after Marilyn's death, 'I can't explain myself or defend myself without revealing things that I don't want to reveal. It's a terrible position to be in, to say I can't talk about it. I just can't tell the whole story.' It was shortly after Marilyn died that another reporter had caught Greenson on the raw, asking him what he knew about her death. He swung back, 'Why don't you ask Bobby Kennedy?'

*John Miner*, the Deputy District Attorney who observed the autopsy on Marilyn Monroe's body, was also the man whom the DA sent to interview Ralph Greenson. During this interview he listened to tapes made by Marilyn Monroe. Miner staunchly honoured his agreement with Greenson that what he heard on the tapes would remain confidential. He told no one, not even his boss, at the risk of a great deal of trouble. He finally relented when he realised how important it was to put the record straight, and first spoke of what he had heard in June 1996.

For those who had any doubts, he confirmed that the tapes indicated that Marilyn had had a relationship with both John F. and Robert Kennedy. Miner, a man of high integrity, admitted to me for the first time that he believed Marilyn had been murdered.

John Miner became a well-known and highly successful Los Angeles lawyer specialising in medical malpractice suits. He still practises in Los Angeles, though he is now semi-retired.

*Arthur Jacobs*, Hollywood's ace publicity man, later became a successful film producer. Adept at keeping out of the limelight he created for his stars, he succeeded in never being questioned on the subject of Marilyn's death in spite of the major role he had played. He died in 1973. Actress *Natalie Trundi Jacobs*, his widow, still lives in Hollywood and remains active in her career.

*Dr Thomas Noguchi* is now Los Angeles County Medical Examiner-Coroner. He has performed autopsies on the bodies of a whole string of famous people, including Robert Kennedy, Sharon Tate, Janis Joplin, William Holden, Natalie Wood and John Belushi. It is small wonder he has become known as the Coroner to the Stars.

When Robert Kennedy was murdered in 1968, the killer was said to be Jerusalem-born Sirhan Bishara Sirhan, who fired at Kennedy from a distance of two to three feet in front of him. Noguchi, however, in describing his wounds indicated that they had been made by a weapon fired at point-blank range from behind. The Los Angeles authorities were furious at Noguchi for tuning what appeared to be a straightforward shooting into a conundrum, another 'Dallas'. They found an excuse to fire him, but Noguchi argued his case in court and won.

Thomas Noguchi told me that he is not averse to the idea of exhuming Marilyn's body to see if present-day techniques will reveal more about her death.

*Jeanne Carmen* retains her youthful looks and is still in demand for fashion photographs. She saw Marilyn and Robert Kennedy together 'at least half a dozen times', she says, and well remembers the occasion when he got angry at seeing her red diary.

Apart from her acting career, Jeanne was – and still is – a professional 'trick shot' golfer, and she and Marilyn had planned a round of golf at Monterey for the day after she died. Jeanne recalls the telephone call she got from Marilyn one day when she was out shopping in Beverly Hills and wanted to know what clothes she should buy for golf.

*Dr Norman Farberow*, *Dr Robert Litman* and *Dr Norman Tabachnik*, the three doctors who made up the Suicide Team, are all still in harness in their respective practices in Los Angeles.

*Milton Rudin* still practises law and remains as tight-lipped as ever on the subject of Marilyn. Los Angeles Police Department's *Sergeant Martin Ionnone*, who took part in the investigation into Marilyn's death, is now Chief of Police at Beverly Hills, while his fellow-investigator, *Detective Sergeant R. E. Byron*, is retired. Neither will speak about their investigation nor anything to do with Marilyn's death. *Dr Hyman Engelberg* is also silent on the subject of Marilyn.

*Ex-Sergeant Jack Clemmons*, the first officer to arrive at the house when news of Marilyn's death was finally reported, is still energetic and works in a construction company. He is always willing to share his memories of that night shift, after which, he reckons, his life was never quite the same again.

*Robert F. Slatzer*, writer and film producer, still lives in Hollywood with his wife Debbie. He has amassed all the available documentation on the Marilyn Monroe case and is one of the few real experts on the subject. He has written two books, *The Life and Curious Death of Marilyn Monroe* and *The Marilyn Files*. The latter formed the basis for a fascinating television programme.

*Police Chief William Parker* never became head of the FBI: J. Edgar Hoover never moved over. Parker earned a national reputation as an outstanding and highly effective chief of police. He died in early 1966 while receiving a rarely bestowed award from the First Marines.

Assistant to the Chief of Police, *Tom Reddin*, is now retired and still lives with his charming wife Betty in Los Angeles.

*Jimmy Hoffa*, *Sam Giancana* and *Johnny Roselli* all died violently. Hoffa simply disappeared, never to be seen again, Giancana was killed by the mob to silence him, and Roselli was killed because he talked. The mob exercised an iron discipline when it came to keeping the secrets of their 1960s relationship with the CIA.

Ace wiretapper *Bernard Bates Spindel* died of a heart attack in 1971, and Hollywood sleuth *Fred Otash* died in 1994.

*Sam Cordova* is the name of a man who nearly got into the pages of the story of the death of Marilyn Monroe. In 1985 Robert Slatzer wrote to the Los Angeles County Board of Supervisors saying that new evidence had come to light in regard to Marilyn's death and asking for the Grand Jury to set up an official investigation. The Board of Supervisors voted unanimously that this should be done. The Grand Jury foreman, Sam Cordova, expressed the opinion that there was reason to doubt the official verdict, said he had found evidence of a cover-up, and called a press conference. On the day that press conference was to be held District Attorney Ira Reiner announced that Cordova had been fired, and the new Grand

Jury foreman immediately and unceremoniously closed down the investigation.

If the 1982 enquiry instigated by District Attorney John Van de Kamp (see Chapter 13) was the 'nearly' investigation, the aborted 1985 Grand Jury must surely have been the 'never'.

*John F. Kennedy* was assassinated on 22 November 1963 while on a visit to the city of Dallas, Texas. Though Lee Harvey Oswald was officially blamed for the murder, few now believe this. It is likely that he was killed by a group made up of oil men, men from the military-industrial complex and others, notably renegade CIA agents including those who killed Marilyn Monroe.

When *Robert Kennedy* was informed by his press agent that Marilyn was dead he showed no emotion, saying only, 'Yeah, it's too bad.' He entered politics and won a seat in the Senate for New York State in January 1965, then went on to receive the Democratic nomination for the presidency in June 1968. His crucial rally was held at the Los Angeles Ambassador Hotel, following which he was shot and killed. Although this was ostensibly the work of a Jerusalem-born immigrant, the real killers were most likely the same group which killed his brother.

The whereabouts of Marilyn's red diary are still unknown. Regardless of its route, if I were obliged to make an intelligent guess as to where the diary finished up, and if Robert Kennedy were still alive, I would echo the words used by Ralph Greenson: 'Why don't you ask Bobby Kennedy?'

# SELECT BIBLIOGRAPHY

BROWN, Peter Harry, and Barham, Patte B., *Marilyn, the Last Take*. Dutton, New York, 1992

CAPELL, Frank A., *The Strange Death of Marilyn Monroe*. Herald of Freedom, Indianapolis, 1964

CARPOZI, George Jr, *The Agony of Marilyn Monroe*. Consul Books, London, 1962

DUNLEAVY, Stephen, and Brennan, Peter, *Those Wild, Wild Kennedy Boys!* Pinnacle Books, New York, 1976

FREEMAN, Lucy, *Why Norma Jean Killed Marilyn Monroe*. Global Right Ltd, Chicago, 1992

GIANCANA, Sam and Chuck, *Double Cross*. Warner Books, New York, 1992

GREGORY, Adela, and Speriglio, Milo, *Crypt 33, the Saga of Marilyn Monroe: The Final Word*. Birch Lane Press, New York, 1993

GUILES, Fred Lawrence, *Norma Jeane: The Life and Death of Marilyn Monroe*. Grafton Books, London, 1986

ISRAEL, Lee, *Kilgallen*. Delacorte Press, New York, 1979

JORDAN, Ted, *Norma Jean: My Secret Life with Marilyn Monroe*. William Morrow, New York, 1989

KENNEDY, Robert F., *The Enemy Within*. Harper and Row, New York, 1960

LAWFORD, Pat Seaton, with Schwarz, Ted, *Peter Lawford: Mixing with Monroe, the Kennedys, the Rat Pack and the Whole Damn Crowd*. Futura, London, 1990

MAILER, Norman, *Marilyn: A Biography*. Warner Paperback Library, New York, 1975

MANCHESTER, William, *Death of a President*. Michael Joseph, London, 1967

MANCHESTER, William, *One Brief Shining Moment: Remembering Kennedy*. Little, Brown, Boston, 1983

MELANSON, Philip H., PhD, *The Robert F. Kennedy Assassination*. Spi Books, New York, 1991

MINER, John, statement to Charles Lawrence in the London *Daily Telegraph*, 31 May 1996

NOGUCHI, Thomas T., MD, with Dimona, Joseph. *Coroner*. Simon and Schuster, New York, 1983

OTASH, Fred, *Investigation Hollywood*. Regnery, Chicago, 1976

PEPITONE, Lena, and Stadiem, William, *Marilyn Monroe Confidential*. Pocket Book, New York, 1980

SCHEIM, David E., *The Mafia Killed President Kennedy*. W. H. Allen, London, 1988

SCHLESINGER, Arthur M. Jr, *Robert Kennedy and His Times*. André Deutsch, London, 1978 and Futura, London, 1979

SCIACCA, Tony, *Kennedy and His Women*. Manor Books, New York, 1976

SHERIDAN, Walter, *The Fall and Rise of Jimmy Hoffa*. Saturday Review Press, New York, 1972

SHEVEY, Sandra, *The Marilyn Scandal*. Arrow Books, London, 1989

SLATZER, Robert F., *The Life and Curious Death of Marilyn Monroe*. Pinnacle Books, Los Angeles, 1975

SLATZER, Robert F., *The Marilyn Files*. Spi Books, New York, 1992

SMITH, Matthew, *JFK: The Second Plot*. Mainstream Publishing, London and Edinburgh, 1992

SORENSON, Theodore C., *Kennedy*. Hodder and Stoughton, London, 1965

SPADA, James, *Peter Lawford, the Man Who Kept the Secrets*. Bantam, New York, 1992

SPERIGLIO, Milo, *Marilyn Monroe: Murder Cover-Up*. Seville, New York, 1982 and Corgi, London, 1986

SPERIGLIO, Milo, *Marilyn Monroe, the Biography*. Arrow Books, London, 1994

SPOTO, Donald, with Chain, Steven, *The Marilyn Conspiracy*. Corgi, London, 1986

STEINEM, Gloria, and Barris, George, *Marilyn*. Victor Gollancz, London, 1987

STRASBERG, Susan, *Marilyn and Me*. Doubleday, London, 1992

SUMMERS, Anthony, *Goddess, the Secret Lives of Marilyn Monroe*. Victor Gollancz, London, 1985 and Sphere Books, London, 1986

WEATHERBY, W. J., *Conversations with Marilyn*. Sphere Books, London, 1977

# ILLUSTRATIONS INDEX

# NAME INDEX

# SUBJECT INDEX